Health Insurance Bargaining

HEALTH INSURANCE BARGAINING

Foreign Lessons for Americans

WILLIAM A. GLASER
Columbia University

GARDNER PRESS, INC. NEW YORK

Distributed by the Halsted Press
Division of JOHN WILEY & Sons, Inc.
New York   London   Sydney   Toronto

Gardner Press, Inc.

19 Union Square West

New York 10003

Distributed solely by the Halsted Press Division

of John Wiley & Sons, Inc., New York

Library of Congress Cataloging in Publication Data

Glaser, William A.
Health insurance bargaining.
Includes bibliographical references and indexes.
1. Insurance, Health.   2. Medicine, State.
I. Title. [DNLM: 1. Insurance, Health—Europe.
2. Insurance, Health—Canada.   3. State medicine—
Europe.   4. State medicine—Canada.   W275 GA1 G5h]
HD7107.G53.   368.4'2'009   78-1442
ISBN 0-470-99398-7

Printed in the United States of America

Book Design by Sidney Solomon
Typesetting in Baskerville on the Linotype
by Service Type Inc., Lancaster, Pennsylvania
Printing and binding by Haddon Craftsmen, Inc., Scranton, Pa.

For Evelyn

Contents

Acknowledgments

The research was carried on at the Center for the Social Sciences of Columbia University. It was also sponsored by the University's School of Public Health and its Center for Community Health Systems.

This investigation was supported in part by grant number 10-P-57847/2-02, from the Social Security Administration, U.S. Department of Health, Education and Welfare, Washington, D.C.

For their readings of the drafts of the manuscript or for comments on its theses, I am indebted to Manfred Kilgus of Sweden; Gordon Hatcher, Lothar Rehmer, and L. G. Williams of Canada; Robin A. Birch and E. Douglas Symes of Great Britain; and the following Americans: J. Paige Clousson, Jay Constantine, David Drake, Paul Fisher, Lewis Freiberg, Clifton Gaus, Warren Greenberg, William Hsiao, Donald Jones, Benjamin Liptzin, Gordon Mallett, Theodore Marmor, Larry Morris, Tom Mura, Francis D. Powell, Paul Rettig, Gerald Rosenthal, Bert Seidman, Richard Shoemaker, Mark Voyvodich, Charles Weller, and Alonzo Yerby.

At the Bureau of Applied Social Research and the Center for the Social Sciences at Columbia University, Madeline Simonson made her usual invaluable administrative contribution to my work.

I am most indebted to the many medical administrators and scholars abroad who were so generous with their time and information. They are listed in Appendix C.

Health Insurance Bargaining

CHAPTER 1

Learning from Abroad

No COUNTRY's domestic problems are unique. When its officials and organizations search for solutions, others in the world have done so before and are doing so at the same time.

While no country is unique, neither is it an exact duplicate of another. Institutions and cultural traits resemble each other in various ways from place to place, but the total mixture in each country is distinctive. Because each society differs in this respect, a complete set of institutionalized solutions for certain social problems cannot be automatically copied in another country.

However, a policy maker can benefit in several ways from looking at other societies as well as his own. First, he gains perspective. A decision maker is usually too harassed to understand his own situation well; he often thinks he is in a crisis, he often thinks he confronts great difficulties unparallelled elsewhere and beyond control. If he knows about other countries, however, he learns which of his problems and organizational features are common elsewhere and which are unusual. The more common problems may be handled by methods suggested from the foreign experiences, while the more unusual features may require some truly original thought. If a country's institutional arrangements and their troublesome outcomes are unusual in the world, the policy maker should be less inclined to accept them as "inevitable" or as "our way of life" and may be emboldened toward contemplating fundamental changes.

The bane of policy making is a preoccupation with each day's immediate demands and a want of imagination. When looking abroad, the policy maker sees a series of "natural laboratories." His own national debates may have generated only a few possible reforms. Abroad, he may learn additional possibilities. The range of different arrangements can stimulate his imagination to think of yet more.

Any major innovation is debated in the abstract beforehand. How it may work out is guesswork, and predictions about effects vary among partisans and vested interests. If something similar to the proposal is already operating abroad, one can see how it works in practice. The identical program with the identical consequences may not be enacted by one's own country, but one can think more realistically about the proposals being considered. Certain outcomes may now seem unlikely, others may come to mind for the first time.

Often a new proposal involves a change in scale or character. For example, a country may have several insurance programs of limited scope and consider unifying them in a national system. Likewise, the insurance programs have been voluntary and the proposal is to make them compulsory. The consequences cannot be visualized within the country's existing experience. Policy research about the *status quo* is irrelevant. One can see different systems only abroad.

FOREIGN PERSPECTIVES FOR THE UNITED STATES

During certain periods in its history, the United States has been attentive to lessons from abroad. Trying to develop new structures of representative democracy, checks and balances, and federalism, the Founding Fathers at the Constitutional Convention and in the ratification debates described foreign models and estimated the probable outcomes if emulated by the new American Republic.* [1] Once the new government was established, the Americans became preoccupied with domestic affairs; they were isolated by wide oceans and felt that their institutions were successful. By the late nineteenth century, the Americans had begun to think that the rest of the world was decaying and could be saved only if it learned from them. The flight of people from the Old World to the New seemed proof that others agreed. During the twentieth century, the United States fought several wars, organized multinational businesses, and conducted overseas programs in technical assistance in order to "save" the rest of the world and teach it lessons.

However, complacence and superiority are now changing. Some scholarly fields have always had an international orientation, and American authors regularly have compared American institutions with those of other

* All notes in this book appear at the end of the chapter to which they apply.

countries, including judgments about how to improve both. For example, several writers have evaluated American industrial relations in this fashion.[2] Not until the national crises in morale during the 1960's and 1970's, however, did American policy makers seriously consider looking abroad for guidance in solving their domestic problems. During the coming years, the United States may regularly use its foreign relations to obtain such practical ideas and information.[3]

NEGOTIATIONS IN HEALTH SERVICES

This book analyzes foreign experiences in an area where the United States is not the most developed in the world; that is, the large-scale organization of medical care. During the coming years, the United States will enact some form of national health insurance, the last developed country to do so. Unhappy experiences with Medicare and Medicaid show that the United States has much to learn. It did not plan nor has it reformed these programs in the light of experiences in other countries.[4] America's usual confidence in its ability to solve its problems by its own ingenuity has begun to wear thin. Its usual form of organizational First Aid, viz., manipulation of government regulations, has not made Medicare or Medicaid any better. Instead of a few coherent plans for national health insurance, there are over a dozen, with little but ideology to determine the choice. No one can predict the consequences of any; the malaise that surrounds the national debate over health lately indicates that all are likely to work out badly. So, for several years, the Congress and Executive Branch have been quick to offer bills but shrink from enacting a law.

In order to plan for national health insurance, Americans have employed their favorite response of commissioning very large amounts of research about existing domestic health services. But all this is beside the point: the essential fact about national health insurance is that it will be a new form of organization, and all preexisting parts will function within it differently from how they operate at present. From another perspective, this research hampers rather than helps decision making: the reports are too voluminous and numerous and often too esoteric in style; their discrete findings are too confusing, and the total result is to accentuate the malaise surrounding the planning of national health insurance.

This introspective research has neglected lessons from other countries where national health insurance has been part of daily life for decades. As a result, the Americans have been paying little attention to several institutional features that are essential to the efficiency and financial stability of national health insurance. The Americans are trying to reinvent the wheel, but without spokes.

One feature that should be self-evident is the need to specify how prices are determined, since national health insurance is a system for the paying of health services. No national health insurance system can function without machinery for negotiating pay rates at the national or regional levels. No private health insurance scheme can long remain viable without it either. Usually the same machinery is used to negotiate the terms of service between the medical profession and the health insurance system.

This book describes the different ways of organizing the confrontation between the medical profession and the public authorities in the principal developed countries. The purpose is to demonstrate the need for such machinery, the different ways of organizing it in different types of political and medical systems, various devices that work well, and other techniques that are troublesome. The book includes recommendations about several possible arrangements that the United States might emulate and others that it should avoid.

Besides offering information and recommendations for the planning of health insurance in the United States, this book demonstrates the value of studying other countries. Appendix A summarizes the numerous ways of drawing lessons from abroad for any troubled domestic policy.

NATIONAL HEALTH INSURANCE AND NATIONAL HEALTH SERVICE

Most systems described in this book are forms of national health insurance. Payroll taxes are imposed on employees and employers, the money is deposited in special funds, and the funds pay doctors, hospitals, and other providers. Usually only the subscribers can draw benefits. National health insurance resembles private health insurance, but its statutory basis and governmental sponsorship increase its scale: the law covers more people than would have joined voluntarily; the national Treasury supplements the sick funds' resources with payments permitting wider coverage of persons, higher benefits, or more effective administration; the law standardizes the benefits and the rules for the entire country or province. The United States will adopt some form of national health insurance instead of a governmentally administered health service.

Of the industrial countries, Great Britain is the only one with a complete national health service, although Sweden is rapidly evolving in this direction. In a health service virtually all essential benefits are provided to all members of the population. Under national health insurance most money comes from the payroll taxes levied on workers and employers. In a health service the government owns the hospitals and creates a structure for ambulatory care. Under national health insurance the preexisting health delivery system is not altered, ambulatory care usually is not organized into any national structure, and the hospitals remain under diverse ownership.

In national health insurance the sick funds and medical associations are always involved in across-the-table bargaining in some fashion. The organization of the sick funds, the organization of the medical associations, and the structure of the bargaining and communication relationship vary among countries. Parliaments and Government Ministries everywhere play roles in setting the ground rules and in approving the results, but the details vary among countries. Several other features differ among nations too, such as the timetable of negotiations, the tone of the discussions, the involvement of political allies, the reliance on automatic formulas, and the number of subjects other than doctors' pay that are negotiated in the same setting. Some countries are more successful than others in their methods of resolving disputes and negotiating agreements, in the economy and clarity of their administration, and in other features.

In a national health service, the Government Ministries face the medical association across the table. As in all public service bargaining, a difficult problem is how to resolve deadlocks and deal with strike threats. Some aspects of the negotiation resemble the arrangements under national health insurance, particularly when government agencies handle the insurance work.[5]

CHARACTERISTICS OF THE COUNTRIES

The countries to be reviewed are Canada, France, Belgium, the Netherlands, West Germany, Switzerland, Sweden, and Great Britain. Britain has a national health service and many Swedish doctors work under such an arrangement, but the other countries have national health insurance. The following are some brief details about the countries that are described in later chapters.

Type of political system

Canada, Germany, and Switzerland are federal countries of varying degrees of centralization and standardization. In all three, the governments, insurance carriers, and medical associations of the provinces have considerable autonomy and conduct much of the negotiations. The outcomes vary among the provinces.

France, Belgium, and The Netherlands are centralized unitary coun-tries. All negotiations take place at the national level, without provincial participation, and the outcomes apply uniformly to the entire countries.

Sweden and Great Britain are centralized and unitary, with some dele-gation of powers and functions to provinces. Centralized national negotia-tions take place in which provincial representatives sit in a single national delegation.

Type of payment

Fees are payments for each procedure. Salaries are fixed annual (or monthly) amounts for a fixed number of hours of service. Capitation is a flat payment for each person on a list; the doctor gives all necessary care for each person on that list. For the countries in this research, the principal methods of payment are:

	General practitioners	Specialists in offices	Specialists in hospitals
Canada	Fees	Fees	Fees, salary
France	Fees	Fees	Fees, salary
Belgium	Fees	Fees	Fees
The Netherlands	Capitation	—	Fees
West Germany	Fees	Fees	Fees, salary
Switzerland	Fees	Fees	Fees, salary
Sweden	Fees, salary	Fees	Salary
Great Britain	Capitation	—	Salary

Holland, West Germany, Sweden, Great Britain, some Canadian prov-inces, and some Swiss cantons have direct payment or "service benefits" arrangements. The sick fund or national health service pays the doctor.

France, Belgium, some Canadian provinces, and some Swiss cantons have reimbursement, "cash benefits," or "indemnity" arrangements. The patient pays the doctor and recovers the money from the sick fund. A few Swiss cantons have sliding scales with service benefits for the lower income groups and cash benefits for the richer.

Parties to the negotiations

The medical profession is represented by a unified medical association in Canadian provinces, Holland, Switzerland, Sweden, and Great Britain; by a unified medical trade union in West Germany; and by several rival medical trade unions in France and Belgium. The French trade union also performs many of the functions of a professional association.

Associations of sick funds negotiate in Belgium, Holland, West Ger-many, and Switzerland. The principal associations collaborate closely in all countries, but Germany has splits. A government agency bargains with the doctors in Canada, Sweden, and Britain. The official sick funds bargain in France, behaving at times like private associations and at other times like government agencies.

In the countries where the negotiating is done by associations of sick funds rather than by a government agency, the government plays various roles. It amends, overturns, or postpones decisions at times in Belgium; it provides usually *pro forma* approval in Holland and Switzerland, and it merely reviews but does not approve the ordinary agreements in Germany.

Organization of negotiations

Great Britain has a special arbitration tribunal to award pay. All the others—including Britain for terms of service—have bilateral negotiations between the medical profession and the sick funds or government. In Holland, Belgium, Sweden, France (for the fee schedules), Germany (for the fee schedule), some Swiss cantons and some Canadian provinces, the discussions take place in standing negotiating committees with fixed representatives from the doctors and public authorities. In Holland and Belgium, these committees are parts of larger organizations to administer health insurance, and they have secretariats. In France (for conditions of service), Germany (for conditions of service and money), some Swiss cantons, Britain (for conditions of service), and most Canadian provinces, the negotiations take place in *ad hoc* meetings of representatives from the opposite sides, without fixed membership or formal procedures.

The bilateral negotiations are routine and calm in style in Holland, Germany, Switzerland, Sweden, and most of Canada. They are more flamboyant in France, Belgium, and Britain. Negotiations in Holland, Sweden, and much of Canada involve the preparation and exchange of voluminous documentation.

Countries vary in the complexity of procedure and number of unexpected occurrences. This difference among countries accounts for the unequal length of chapters in this book. Small countries with complicated procedures (such as Belgium) get more space than large countries with simple negotiating systems (such as France).

TERMINOLOGY

Throughout this book, I shall retain the foreign language names and abbreviations for organizations of doctors, organizations of sick funds, and certain other institutions. I think this essential for accuracy: An English title or word can refer to several possible things in the foreign country, and I am often confused by English language texts that describe another country completely in English. Appendix B to this book contains a complete glossary of the titles and abbreviations.

NOTES

1. William H. Riker, "Dutch and American Federalism," *Journal of the History of Ideas*, Volume XVIII, Number 4 (October 1957), pp. 495-521. The Founding Fathers' extensive discussions were often based on incomplete or inaccurate sources and, as Riker notes in the case of federalism in Holland, many of their inferences were mistaken.

2. Possibly the best book describing how America can learn from other countries combines contributions by American and European specialists in industrial relations. Walter Galenson (editor), *Incomes Policy: What Can We Learn from Europe?* (Ithaca, N.Y.: New York State School of Industrial and Labor Relations, 1973).

3. Jimmy Carter, speech to the Foreign Policy Association, 23 June 1976; and Zbigniew Brzezinski, *Between Two Ages* (New York: The Viking Press, 1970), p. 258.

4. I predicted certain trends and problems in Medicare in the light of foreign precedents in " 'Socialized Medicine' in Practice," *The Public Interest*, Number 3 (Spring 1966), pp. 90-106. But Medicare turned out less stable and more wasteful because the United States did not organize it like national health insurance programs elsewhere.

5. Comparisons between national health insurance and a national health service appear in William A. Glaser, *Paying the Doctor* (Baltimore: The Johns Hopkins Press, 1970), Ch. II. That book contained many details about fee-for-service, salary, and capitation that I will not repeat in this new manuscript. A valuable overview of medical services abroad is in Milton I. Roemer, *Comparative Natiinal Policies on Health Care* (New York: Marcel Dekker Inc., 1977). A good overview of how health insurance and health services work in several of the European countries described in the present book is Alan Maynard, *Health Care in the European Community* (London: Croom Helm Publishers, 1975).

CHAPTER 11

CANADA

LONG before the enactment of obligatory national health insurance, most Canadian provinces had insurance plans (in addition to the usual private commercial coverage) that the provincial medical associations sponsored or approved. The medical profession guaranteed almost the entire range of services in office, hospital, and home. Doctors were paid by fee-for-service according to fee schedules written by the provincial medical association. Doctors accepted direct payment from the sick funds as payment in full. If the sick funds lacked the money the doctors agreed that fees would be prorated.[1]

At times Canada has been ruled in a highly centralized fashion; at other times, because of the political maneuvers of the provinces and the constitutional decisions of courts, the national government's powers have been limited and the provinces have been responsible for most domestic programs. National health insurance is now administered by the provinces, with the national government setting minimum standards and contributing money. This decentralized pattern probably would have developed as a result of recent Canadian constitutional practice alone. In addition, it was determined by the way that the doctor-sponsored plans had evolved earlier.

The medical profession's insurance program was encouraged by the Canadian Medical Association (CMA), its national spokesman. It was actually created and administered within each province, with the planning and administrative participation of one or more of the provincial medical groups, such as the provincial branch of the CMA or the College of Physicians and Surgeons. The CMA called nationwide meetings to enable the provincial health insurance officials and the provincial medical associations to share experiences. During the late 1940s and early 1950s, CMA sponsored the Trans Canada Medical Plans (TCMP), uniting them in a loose association. The TCMP staff encouraged creation of new provincial programs where they were still lacking. (To help the reader remember the abbreviations and foreign words, a glossary appears in Appendix B.)

In addition, Canada had several for-profit and nonprofit insurance programs for inpatient hospitalization. Some plans covered doctors' fees too. During the 1940s and 1950s the hospitalization plans were converted into official insurance, administered by the provinces and subsidized by the national government. Medical care insurance for doctors' fees experienced the same transformation and expansion a few years later.

THE PROVINCIAL INSURANCE PROGRAMS

The Medical Care Act of 1966 empowered the national government to give grants-in-aid for about half the costs of provincial insurance plans meeting certain minimum criteria. All medically required services must be covered without exclusions and without substantial financial barriers. All Canadian residents must be eligible. The insured person must not lose coverage when changing dwellings or jobs. The plan must be administered on a nonprofit basis by a public authority accountable to the provincial government. Canadian Medicare (i.e., the national government's medical care insurance program) began with two provinces in 1968; by 1972, all 10 provinces and 2 territories participated.[2]

In many countries, nonprofit or cooperative sick funds become the carriers of national health insurance. Their finances continue as before, stabilized by a steady flow of payroll taxes. The government has statutory authority to specify the characteristics of the sick funds. However, in Canada the wording of national and provincial laws gives the provincial governments great power to control and reorganize the carriers. Nearly all money comes from general budgetary appropriations, from both Ottawa and the provincial governments, thereby giving government more leverage in Canada than in other Western countries. Some provinces made one or several private carriers the administrator(s) of the program, often with extensive revisions that made them virtually public agencies. In other provinces, either at the start or after a period using private carriers, the province created a government department to administer health insurance. Usually it is called a "Commission" or a "Plan" and it ties into the government structure in various ways: in most provinces, it reports to the Ministry of Health (or Social Affairs) and also submits to financial and budgetary review by the economic and fiscal department; the degree of administrative control by the provincial Ministries of Health varies, so that some Commissions appear quite autonomous in practice. Policy decisions about health insurance, however, are made either in the responsible Ministry or in the Cabinet on recommendation of a Ministry. Usually medical insurance and the older hospitalization insurance are administered by different agencies, thereby producing some organizational problems.[3]

Medicare was originally intended to be a form of health insurance and it is still called "insurance." But it has evolved into a system that may not be insurance at all: Unlike the European programs, it lacks carriers with fixed funds, it is supported in most provinces by general revenue rather than by premiums and payroll taxes, and every citizen is covered. It is not a national health service either, since the doctors and hospitals remain independent. Instead, Canada has a system of public purchase of medical services. (In keeping with Canadian custom, I will call the system "insurance," but clearly it differs.)

In 1977, the national and provincial governments negotiated new administrative and financial arrangements. The provinces will have greater responsibility for medical and hospitalization insurance. Instead of the large conditional grants of earlier years, Ottawa will give the provinces smaller block grants—i.e., money for general purposes but with no detailed conditions. The provinces will pay for their own programs by means of their original taxing powers plus larger shares of the country's personal and corporate income taxes. The provincial programs may now become far more heterogeneous in administration and in standards.[4]

THE MEDICAL PROFESSION

The provincial divisions of the Canadian Medical Association fostered the plans inTCMP and wrote the fee schedules. They still represent the doctors in the insurance programs in all provinces except Quebec, but bargaining has replaced the earlier domination. The provincial medical associations resemble those in the United States in all their other functions and organizational characteristics: they have annual (or occasionally more frequent) plenary meetings; they have democratically elected leaderships and permanent secretariats; they publish professional journals and other papers; their meetings discuss scientific and professional matters; they conduct refresher courses; and so on. They have one task and machinery that is absent among their American counterparts; viz., one or more committees of members with staff employees who specialize in health insurance, update the fee schedule, and bargain with the sick fund. This office and an often large staff are located in each provincial capital.

The Canadian Medical Association is a federation of ten provincial divisions. It continues many functions it exercised under TCMP: helping the provincial associations exchange information, representing the entire national profession in dealing with the national government over legislation and financial policy, and speaking for Canadian doctors in the mass media. It also holds meetings, publishes a journal, and fosters clinical as well as professional developments. It may expand its research capabilities during the coming years in order to strengthen its voice in health policy and help the provincial negotiators. CMA and its provincial divisions have enrolled about 26,000 of the 31,000 Canadian doctors who are eligible. It has an annual meeting of all members; a 210-member elected General Council that governs; a 21-member Board of Directors that implements decisions of the General Council; special committees; and a secretariat located in Ottawa.[5]

The multipurpose professional associations represent the doctors in all provinces except Quebec. During the 1960s the Quebec provincial division of the Canadian Medical Association seemed ineffective: it appealed to the English-speaking doctors, but most were French-speaking; it was oriented toward the specialists, but the many general practitioners, the majority of the membership, were having economic problems. The only other important organ with wide membership in Quebec was the College of Physicians and Surgeons, but it was a governmental disciplinary body, inappropriate for fighting pecuniary battles. The doctors organized two medical trade unions on the French model, the *Fédération des médecins spécialistes du Québec* (FMSQ) and the *Fédération des médecins omnipraticiens du Québec* (FMOQ). All doctors participating in health insurance are represented by the federations and their dues are checked off from their payments under health insurance.

THE NEGOTIATING SYSTEM

Other countries with national health insurance usually have a general contract between doctors and sick funds and a hierarchy of other agreements. They require a standing consultative machinery to create, amend, and interpret the general contract and to work out the short-term agreements. These standing commissions meet regularly or on call.

Much less is negotiated in English-speaking Canada. Many of the principles and details concerning the roles of doctors in health insurance are stated in these contracts abroad but are included in the statutes and regulations of the provincial government in Canada. Therefore, the medical association can influence them only by appealing to the health Ministry or Cabinet of the provincial government, not by bargaining with the provincial insurance plans.

In long-established national health insurance systems in Europe, the official fee schedules almost always began as guides written by the medical associations for the instruction of their own members. When private health insurance spread, the medical associations encouraged members to follow these charges, so patients' care would be paid for predictably, either in full or with minimum cost sharing. Eventually these became official and binding, and they became important parts of the negotiating agenda in the standing committees of doctors and sick funds. The funds may defer to the medical association's expertise, but there is no doubt that the sick funds have full rights of coauthorship.

Canada is well along in this evolution, with considerable variations among provinces and visible movement in each successive round of negotiations. Once fee schedules in all provinces were only the association's informal guidelines to its members. Then they were used to regulate payment in full or in part under TCMP, according to usage in each province. Since TCMP was the doctors' creation, the fee schedule was a form of professional self-government.[6] During the early years of Medicare, the fee schedules continued to be written by special committees of the provincial medical associations, and were accepted by the administrations of the health insurance plans as their schedules for paying doctors' bills. The sick funds or insurance plans requested changes by letter, but they did not participate in the committee meetings that wrote and revised the documents.[7] (In Quebec from the beginning of Medicare, the entire fee schedule was written by negotiators from the medical syndicates and the government.)

Negotiating sessions have existed in all provinces from the start of Medicare, if only to settle the amount of money to be paid doctors during the next year or two. In most provinces these are *ad hoc* meetings rather than standing negotiating committees. Where a standing committee exists (as in Ontario) it may discuss other aspects of health insurance. Where the structure of the fee schedule was left to the medical association the negotiators usually discussed only the total amount of money and regulations concerning payments, but not relative values among specialties and acts. This distinction has proved untenable; because it was paying the money, the provincial government needed to negotiate rules, and this required discussion of many items in the fee schedule. In bargaining sessions, more aspects of the fee schedules were discussed. Now, in several provinces, the entire document is negotiated, as in Quebec and in Europe, and movements in this direction are evident everywhere else in Canada. (The provincial medical association may still have its own fee schedule, but in an increasing number of provinces, it is based on the payment schedule agreed upon by negotiators, instead of the earlier pattern, wherein the insurance plan's payment schedule was based on the association's fee schedule.)

Since most provinces lack standing machinery to deal with the entire range of relationships between doctors and health insurance authorities, yet another group must be involved to deal with utilization control and sanctions against doctors who abuse billing. The provinces have many different arrangements: in some, the medical association takes complaints from the insurance authorities and has its own committees; in some, the insurance authorities administer control; in others, special joint machinery is created.

Several Canadian provinces are examples of a probable future worldwide trend to feed back data about the performance of the system into decision making. Negotiators for sick funds and for governments in the world dream of the day when they can detect sudden increases in utilization and incomes and when they can make their payment offers accordingly; doctors wish current knowledge of trends in the costs of practice so net incomes do not drop. All this requires full statistical information and rapid feedback. So far only Canada has had both the complete billing of the population to form the data base and the computing power to process it. Information about utilization and costs is based on the machine-readable data files of bills in each provincial insurance plan. Earnings and practice costs of doctors are calculated from coded and grouped income tax records of Revenue Canada (Taxation). Several statistical offices in the Department of National Health and Welfare supply the tabulations to the provincial governments and to the provincial medical associations, supplementing data of the provincial organizations.[8] If it appears that total health spending has been rising rapidly and/or if doctors' net incomes after practice costs have been growing quickly, the negotiators for the government and sick funds offer no or very low increases in fees.[9]

Ideally, feedback about the state of the system should be immediate. However, negotiators must work with data that is a few (usually two) years late, because many steps must be followed. Before Health and Welfare Canada can supply tables about utilization and costs, the insurance offices throughout each province must keypunch and merge all bills; data tapes must be prepared for each year; and (because Ottawa's tables compare the provinces and generalize about the entire country) nearly all provinces' tabulations and data tapes must be delivered. Before Health and Welfare Canada can supply tables about doctors' incomes, all tax returns for all Canadians must be keypunched and merged for that year. Revenue Canada must complete its higher priority data management and tabulations; and Revenue Canada must run the special tables about doctors. The usual bureaucratic grumbling arises: The negotiators say that Health and Welfare Canada is too slow, while that office points to late deliveries by the provincial plans and by Revenue Canada. In addition, several negotiators for the medical associations suggest an ulterior reason why Health and Welfare Canada does not speed up: The most recent data, they say, would show that doctors' costs are now rising much faster than their incomes. As a result, the Canadian Medical Association will soon institute its own regular national surveys of doctors' costs and incomes, so that it can place more recent figures on the table.

The medical association is experiencing an evolution quite common in federal systems. At one time effective power in making decisions and in negotiating agreements rested exclusively with the provincial association. The CMA's headquarters helped them with ammunition from its staff of researchers and publicists. However, as in other federal systems recently, anti-inflation and incomes policies have been imposed by national governments, and the medical profession tries to respond in a unified way. The CMA has held annual meetings of all the provincial negotiators to share information and negotiating tactics, to guard against the more stringent application of Ottawa's income ceilings in some provinces than in others, and to develop lobbying strategies against the national government's regulations. Negotiations continue to be confined to the provincial level, because no national spokesman exists for all the insurance plans.

NEGOTIATIONS IN ONTARIO

The organization differs a bit from that of other provinces: medical and hospitalization insurance are united instead of divided; they are administered by one agency (the Ontario Health Insurance Plan or OHIP) within the Health Insurance Division of the Ministry of Health. During the first years of Medicare private insurance companies were carriers and they collected premiums from subscribers. The private carriers have since been superseded by the government agency OHIP but premiums are still collected for part of the plan's income. (This results in the lapsing of coverage if someone's premiums are not paid continuously, an anomaly that national health insurance is supposed to eliminate.)

Money

During the 1970s Ontario experienced a general movement to limit the customary monopoly of professions over their own field of work and over their activities, and to involve the general public in their government. The Ontario Medical Association (OMA) created a special study to re-examine itself. The report recommended machinery to fix fees that would no longer be dominated by doctors but would include representatives of the public interest.[10] The report did not picture the new committee as a bilateral bargaining site, of the kind long taken for granted in European national health insurance, and the result differs from that pattern. A European style bargaining committee is legally appropriate when the sick funds are entities other than sovereign government agencies: They can enter into contracts with a private organization (such as a medical association), and they are bound to obey the results of appeals to the courts. A government, however, (such as the Ministries administering health insurance in Ontario) is reluctant to be bound by contracts in this fashion. The solution in Great Britain is compulsory arbitration of the payment disputes between the doctors and a Ministry by a Royal Commission appointed by the Queen.

Ontario's Joint Committee on Physician Compensation was created in late 1973. The membership is:

1. Three representatives from the Ontario Medical Association (OMA). At present, they are two of the OMA's leading physicians and a lawyer who advises OMA on negotiations. Until 1978, the entire team consisted of physicians.

2. Three representatives from the government of Ontario. At present they are the Assistant Deputy Minister for Finance and Administration of the Ministry of Health (i.e., the financial overseer of OHIP); the Assistant Deputy Minister in the Social Policy Secretariat; and the Secretary of the Management Board (which makes budgetary decisions for the entire provincial government).

3. A neutral chairman recommended by the two sides. At present he is Harold Clawson, a former steel executive and a lawyer with long experience in labor negotiations. The committee is customarily called the "Clawson Committee."

The Committee is appointed by the Premier of the Province of Ontario. It reports to the Premier and Cabinet.

Standing bilateral negotiating committees in Europe often have neutral chairmen. Sometimes (as in Holland) their roles are limited, to ensure against partisanship and to foster a calm atmosphere. In other European countries (such as Belgium), the neutral chairman plays a conspicuous and creative role. He does so in Ontario's Joint Committee. He serves for two years and may be reappointed if the OMA and Government agree. He does not vote in the unlikely event of a roll call, but he is an active manager and mediator: he administers and supervises the Committee's affairs, he participates actively in discussions, he commissions research and edits research reports, he can hire consultants of his own choice (their fees are paid by the Government of Ontario), he can mediate between parties, he may organize separate or joint meetings with the parties in whatever manner will promote agreements, and he can make recommendations to the separate sides or to the full committee. The group can organize its own secretariat and can call upon any agency for statistical or administrative support. (At first the Committee had an executive secretary who also taught at the University of Toronto. At present its administrative and statistical work is done by the Data Development and Evaluation Branch of the provincial Ministry of Health.)

The Clawson Committee's principal task is to award higher pay to doctors, at least once every two years. It can comment on the structure of the fee schedule, once the exclusive prerogative of OMA. It can recommend alternative payment systems (other than fee-for-service), whether physician extenders should be used and reimbursed, how to manage new trends in medical technology and productivity, and how to distribute medical services geographically. However, in its short life, the Clawson Committee has focussed on fees and has not yet studied broader policy matters.

One of OMA's organs is a Committee on Economics. It deals with the economic position of the medical profession of Ontario, and particularly whether economic trends in practice costs and other matters are hurting doctors. It drafts recommendations to the Board of Directors of OMA on the need for higher fees. Under Ontario's Health Insurance Act of 1972, OMA must notify the Minister of Health six months before a proposed increase in fees, and the Minister then arranges discussions. This communication now takes place in the Clawson Committee. The Board of Directors of OMA (or its supreme governing council) asks for an overall increase in fees of a certain percentage, such as the 12% requested for 1974 and 1975. The OMA Committee on Economics and its secretariat prepare papers about the movements in the costs of medical practice, the Canadian Consumer Price Index, and the Canadian Index of Average Weekly Wages and Salaries. Most data come from the aforementioned tabulations from Health and Welfare Canada, Revenue Canada, and other public sources, but the OMA secretariat occasionally conducts special sample surveys of Ontario doctors to learn details about practice costs. (A weakness of the reports from Revenue Canada is that practice costs are totals and are not itemized.) The three OMA representatives meet separately from time to time, to be briefed by the Committee on Economics and by the OMA secretariat.

The Ministries and their three representatives on the Clawson Committee confer, look at OHIP data about utilization trends,[11] and study the economic reports from Ottawa. They may offer low or no increase in fees if they believe that doctors' net incomes have remained the same or have risen because of higher utilization or because of the generosity of the last award.

The chairman of the Clawson Committee has power to commission and introduce research reports that are less self-interested. As part of the fight on inflation a new but temporary consideration that must now be included in its decisions is the limits on wage increases in Canada. At the time of this writing in 1977, doctors cannot receive pay increases resulting in an average annual rise in net income for the profession of more than $2400.[12] The Clawson Committee sends the Premier of Ontario a memorandum with its award (stated as a percentage over current fees) and a summary of the economic variables that determined its decision.

Up to now, the Clawson Committee has been able to make each of its decisions within several months, by means of a tireless schedule of meetings. It held over 20 meetings in late 1973 and early 1974. Prolonged deadlocks have occurred in other provinces but the mere existence of a standing committee and the independent power of the chairman probably make stalemates less likely in Ontario. The binding character of the system was demonstrated in 1975. The OMA Board of Directors decided that its negotiators had accepted an award for 1974–1975 that was too low, OMA asked that negotiations be reopened, so the Clawson Committee met again. The government's members on the Committee, however, continued to defend the award as proper, they refused to increase it, and OMA reaffirmed the earlier decision under protest. (OMA's leadership then had to "take the heat" from its aggrieved members.)

A fundamental question in any payment system is whose word is final. At present, the Ontario situation is not clear-cut. The Clawson Committee—and particularly its chairman—has been functioning as an agency of final resort, but formally it is only a mediator. A disappointed party—usually the doctors—has no clearly defined place to appeal except to ask the Clawson Committee to reconsider. After receiving several awards that were lower than the annual rises in general prices, several spokesmen for OMA in 1977 called for creation of an arbitration panel, similar to those common in other sectors of the Ontario government. They approached this idea gingerly, however, for professionals usually do not like to turn their fate over to outsiders.

Allocating the award

Instead of an across the board increase in every fee, the award is distributed differently among specialties. This requires revising the relative values in the fee schedule. During its first years, the Clawson Committee has left this delicate and complicated task to OMA. Both the Association and the government agree on goals: Increases in fees should be distributed so that differentials in incomes among specialties are reduced. (Were they to disagree, the Clawson Committee might take jurisdiction over the fee schedule for the first time.) This work involves considerable negotiation within the medical profession, since the better paid specialties do not like equalization formulae and the lesser paid ones favor more generous ones.

The OMA Committee on Economics—with a large membership from many specialties—conducts this difficult job. It solicits advice from the OMA Sections representing different specialties, some of which have their own Committees on Tariff, and uses several able members of the OMA secretariat. It distributes an award of the Clawson Committee in three parts: increases of the costs in each specialty; an equalization formula, with more money going to the lower paid specialties; and a small flat increase for all specialties.[13] Before the disparity formula is applied and a new fee schedule is printed, to guide OHIP payments during the next year, it is approved by the Council of OMA.

The procedure in 1974 illustrates the disparity formula in action. The Clawson Committee awarded the medical profession an increase of 7.75%. The portion for honorarium after practice costs went up more for the much worse paid specialties and less for the much better paid. Only a few specialties were affected: The average 1973 net income of all full-time specialists was $50,650, and the corrections were applied to fields earning more or less than a 10% deviation (i.e., to specialties averaging less than $45,600 and to those averaging more than $55,700). The differences between the specialty's average and the limit was taken and divided by two, and the deviation from the limit was calculated as a percentage. For example, for orthopedic surgeons in the 1973 data:

$$\frac{\text{(average income)} - \text{(limit of the formula)}}{2} = \frac{\$60,147 - 55,700}{2} = \$2,200$$

$$\frac{\$2,200}{\$60,147} = 2.5\%$$

Then the amount of the average deviation was calculated to bring the average orthopedic surgeon into line with the mainstream of the medical profession:

$$\frac{\text{(total payments to all orthopedic surgeons in 1973)}}{\text{(total number of orthopedic surgeons)}} \times 2.5\%$$

$$= \left(\frac{13,273,644}{205}\right)\left(\frac{2.5}{100}\right) = \$1,619$$

In other words, the average orthopedic surgeon was earning $1,619 more than the average specialist under the fee schedule in 1973. Some specialties earned more, some less, others fell within the range of those not to be changed. The underpaid group's net honoraria in each of its fees went up more than 7.75%, the average group by about 7.75%, and the overpaid groups less, depending on each specialty's distance from the average.

Reducing disparities is a worthy idea but is resisted by the wealthy and powerful specialties. Therefore, the formula in 1974 in Ontario was developed hesitantly: The range defining high and low fields and the halving of the deviation limited the scope. Only five specialties had their fees altered under the formula. Proposals to equalize incomes in other provinces have also encountered protests from the better paid specialties, and reforms have been cautious.[14]

Fee schedule

The clinical content of the fee schedule is written entirely by the Committee on Tariff of OMA. Its thirteen members come from different specialties and from different parts of Ontario. It meets once a month for two (or occasionally one) days. When the interests of a particular specialty are discussed, leaders of that section attend. Occasionally others with a special interest in interpretation of the fee schedule attend, such as the Secretary of the Medical Review Committee of the College of Physicians and Surgeons of Ontario.

The Committee on Tariff has not needed to write a completely new document for several decades, although it might during the coming years. It continually updates the existing fee schedule by adding new acts, revising the wording of old ones, and issuing memoranda explaining usage. The new interpretations are published in the *Ontario Medical Review* and in supplements that are printed in new editions of the fee schedule. Whether a doctor is guilty of abuse in his health insurance billing often revolves around the meaning of particular items; these may be fought over in court, and therefore—much to its regret—the Committee has had to produce a steadily larger and more legalistic documentation.

Because it writes the final fee schedule, it is the Committee on Tariff that must interpret and apply the Economics Committee's formulas for distributing the Clawson Committee's award. It must settle the relative values among specialties and among individual acts. Some battles lost in the Committee on Economics and OMA Council are reopened in the Committee on Tariff, particularly if the victory was narrow. This has increased the Tariff Committee's work lately. Recently the Committee has been rewriting entire sections of the fee schedule in a new vocabulary of relative values, such as the section on laboratory tests. The Committee's work must be approved by the Board of Directors of OHIP. The OMA secretariat writes the new fee schedule, with the new amounts in Canadian dollars.

OHIP never meets with the Committee on Tariff and officially does not participate in the writing of the fee schedule. However, since the staffs of OMA and of OHIP are friendly, drafts of the new schedule are shown, and OHIP's staff has a chance to raise questions and offer suggestions before it is printed. The medical director of OHIP occasionally sends official letters or makes official phone calls, to ask for changes or explanations. The OMA is responsive to OHIP's advice, but nevertheless OMA writes the schedule; it is not yet negotiated, as in Europe, but it will be eventually. The schedule still contains items that OHIP will insist on changing in a negotiated system.

If the medical staff of OHIP deems an act not medically necessary, it may recommend that OHIP not pay for it. The Management Committee of the Ministry of Health must concur; the Ministry's legal branch writes a regulation, and the Regulations Committee of the Cabinet of the Province must then agree. Such an act would stay in the fee schedule, but the doctor must charge the patient privately. (Such exclusions are few: examples are cosmetic surgery and certain forms of psychotherapy.) One task of the Committee on Tariff is to formulate the OMA's case why an act is medically necessary and should be paid by OHIP. As the principal use of the fee schedule is to guide doctors' billing of OHIP, OMA prints it with the OHIP code number for each item. OHIP formally adopts the OMA fee schedule and its supplements for its own payments by an executive order of the Minister of Health.

NEGOTIATIONS IN QUEBEC

Unlike English-speaking Canada, Quebec did not have a big TCMP program. Therefore, it did not have nonprofit funds and a payment method that could be taken over by Medicare. Nor did Quebec have a long history of responsibility by doctors for making health insurance succeed, a willingness to restrain demands upon the budget. The medical profession and the provincial government have had to grope for satisfactory relationships, several conflicts and deadlocks have occurred, and the situation is not yet resolved.

The Insurance Board

Quebec had several commercial and nonprofit health insurance schemes before the mid-1960s. The gaps were substantial and were important reasons for the campaign for public health insurance. A temporary but highly successful measure was the Medical Assistance Plan of 1966 (the *Régime de l'Assistance Médicale*), which provided medical care for persons on welfare assistance. The plan was administered by an agency within the Ministry of Health of the Province of Quebec. (It would be highly instructive for Americans to learn why this counterpart of their Medicaid worked so much better in Quebec.)

When Medicare was organized in Quebec in 1970, the machinery of health insurance was neither the public nonprofit sick fund system of much of continental Europe nor a conventional department of a Ministry. It is administered by the Health Insurance Board (*Régie de l'Assurance-Maladie du Québec*), a public corporation under the Civil Code of Quebec. The board has 14 members appointed by the Lieutenant Governor: two from business; two from labor; one from a consumer organization; four from the health professions (the heads of the syndicates or associations of general practitioners, specialists, pharmacists, and optometrists); one from the hospital association; two from within the government (at present the Assistant Deputy Minister of Finance and an official of the Ministry of Social Affairs); and two of the senior managers of the Board's work. The inclusion of both the doctors and their adversaries might make the governing Board a battleground over doctors' pay, but the organization is limited to administration of health insurance. The Ministry of Social Affairs makes policy for the *Régie,* including all negotiations with the medical profession over pay.

Medical profession

Unlike the English-speaking provinces, Quebec never had a provincial division of CMA with widespread membership. Its CMA affiliate consisted of English-speaking specialists around Montreal. The bulk of the Quebec doctors in organized medicine were identified either with the College of Physicians and Surgeons or with various special associations. No organization was well suited to represent the entire medical profession in economic bargaining with the government and sick funds. The general practitioners (GPs) in particular were left out: they had serious economic problems before being rescued by Medicare; the new hospitalization law was working to their disadvantage by giving more of the inpatient work to specialists; the College and the other associations were dominated by specialists and neglected the GPs. A sore point was a fee schedule recommended by the College for health insurance and private practice during the early 1960s: For the same act, a specialist was paid more than a GP.

A solution was suggested by the half-forgotten Professional Syndicates Act of Quebec, authorizing organizations of a Latin European rather than Anglo-Saxon type: All members of an occupational group can be assigned to a common bargaining agent if they enroll voluntarily, pay an entrance fee or (whether voluntarily or by compulsory taxation) pay dues. Small syndicates of GPs had existed in Montreal and a few other towns before the 1960s and a province-wide *Fédération des médecins omnipraticiens du Québec* (FMOQ) was created in 1962. When the Medical Assistance Plan began in 1966, the Ministry of Health recognized FMOQ as the bargaining agent for all Quebec GPs, and in 1967 the Ministry agreed to a dues checkoff for FMOQ from all payments to GPs by the Plan. Energetic leadership by the FMOQ won over doubters within the profession, and a revolt against such a compulsory syndical system by some GPs gained little support. In order to bargain with equal effectiveness with the Medical Assistance Plan, the specialists—formerly organized as a series of separate licensing and disciplinary groups within the College of Physicians and Surgeons—created the *Fédération des médecins spécialistes du Québec* (FMSQ) in 1965.[15]

A doctor can be exempt by not paying voluntary dues and by not taking patients, under either the old Assistance Plan or under Medicare. Then he has no flow of official payments from which dues can be deducted. In Quebec under Medicare, he formally notifies the *Régie* that he will not participate.

Both FMOQ and FMSQ have governing councils elected by the constituent sections, but their structural organizations differ: since FMOQ is homogeneous, its sections represent doctors from 16 different regions of Quebec and three groups of salaried general practitioners; FMSQ's sections represent the different specialties. A governing board in each federation makes decisions between meetings of the Council. Both federations are led by a full-time President and by large secretariats located in Montreal. Both represent doctors in dealings with the Quebec government beyond health insurance, such as the rights of doctors in hospitals. Both organizations have added professional functions, such as post-graduate education. Because other associations do not exist for GPs, FMOQ in particular has expanded its role beyond economic representation: it discusses health policy and clinical matters at its conventions and study seminars, oversees new trends in education and works with programs in general practice at medical schools; conducts studies of the health needs of Quebec; and publishes Canada's leading French-language journal on professional medical affairs.

When the Medical Assistance Plan began in 1966, FMOQ and FMSQ sat together at the bargaining table. Possibly they might have merged into a Confederation, as in France. Collaboration, however, quickly broke down over the specialists' customary expectation of higher status: They wanted two and not one fee schedule, with higher payments to specialists. The price of division was paid in 1970: The GPs found Medicare much to their benefit, indicated they would sign an agreement, and therefore would enable it to begin. The specialists opposed many of its provisions, struck in protest and (in part because Medicare would probably operate with the GPs) ultimately surrendered.[16] Since then, the two federations have negotiated separately with the Ministry of Health (now merged into the Ministry of Social Affairs). Since they realize, though, that divisions can result in expensive victories by the government they coordinate informally.

Unlike Ontario, Quebec lacks a supra-Ministerial commission with an independent chairman, whch can conduct negotiations between government and a professional association and which can propose a settlement in case of deadlock. Instead, the Ministry faces the doctors and can invoke the sovereignty of government as the last word. If the doctors strike against the absence of further concessions, the government in theory can declare such a strike illegal, can arrest striking doctors, and declare the federations to be illegal conspiracies.[17] The only hope of the doctors is to appeal to the ultimate sovereign—i.e., the support of their position by the electorate, which then installs a new government. Threats often succeed, since voters turn against incumbent governments that cannot avoid major strikes in industry and noisy fights with doctors.[18] Governments often make concessions to the doctors in order to buy peace.

Health insurance in Quebec (as in other parts of Canada) depends on a provincial statute. FMOQ and FMSQ participated in the deliberations of the commission that planned Medicare in Quebec.[19] FMOQ and FMSQ commented on drafts of the statutes and administrative regulations, the provincial government made a few changes (particularly to appease the specialists), but ultimately the Cabinet and provincial legislature can pass what they think best.

Conditions of service

As in Europe, but unlike Ontario, basic negotiations create a convention (an *entente*) between the doctors and the administration of the sick funds. These are written by the cores of the negotiating teams that also settle the fee schedules and the monetary values of the tariffs. The negotiations that created the original *ententes* (for the Medical Assistance Plan in 1966 and for Medicare in 1970) occupied several sessions apiece, and the core negotiators alone attended: for the Ministry of Health, several members from the Division specializing in relations with the doctors and other professionals, a lawyer from an outside consulting firm, and a practicing physician who is a consultant. (In the present Ministry of Social Affairs, the key Division is called the *Direction des professionnels* in the *Direction général des relations professionnelles*. The head of the *Direction des professionnels* is the chief negotiator for the government.) The core negotiators on the *entente* for each medical federation consist of its President, another senior staff member, and consulting attorneys from the federation's law firm. FMSQ adds senior persons from several of its sections. If special topics are discussed, leaders of any sections particularly involved will be added: radiologists, for example, when FMSQ and the Ministry debated their status in proposed amendments to their *entente* during the late 1960s; leaders of the section representing health center doctors when FMOQ and the Ministry struggled at length over their status during 1975 and 1976.

The Ministry met with both medical negotiating teams together in 1966. Since then the Ministry has met separately with each team. The *ententes* are compatible with each other and cover many of the same topics, but their wording and outlines differ. (They can be found in the two *Manuels des professionnels de la santé,* distributed by the *Régie* to all GPs and specialists.) To prevent the Ministry from "dividing and conquering" them, each federation now avoids signing its *entente* until the other has agreed with the Ministry on its own, and therefore both *ententes* run simultaneously. FMSQ and the Ministry did not sign a new *entente* during 1975 and 1976, while FMOQ and the Ministry had a long deadlock over whether FMOQ should be recognized as the collective bargaining agent for all doctors working in the government's new health centers. Deadlocks are common, and new *ententes* may not be signed for years after old ones have expired. Meanwhile, the *Régie* continues to work as if the previous *entente* were still in effect. During the life of an *entente,* the negotiators may agree on amendments during meetings where other matters (such as fees) are on the agenda.

Among the topics in an *entente* are: right of all doctors to participate in insurance practice; methods for not participating, recognition of each federation as the bargaining agent; dues checkoff; types of medical work that are governed by specific agreements between the federation and the Ministry, therapeutic freedom for the doctor; administration of billing, utilization control; payment method; resolution of disputes; and so on. FMOQ's *entente* includes the Ministry's pledge to pay GPs and specialists the same amounts for the same work. (FMOQ would prefer to make this commitment permanent, by adding it to the statute. The Ministry resists making such an expensive obligation irrevocable.)

Before negotiations begin and between sessions, each side discusses its position internally. Within the two federations, the Boards of Directors meet. Within the Ministry of Social Affairs, the negotiators consult with the *Comité du mandat,* consisting of the Deputy Minister responsible for relations with the health professions, the Deputy Minister responsible for relations with hospitals, several lawyers from the *Régie,* the head of the private accounting firm that guides the Ministry's payment strategies, and several other persons, depending on the topic. Occasionally the Minister attends. The *Comité* is concerned with all aspects of health insurance, but particularly with the work of doctors. It drafts regulations and proposed laws dealing with doctors, and it develops the Ministry's negotiating positions. It meets every other week throughout the year, more often during negotiations.

Money

The detailed economic arguments of the Ministry are drafted by the accountants from a private firm that has long worked closely with it. (A partner chaired the Commission that drafted Medicare in Quebec, and he later became Minister of Health.) They are assisted by several statisticians employed by the Ministry, who provide liaison with the *Comité du mandat* and also obtain helpful data from government files, such as the computer output from the *Régie*. The accountants retained by the medical federations and by the Ministry lead the negotiations over money and sometimes meet each other in small sessions. The Ministry faces FMOQ and FMSQ in separate negotiating sessions, but the two federations keep each other informed. In each round of negotiations, each accounting firm prepares lengthy economic memoranda justifying its case. The usual data about doctors' incomes and practice costs come from Revenue Canada; the costs and utilization of services from Health and Welfare Canada, and about living costs and wage movements from other Canadian sources. In addition, both sides get utilization data from the *Régie*. The accountants for FMOQ and FMSQ conduct special investigations of the costs of practice. The position papers by the doctors usually do not itemize trends in costs of individual items in doctors' practices (as do the memos in Holland, for example), but they group costs in general. The sides usually do not exchange their long position papers but sometimes exchange shorter summaries. Each side's verbal arguments are preserved in detailed minutes.

The fees had been set in 1970 so that the average GP would have earned about $48,400 before expenses and the average specialist about $52,300. The Ministry budgeted for a *masse monétaire* consisting of these figures multiplied by the number of practitioners. During the first year the gross earnings were higher ($49,900 for GPs and $59,700 for specialists) because of utilization higher than expected, and they rose further each subsequent year. Earnings after practice costs also exceeded expectations. Therefore, the Ministry refused to grant higher fees after 1973 in response to the doctors' complaints that everyone else had gotten a rise in unit prices after 1970. The deadlock was continuing when the national government's anti-inflation guidelines were announced, limiting the highest income groups in Canada to an annual increase of $2,400. The Ministry debated whether even that was too much. Meanwhile, the doctors fumed that they had gone so long without higher fees that the *Régie* had built up a budget surplus that was rightfully theirs.

Fee schedule

Since Quebec's TCMP program was limited, the province never had a widespread fee schedule before the late 1960s. The provincial TCMP program and the private insurance carriers often used the Ontario Medical Association's fee schedule as a guide for reimbursing patients, not for paying doctors directly in full. Quebec's College of Physicians and Surgeons proposed a fee schedule of its own during the early 1960s, but the general practitioners protested that it benefitted the specialists at their expense; that issue was a principal reason for the formation of local syndicates and of FMOQ itself. When the Medical Assistance Plan went into effect, it needed a complete fee schedule. By then, FMSQ existed, it was pledged to cooperate with FMOQ, and a Committee on Tariff and the specialty sections within FMSQ drafted a long fee schedule that was acceptable to FMOQ too. The Ministry of Health agreed to pay both GPs and specialists according to the same schedule at the same prices. Later, FMSQ had second thoughts about this arrangement—particularly when Medicare extended health insurance to virtually all ambulatory care—but the Ministry and FMOQ retained it. The long fee schedule continues under Medicare, it is used to pay GPs as well as specialists by direct payment from the *Régie,* and GPs get the same prices for the same acts. The fee schedule (the *cahier des prestations*) is an appendix to each *entente.* Because two *ententes* exist, the fee schedule is printed twice: one for GPs and an almost identical document for specialists. They are printed by the *Régie.*[20]

Some revisions have been made since the start of Medicare in 1970. usually they are discussed between the Ministry and FMSQ, with the specialists' federation keeping the general practitioners fully informed. Some items may be redefined, such as the content of the office visit, under discussion in 1976. New ones may be added. Some may be reduced in value, such as the unexpectedly profitable injections for varicose veins, whose value was cut in 1974. (In making a case that some acts may be overpaid, the Ministry introduces the *Régie's* utilization tables, showing excessive billing.)

In Quebec, as in many other Canadian provinces, reduction of differentials in income among specialties is a policy of both the medical association and of the government. In Ontario, the negotiators agree only on the amount of money and leave to OMA the complicated task of deciding the relative income goals of specialties, producing an equalization formula, and dividing the award across a new fee schedule. In Quebec, all of this is included in the negotiations between the Ministry and FMSQ. Besides debating the size of an increase in fees, they must also agree on the relativities among specialties. Ultimately, the accountants on both sides must write the relative values for the new fee schedule.[21] Because so much had to be negotiated with both the GPs and the specialists about new *ententes* and new fees and because no agreements were signed until all the essentials were settled, the negotiations dragged on for years.

OVERVIEW OF THE CANADIAN NEGOTIATING SYSTEM

Because of Canada's proximity to the United States many Americans have been led to believe that it is the most important model for the United States. Canada has many valuable attributes that Americans can study with profit. However, several important structural aspects differ from those that the United States is likely to adopt in the future.

Canada has nationalized the carriers, while the United States is likely to allow the nonprofit funds—and perhaps the for-profit insurance companies—to play a big role. As a result, Canadian doctors must negotiate with governments, and such a relationship is usually unequal. Government has the final say and sometimes follows austere income policies. In most provinces, the terms of service are defined not by negotiated agreements but by regulations of the government. The example of Canada and several other countries suggests that at times negotiations between doctors and governments are particularly susceptible to deadlock and bitterness.

Because Canadian provincial governments took over the carriers and because payments originate primarily out of general tax revenue, certain other features of Canadian health insurance—outside the scope of this book—also differ from the outcomes that are likely to occur in the United States. For one, budget review and operating payments to hospitals are simpler in Canada, as they are done entirely by provincial Ministries of Health, while in Europe and in the United States (in the future) payments are distributed across several sick funds.

Most federal countries are moving toward greater centralization and standardization, but Canadian health insurance has been moving in the opposite direction. The different financial capacities and priorities of the provinces in bargaining over different benefits and over different levels of fees mitigate against centralization. One of the weaknesses of American Medicaid is Washington's difficulty in overseeing a wide variety of state programs; an American national health insurance is likely to be more uniform. If so, there would have to be some place for negotiation about guidelines between national leaders of the doctors and of the carriers.

In other respects, however, Canada is highly relevant to the United

States. Doctors remain in offices, and—in order to earn their cooperation—governments avoid using official health insurance as a lever to reorganize their practices. They are paid by fee-for-service, the method they prefer and that yields the most detailed records about work. Several provinces have sophisticated methods of data processing and utilization review.

STRONG POINTS IN THE CANADIAN NEGOTIATING SYSTEM

Each chapter in this book concludes with summaries of the strengths and defects in each country's bargaining setup, as lessons for what might be emulated or avoided in the United States. These summaries will be brief, and the final chapter will contain a longer statement about possible negotiating arrangements for national health insurance in the United States. The summaries present a few highlights and are not exhaustive lists of all the advantages and problems within each country.

The decentralization of the Canadian system produces a patchwork of provincial programs rather than a single national insurance scheme, but it also offers some advantages in negotiation methods. Local issues can be settled according to bargaining procedures that have been customary in that province. A deadlock in one province can be settled there and need not involve everyone in the country. If a federal system like Canada's needs to settle nationwide guidelines in health insurance as well as issues within each province, national bargaining on those issues might be conducted between CMA and the Ottawa government, as well as continuing the present provincial negotiations.

Canada's negotiation system has certain advantages lacked by other countries. In health insurance in many nations, the medical profession is frustrated because it meets representatives of the sick funds but not the *éminences grises* in the Ministries. By nationalizing the carriers, Canada resolves the ambiguity: The government makes policies and is overtly the adversary in negotiations. However, this creates a new dilemma that Canada shares with other countries with national health services: Can a group of citizens (like doctors) ever bargain freely with the sovereign, or does the latter unfairly have the last word? Likewise, is a democratic sovereign so preoccupied with avoiding social disorder and buying off the elites (such as doctors) that it is a weak adversary and will surrender too easily? The Clawson Committee in Ontario is one excellent solution in lieu of arbitration: It is a standing negotiating committee, headed by a skilled mediator with an independent reputation, and its members follow customs of courtesy and cooperation.

Compared to the sometime tempestuous situation in Europe, Canadian bargaining is businesslike and productive. Several European countries are handicapped by a lack of facts; but the Canadian bargainers are well supplied, although the information may not be as current as they would like. Data on utilization, price trends, and incomes are fed back into the negotiations from efficient computing systems that cover all the transactions in a province, in a style that can be emulated by other countries in the future.

Like other countries in the negotiation of medical pay, Canada has the custom of extending the old contract if it has expired, but if negotiations have not yet yielded a new one. Therefore, unlike the situation in industrial relations, the medical profession does not automatically strike and the province does not face a crisis when the old contract ends. This should eliminate from the health services the extreme pressure and haste that often characterize the rest of industrial relations in North America; but habit is so ingrained that the negotiators for Canadian Ministries and medical associations often have all-night bargaining sessions when they are close to a settlement. The health care negotiators in other countries conduct such marathons less often.

PROBLEMS IN THE CANADIAN NEGOTIATING SYSTEM

The Canadian negotiating system has several organizational problems. Some eventually are corrected. For example, a few years ago the provincial governments and the carriers were unable to review and influence the content of the fee schedules. They are now, however, becoming part of the agenda for negotiations.

A few problems seem to be increasing. Each province is developing its own fee schedule, making it increasingly difficult to calculate comparable data for medical care throughout the entire country. Provincial negotiators are free to rewrite the fee schedule at times, thus ruining the calculation of the time series.

A few provinces may have special difficulties, but the decentralized structure of the negotiations means that these problems are not likely to spread widely. For example, Quebec seems to have a problem in its negotiating system that will remain peculiar to Quebec—and, also to France, which was the model for its negotiation system. In Quebec, as in France, all the conditions for service during a forthcoming period are spelled out in an *entente*. No *entente* can be signed until all issues are settled. One remaining issue can delay the entire *entente,* even for years. Thus an intransigent group insisting on one clause has a potent veto over new arrangements for everyone else until it gets what it wants.

Splits within the medical profession are troublesome in some countries, where two trade unions compete to represent the same doctors. As later chapters will report, such rivalries work to the advantage of the sick funds in France and to their disadvantage in Belgium. However, the division in Quebec is between two different groups, the specialists and GPs. When Medicare was being launched, the rivalry worked to the disadvantage of the specialists, just as a "separate peace" between the British government and the specialists enabled the National Health Service to begin there. Generally, however, the FMOQ and FMSQ have cooperated, the Quebec government has avoided playing one off against the other, and the potential for instability has been avoided.

NOTES

1. On the history of the doctor-approved plans and their organization on the eve of Medicare, see C. Howard Shillington, *The Road to Medicare in Canada* (Toronto: Del Graphics Publishing Department, 1972); and Malcolm Taylor, *The Administration of Health Insurance in Canada* (Toronto: Oxford University Press, 1956). On relations with the medical profession, see Shillington, especially Chs. 5, 10, 14, and 18.

2. Descriptions of Medicare appear in *Questions and Answers—The Federal Medical Care Program* (Ottawa: Health Insurance Directorate, Health Programs Branch, Department of National Health and Welfare, 1974); *Government Controls on the Health Care System: The Canadian Experience* (Washington: Lewin and Associates, 1976); and Robin F. Badgley et al., *The Canadian Experience with Universal Health Insurance* (Toronto: Department of Behavioral Science, University of Toronto, 1975; distributed by the National Technical Information Service, Springfield, Virginia). The legislative history and early implementation are described in Malcolm G. Taylor, *Health Insurance and Public Policy* (Montreal: McGill University Press, 1978).

3. The melange of different arrangements is described in the report by Lewin and Associates, *Government Controls on the Health Care System* (note 2, supra).

4. The change in financing is described in "The New Federal-Provincial Fiscal Arrangements," *Monthly Review of the Bank of Nova Scotia*, March 1977. The possible consequences are predicted in "Bill C-37 Signals Federal Hands Off Policy in Health Care Delivery," *C.M.A. Journal*, Volume 116, Number 7 (9 April 1977), pp. 809-812.

5. The history of CMA and of other professional institutions appears in H. E. MacDermot, *One Hundred Years of Medicine in Canada* (1867-1967) (Toronto: McClelland and Stewart, 1967); Malcolm G. Taylor, "The Role of the Medical Profession in the Formulation and Execution of Public Policy," *Canadian Journal of Economics and Political Science*, Volume XXVI (February 1960), pp. 108-127; and J. W. Grove, *Organized Medicine in Ontario* (Toronto: Queen's Printer, 1969).

6. The history of fee schedules in Ontario is described in Milan Korcok, "Medical Dollars and Data: Collection Recollections," *C.M.A. Journal*, Volume 112, Number 5 (8 March 1975), pp. 623-624.

7. Full and equal bargaining of fee schedules was so unfamiliar an idea during the early years of Medicare that a group of specialists in health insurance administration recommended that the financial relations between doctors and sick funds "should be discussed and if possible agreed upon, by the provincial medical association and the insuring agencies" but "that within the agreed change in total fees, the allotment of individual changes to fee items and assessment rules should remain the responsibility of the medical association." "Task Force on Price of Medical Care," *Task Force Reports on the Cost of Health Services in Canada* (Ottawa: Department of National Health and Welfare, 1970), Volume 3, pp. 175-176. In other countries by this time, it had long been taken for granted that the content of fee schedules and the monetary level of fees were linked and that both must be negotiated. In 1976, fee schedules created unilaterally by medical associations were made illegal under Canadian antitrust laws.

8. Eventually the figures from all provinces are published by the Department. The most recent editions are *National Health Expenditures in Canada 1960-1973* and *Earnings of Physicians in Canada 1962-1972.*

9. "Price Changes—Physicians' Services" (Ottawa: Medical Economics and Statistics, Health and Welfare Canada, 1975).

10. Edward A. Pickering, *Special Study Regarding the Medical Profession in Ontario* (Toronto: Ontario Medical Association, 1973), pp. 103-111.

11. Eventually some are published by the Ontario Ministry of Health, under the titles *Statistical Report on OHIP Medical Experience* and *OHIP Practitioner Care Statistics*. Numbers of individual acts in the fee schedule are listed in voluminous computer printout but are not published.

12. *Highlights of the Government of Canada's Anti-Inflation Program* (Ottawa: Government of Canada, 1976), p. 8.

13. For a discussion of income differences by a former chairman of the Council on Economics, see D. D. Gellman, "Medicare, Medical Income Disparities and Fee Schedule Changes," *C.M.A. Journal,* Volume 105 (18 September 1971), pp. 651-657. The recent equalization formulae are described in Milan Korcok, "Medical Dollars and Data: Collection, Recollection," *C.M.A. Journal,* Volume 112 (1975), pp. 771-772, 899-902, and 995-996; and report of the Committee on Economics, *Ontario Medical Review,* March 1975, pp. 148-149.

14. See for example, the experience in British Columbia, described in *Government Controls on the Health Care System: The Canadian Experience* (note 2, supra), Volume I, page 2-25. The cautious disparity formula suggested by FMSQ of Quebec appears in *ibid.,* page 2-24.

15. The creation and early work of the medical syndicates are described in Michel Vaillancourt, *Le syndicalisme des médecins du Québec* (Montreal: unpublished thesis for the M.A. in Industrial Relations, University of Montreal, 1966), and Gilles Dussault, *La profession médicale du Québec (1941-1971)* (Quebec City: Institut supérieur des sciences humaines, Université Laval, 1974), esp. Ch. 2.

16. Described in Malcolm G. Taylor, "Quebec Medicare: Policy Formulation in Conflict and Crisis," *Canadian Public Administration,* Volume XV, Number 2 (Summer 1972), pp. 211-250. The specialists' strike failed for other reasons too.

17. As it did, in order to break the specialists' strike in late 1970. *Ibid.,* pp. 239-246. The provincial government had exceptional powers at that moment: both Quebec and Ottawa had been given emergency authority to combat a sudden flurry of urban terrorism.

18. No Canadian politician can forget that the long-lived Socialist government of Saskatchewan that fought the doctors at the start of the first provincial medical care plan was defeated at the next election. Shortly after the national strike of doctors in Belgium, the national Cabinet collapsed. Declines in its popular vote in the 1961 and 1965 *Bundestag* elections were important reasons why the Adenauer Cabinet abandoned its bill to amend German health insurance and why it gave the doctors what they wanted. Events in Saskatchewan are described in Robin F. Badgley and Samuel Wolfe, *Doctors' Strike: Medical Care Conflict in Saskatchewan* (Toronto: Macmillan of Canada, 1967). Events in Belgium and Germany are described in Chapters IV and VI of this book, *infra.*

19. Report of the Commission of Inquiry on Health and Social Welfare (the Castonguay-Nepveu Commission), *Health Insurance* (Quebec: Official Publisher, 1967 and 1970).

20. The history of fee schedules in Quebec is summarized in Raymond Robillard, *Medicare, The M.D.'s and You!* (Montreal: privately printed but circulated by FMSQ, 1970). Besides having to publish two fee schedules, the *Régie* has the additional expense of printing each in two languages.

21. During the negotiations, of course, each side suggested equalization formulae. One by FMSQ appears in *Government Controls on the Health Care System: The Canadian Experience* (note 2, supra), Volume I, page 2-24.

CHAPTER III

France

THE SICK FUNDS

HEALTH insurance carriers have existed for many years in France and have been reorganized several times. In most countries, existing private for-profit or cooperative sick funds are made the carriers for national health insurance. The many cooperative funds (the *sociétés mutualistes*) played this role during the first decades of national health insurance in France. However, after World War II, a few semiofficial funds (*caisses*) were specially created. The *mutuels* survive, providing additional benefits not covered by the official scheme.[1]

In short, nearly all French citizens—whether employed or retired—are covered under national health insurance. Most are governed by a "general regime" for employees (*travailleurs salariés*). Farmers and self-employed persons are covered by two other regimes. The three are becoming nearly identical in benefits and in administration and will unite during the coming years. Each regime is a hierarchy consisting of a single national office (a *caisse nationale*), a set of regional coordinating offices, and many local offices (*caisse primaire*). The *caisses primaires* handle all grassroots administration, such as enrolling individuals, keeping their records, and paying benefits.

Since France has a cash benefits system—i.e., the patient pays the doctor and recovers most of the fee from the sick fund—the *caisses primaires* do not deal with physicians directly. It is the three national offices that

34

negotiate with the medical profession: the *Caisse nationale de l'assurance maladie des travailleurs salariés* (CNAMTS), the *Caisse centrale de secours mutuels agricoles* (CCSMA), and the *Caisse nationale d'assurance maladie et maternité des travailleurs non salariés des professions non agricoles* (CANAM, also colloquially called the "non-non").

For several decades, the sick funds were ruled by their subscribers. The governing bodies were elected and then they picked the officials. Because most subscribers were workers, the political parties affiliated with the Left and with the trade unions won large majorities.[2] In 1967, the De Gaulle Government tried to replace the spirit of class conflict that had long surrounded social security with a new style of social partnership. The governing board would no longer be elected but would consist of equal numbers of representatives from the rival social forces, viz., nine from the trade unions and nine from the employers' association. In addition, the governing council includes two representatives from other social insurance bodies, two from dental and pharmaceutical commissions, and two from government ministries. Once dominated by the trade unions the *caisses* may now be more responsive to the employers, since their representatives are more unified: All come from the *Conseil national du patronat français,* while the nine workers' spokesmen come from five different (and somewhat rival) labor federations.[3]

In the past the negotiating position of the sick funds was complicated by the need to coordinate many different organizations. The French situation has become steadily simpler: Now the general regime is so large that CNAMTS effectively sets the negotiating strategy for all three. After the three regimes are merged, coordination will no longer be necessary. (Before 1968, when the sick funds were more numerous and no one fund dominated the scene, the task of developing a position and bargaining with the doctors was performed by a special coordinating office, the *Fédération Nationale des Organismes de Sécurité sociale* (FNOSS).)

The new system for producing a common policy about social security and a common bargaining position has proceeded hesitantly, in large part because the employers have not yet formulated positions about medical care. Usually it is the trade unions and the Left that have thought extensively about health insurance. Before its enactment, employers usually are opposed to health insurance; often they are allied with the medical association. After enactment of national health insurance, employers usually take a narrow view, concerned primarily that costs will not go too high and the social security taxes will not burden them excessively. It is rare that the employer class in any country develops comprehensive and positive policy about medical care. Although its role in CNAMTS requires it to think more broadly, the association of French employers has yet to go much beyond a limited concern with costs.[4] Perhaps in the future, CNAMTS negotiators will face the doctors with mandates for creative actions, but this has not happened yet.

If they could decide how to use their power, the representatives of the employers' association could easily dominate CNAMTS and the sick funds' side in the negotiations with the doctors. Within CNAMTS, the representatives of the workers are divided among several rival unions, and some vote with the employers occasionally. The employers can look for support to a government that has been ruled by conservatives for several decades.

THE MEDICAL PROFESSION

Many medical societies exist for scientific and professional matters.[5] Medical trade unions or "syndicates" originated in the 1880s. When national health insurance was enacted in 1928, they formed a national association (*Confédération des Syndicats Médicaux Français*) to campaign publicly against adverse legislative developments in health insurance and also to lead the bargaining with the sick funds over fees and conditions of service. A member belongs to a syndicate for his occupational category —i.e., one for either GPs, twenty-two specialties, or a category of employment. In addition, all the members in a region are classified as belonging to a regional division of the *Confédération*.

The governing bodies of the *Confédération* consist of representatives elected from the regional divisions and from the syndicates. The larger divisions have more representatives than the smaller. The general assembly (*Assemblée générale*) deals with the overall policies of the *Confédération* and directs the council. Its several hundred members meet at least once a year. The council (*Conseil d'administration*) governs the association between meetings of the assembly and discusses all policies in detail. Its several dozen members meet at least four times a year. A secretariat of over 30 members performs the work of the *Confédération*, with headquarters in Paris. It is headed by a president, six vice-presidents, a treasurer, and a deputy treasurer. The president is full-time, chairs the council meetings, leads all negotiating teams, and is the most prominent spokesman for French medicine in health policy.[6]

As long as the *Confédération* was militant toward the government and sick funds, it was united. However, during the 1960s, it was forced to accept price ceilings on fees and to compromise with the sick funds in other ways. Devotees of unfettered private office practice in Paris, Lyons, and along the Riviera first protested and then took their syndicates out of the *Confédération*. They formed the rival *Fédération des Médecins de France*. Accurate figures are kept secret—each side claims a large membership to strengthen its relations with the rival medical group and with the sick funds—but the *Confédération's* constituent syndicates may enroll 60% of all French doctors, while the *Fédération* may represent 15%. (The remaining doctors belong to neither.)[7] While the *Fédération* is numerically small, its importance is great because of the location of its membership (concentrated in Paris and Lyons) and because its conservative views are shared by the *Ordre National des Médecins,* the compulsory and official agency that defines and enforces medical ethics.

Besides the problems of harmonizing the actions of several rival spokesmen for providers, each organization has tasks of internal coordination. These are greatest for a large and heterogeneous association, such as the *Confédération.* A fundamental rivalry exists between general practitioners and specialists in every country. The *Confédération* must work out agreements on a common set of demands that both GPs and specialists will support before meeting with the sick funds. A recurrent issue is whether the fees of GPs and specialists should rise at the same rate, or whether the GPs fees should rise more quickly, thereby narrowing the large difference in their incomes. The question arises every year between representatives of the GPs and specialists within the *Confédération's* governing council, on the eve of the annual request for higher fees. The council includes more representatives of GPs than it had twenty years ago, and the monetary differentials between GPs and specialists have narrowed.

AGREEMENTS AND OTHER DOCUMENTS

Each step in the negotiations produces a considerable quantity of paper. The parties may have had to compromise conflicting positions in their home organizations, so their position papers inform their constituents and stabilize their own negotiating positions as well as inform their adversaries. In order to maintain a calm and factual atmosphere and to record tentative agreements, mimeographed minutes are kept for many meetings. Final agreements often are preceded by successive drafts annotated with comments by the parties.

Engagement national

This statement is the Cabinet's philosophy of medicine, setting the keynote for the revision of social security laws and for the next convention. Because of the class conflict that has surrounded French social security and because of the perennial distrust and hostility by the doctors, such statements are issued periodically, particularly when major changes are pending. The *engagement* of 1971 was designed to reassure the doctors and promised that: the government will not interfere with private practice fee-for-service direct payment by patient to the doctor; doctors who agree to the rules and to the fee schedules will obtain pension and tax benefits; the government and medical profession will collaborate in helping groups, in strengthening general practice, in improving the geographical distribution of medical services; and so on.

Code de la Sécurité sociale

The social security laws are enacted by the National Assembly and the Senate and are signed by the President of the Republic. The statute prescribes how the convention shall be negotiated and made official. As concessions to ensure its cooperation, the law affirms several articles of faith of the medical profession, viz., rights of individual private practice, free choice of patient by the doctor, professional secrecy, direct payment by the patient to the doctor, right of the doctor not to participate in national health insurance, and so on. A few duties of doctors are included, such as the obligation to avoid waste and abuses. The law prescribes disciplinary procedures against doctors charged with abuses.

Common declaration of intentions

The negotiations for a new convention often are preceded by passionate statements by the medical syndicates and by political figures of the Left. CNAMTS may reveal an initial negotiating position which—while it lacks rhetoric—is full of proposals that are anathema to the doctors, such as the wider use of health centers and of third-party payment. To reduce the temperature of the negotiations and demonstrate that a new convention can ultimately be written, the two sides sometimes issue a progress report with tentative agreements. Negotiations are less likely to be upset by a reopening of matters after they have been settled in the declaration. Such a joint statement was issued during the turbulent discussions of 1975.

Convention nationale

The agreement of 1971—which lasted until 1975—began with statements of principles by both sides individually and jointly: the free practice of medicine by doctors, free choice of doctor by the patient, freedom of prescribing by the doctor, the direct payment of the doctor by the patient, fee-for-service, and the need for fiscal economy.

The convention of 1971 then listed many specific rules about: rights of any doctor to practice under or withdraw from health insurance; how to fill out bills, many rules about acts that may or may not be billed separately, procedures for developing profiles of doctors, detecting overutilization, and exercising control over this and other abuses; how to determine and revise the fees (the *tarifs conventionnels*); composition and powers of standing committees; the right to charge more than the official *tarifs*; and many other topics.

Nomenclature

This is a detailed list of procedures and their relative values. Some bear the number 15, some are 20, some 80, others up to 250. The numbers are coefficients and not units of money. Negotiating committees fix the coefficients according to the relative time or difficulty of the acts.

Each section of the *Nomenclature* has a "key-letter" or *lettre-clé*. Several are:

C = office visit
C_s = office visit with a qualified specialist
V = daytime home visit
V_s = daytime home visit with a qualified specialist
K = procedure by a surgeon or by another specialist
Z = procedure by a radiologist

Most of the *Nomenclature* has the key-letter K.

Instead of rewriting the *Nomenclature* each year in new prices, the negotiators fix new values (*tarifs*) for the key letters. The new fee for each act is calculated by multiplying its coefficient by the new value of the key letter. For example, if K = 7.20 F., then an act rated K40 is paid 40×7.20 F. = 288 Francs while an act rated K120 is worth 120×7.20 F. = 864 F.[8]

FORMAL STRUCTURE OF THE NEGOTIATING SYSTEM

Since World War II, the relationships among sick funds, medical syndicates, and government agencies have been redefined several times.[9] The following is the system since 1970.[10] The basic rules are defined by the social security laws. The present negotiating structure and other ground rules appear in a statute incorporated into the social security code in July 1971, with a further revision on one point in June 1975.

The introduction of this bill in Parliament had been preceded by a

declaration of the government's philosophy about the practice of medicine in France, the health insurance system, and relations between the
government and the medical profession. This *engagement national* was
issued by the entire Cabinet in May 1971.

Writing the convention

Pursuant to the law, bilateral negotiations are held between representatives of the sick funds and of the medical profession. They produce
the national agreement (the *convention nationale*) governing relations
between the sick funds and doctors for the next several years. CNAMTS
once spoke for the other sick funds, but CCSMA and CANAM now participate in the negotiations equally and sign the *convention* too. Only the
Confédération spoke for the doctors during the meetings in 1971, but both
the *Confédération* and the *Fédération* participated in 1975. The *convention nationale* deals with many aspects of doctors' work under national
health insurance and is described on a previous page; by reference, it
incorporates the *Nomenclature*. An appendix to the *convention*—updated
by the same negotiators at least once a year—is the list of prices in francs
fixed to the relative values scale (the *tarifs conventionnels*).

France lacks a standing negotiating committee for the *conventions*. (It
has one for the *Nomenclature*.) The negotiators for the sick funds and
medical associations do not have any fixed membership. In practice, because of the importance of the *conventions* and the frequently explosive
atmosphere, each side sends its leading officials. For example, CNAMTS
is usually represented by its director, its chief medical officer, and the two
members of the department of the national secretariat specializing in
relations with the medical profession. They formulate the policy of
CNAMTS about the next *convention* in consultation with the *Direction de
la sécurité sociale* within one of the Ministries (Labor until 1977 and Health
thereafter) and in consultation with the governing board of CNAMTS.
They receive regular reports about utilization and costs of social security
from the *Direction de la sécurité sociale* and from their own statistical
office and therefore they can develop a strategy about any provision of the
convention that might be expensive. The staffs of CNAMTS, CCSMA,
and CANAM coordinate their positions through informal contacts.
CANAM has less money than CNAMTS and must beware lest CNAMTS
make excessively expensive concessions.

The leaders of the *Confédération* develop the medical profession's
proposals for a new *convention*. They inform the annual General Assembly of their intentions, and delegates have the chance to comment and
suggest additional goals. The *Conseil* of the *Confédération* plays a very
involved (and often militant) role during the negotiations; it discusses

the leadership's initial negotiating documents and meets several times during the negotiations, to hear about progress, guide the *Confédération's* leaders, and (at the end) authorize the President to sign the *convention*. Often the *Assemblée Générale* is reconvened to debate the proposed *convention*, because of the document's crucial importance to the medical profession.

The development of the *Confédération's* original positions and its reactions to the progress of negotiations are highly visible. Meetings of the *Assemblée Générale* are open. Many policy documents and minutes of all meetings of the *Assemblée* and *Conseil* are published promptly in the *Confédération's* own journal and in newspapers about medical affairs, in order to keep the public and the medical profession informed. In late 1975, the President of the *Confédération* mailed a summary of his proposed negotiating demands for the forthcoming *convention* to every doctor in France and asked for comments. Therefore, the *Confédération's* public and private positions correspond. Its leaders do not start negotiations with many bombastic demands that they expect to concede away quickly.

The *Confédération's* negotiators are the President, other senior members of the full-time staff at headquarters in Paris, and (occasionally) practicing doctors who are active in the *Conseil*. They are supported by statisticians and other members of their staff.

The *conventions* (and the preparatory declarations of intentions) are long and detailed. Many clauses are worked out by small informal groups. Staff members may draft individual sections together. Large impasses are often resolved by conversations among the leaders, assisted by Paris' greatest contribution to the building of consensus, *haute cuisine*.

Each *convention* lasts four or five years. Usually it includes a clause bidding the parties to begin negotiations for the next one six months before the expiration date. There is no fixed schedule of meetings. Often deadlocks occur, meetings are suspended for a while, and a new *convention* is signed only after the previous one has expired. The President of each of the three sick funds and the President(s) of the medical association(s) sign the *convention*.

When providers have several competing spokesmen, a problem is who shall have power to negotiate and sign a binding agreement. Originally the social security law provided:

The relations between the *Caisses primaires d'assurance maladie* and the doctors are defined by a convention concluded between the [three national *Caisses*] and the most representative national syndical organization(s) of doctors.[11]

In response to a legal challenge by the *Fédération* that it was one of the "most representative" national syndicates but had not been an original negotiator of the convention of 1971, the Council of State in early 1975 declared the convention illegal. There followed a debate over the criteria for representativity and for eligibility to negotiate and sign the next convention. How can decisions be made in a pluralist society: by one organization, or by several; by majority action or by proportional representation? Can a smaller group bind an entire class, if its membership is more dispersed than a larger one? Can any group exercise a veto?[12] Leaders of the *Confédération* said that only it could be considered the "most representative" syndicate, since it had by far the largest and broadest membership. The Cabinet then resolved the problem in the manner most feared by the *Confédération*: The law was amended so that the convention could be negotiated between the sick funds and "one or several of the most representative national syndicates of doctors in the entire country." This might allow the government and the sick funds to pick one major medical syndicate to negotiate a legally binding agreement, while ignoring the others. However, the government must conduct a study of who is "most representative" on the eve of each round of negotiations, using such criteria as total membership, independence, membership dues, experience and age of the syndicate, and professional composition.

The *Confédération's* fears were quickly vindicated. In 1975, the *Fédération* offered to sign a *convention* with the sick funds, when the *Confédération* was still trying to change one clause. The sick funds refused to change the clause, and the *Confédération* signed under protest. In 1976 the *Fédération* agreed with the sick funds' fees, and the *Confédération* refused, throwing the insurance system into a crisis.

The agreement by the negotiating parties does not make the *convention* official. It is only "advice" and not a "decision." Rather, the final step is a decree (*arrêté*) signed by the Ministers of Labor, Health, Finance, and Agriculture. (Labor, because the *Direction de la Sécurité sociale* was long located within it or was closely affiliated with it; Agriculture, because of its special interest in the sick funds for the farmers.) If no *convention* is developed by the negotiators for official enactment, the interministerial *arrêté* can extend the previous one (the usual solution) or can impose a new set of rules.[13]

Writing the fee schedule

The relative value scales of fees (the *Nomenclatures* for several health fields) are written by a standing body, the *Commission permanente de la Nomenclature générale des actes professionnels des médecins, chirurgiens, dentistes, sage-femmes et auxiliaires médicaux*. Its composition is fixed by law and varies on the provider side, according to the profession whose fees are being debated. When doctors' fees are discussed, its composition (in 1977) is:

Organization	Number of representatives
A neutral chairman named by Ministry of Labor	1
Sick funds:	
CNAMTS	4
CCSMA	2
CANAM	2
Medical profession:	
Confédération	5
Fédération	1
Ordre des médecins	1
Haut comité médical	1
Ministries of:	
Labor	3
Health	3
Agriculture	2

Representatives of dentists, nurses, midwives and other groups are also members. If the meeting deals with the *Nomenclatures* of several occupations, all attend. Since the discussions of doctors' work cover technical matters of clinical practice most (but not all) participants are doctors.

The detailed efforts are done in working groups, which report to the full *Commission*. The *Commission's* agenda therefore consists almost entirely of their recommendations.

Work on the *Nomenclature* for doctors need not follow the same cycle as work on the *convention*. At a time when the leaders of the various groups come together to negotiate a convention, they may recommend a new look, and a general revision then may be set in motion, as it was during the early 1970s. The *Commission* then decided to write a completely new *Nomenclature*, classifying acts by parts of the body and not by clinical specialty, incorporating modern clinical ideas, and combining separate small acts into more broadly defined global acts. As it usually happens in the work on fee schedules, much of the impetus came from the medical association's twenty-two specialists' syndicates, the general practitioners' syndicate made many suggestions, the *Confédération's* council backed these ideas, and the council sent members of these groups as the *Confédération's* representatives on the fifteen working parties of the *Commission*. These working groups performed the detailed preparation of the *Nomenclature*. Besides representatives from the *Confédération*, the working groups included representatives from the sick funds and observers from several Ministries. Additional technicians and practicing doctors were invited to attend, if special points could be resolved more easily. For the next two years, the groups and smaller working units met; at busy times, they conferred once or twice a week.

Since issue of the new *Nomenclature,* the *Commission* and the working groups continue to meet. The groups meet whenever the volume of work justifies it, and the full *Commission* assembles about once a month. A working group collects complaints about ambiguities in the definition of certain items or in the wording of the fee schedule's instructions; it learns from the doctors' grapevine or from the sick funds about parts of the fee schedule that seem to be used improperly; it hears that certain acts are undervalued (according to the doctors) or overvalued (according to the sick funds); or it considers inserting new procedures. The representatives from the sick funds are very concerned about the mounting costs of health insurance and therefore resist increasing any relative values; changes in coefficients usually are confined to reductions.

The *Nomenclature* becomes official when it is issued as an *arrêté* over the names of the Ministers of Labor, Agriculture, and Health. Any revisions are also issued as *arrêtés.* The formality is necessary to give it the force of law: It can be invoked as a basis for price controls in the absence of a *convention.* Sometimes the Ministers revise the recommendations of the *Commission,* on the advice of the *Direction Générale de la Sécurité Sociale.*

Negotiating the tarifs

Every autumn, the parties that negotiate the *convention* come together to fix the financial value of the key-letters. During the years when they negotiate a new *convention,* they include pricing the key-letter as part of the agenda. During other years, they take the opportunity to discuss how the *convention* is working out in practice; occasionally they prepare a statement amending or clarifying the *convention.* The key-letters are given values for the next year that begins in January.

The *Confédération* and *Fédération* prepare their cases for more money with the help of their own economists. (The *Confédération* has a department for economic research in its Paris secrétariat.) The two rivals coordinated their recommendations in 1974, lest they undercut each other when confronting the sick funds. (These arrangements broke down in 1976.) As in other negotiating demands, the positions are discussed by the general assemblies of the two associations (if they happen to be in session then) and by their governing councils. The proposed new financial values of the key-letters are then published before the meetings with the sick funds. The requests have been restrained and realistic during the 1970s. The profession has not made excessive demands merely to be in a position of claiming that it was willing to compromise.

To the negotiation meetings, each side brings its statisticians, armed with competing documents about practice costs, living costs, and future economic prospects in the country. Since 1971, the system has included machinery for negotiating sets of economic facts that would lead to annual agreements about the *tarifs*. A *Comité d'Experts Tripartite* consists of economists and statisticians from the sick funds, the medical syndicates, and the Ministries of Health and Finance. The statisticians from the *Direction Générale de la Sécurité Sociale* provide the secretariat. They are supposed to produce joint reports with time series about utilization, time series about total expenditures and estimates of the probable total costs to the sick funds of alternative increases in the fees. Occasionally the group has agreed and forwarded a joint report to the negotiators of the *tarifs*, such as one about dentistry in 1973. At other times it has deadlocked, as in a dispute in 1975 over the size of practice costs and over the profitability of proposed increases.

The negotiators sometimes propose tying the values of key-letters to general economic indicators—as in several small European countries—but they cannot agree about the measures. The sick funds suggest the general consumer price index issued regularly by the official *Institut national de la statistique et des études économiques* (INSEE). But, the *Confédération* believes, the result would be to reduce doctors' real incomes. Practice costs have been going up faster than general prices, they say. They have recommended an index of the costs of medical practice, as a partial basis for calculating changes in the key-letters. The sick funds and the government consider such an arrangement inflationary. However, several statisticians at the sick funds and in INSEE have experimented with various indexes of practice costs, and the negotiators might seriously consider such a device in the future.

Effects of divisions within the medical profession

In the unusual situation with two rival provider associations, several outcomes are possible: they may radicalize each other in the competition for members (as in Belgium); or, one may undercut the other by making deals with the common adversary. Both have occurred in French medical politics, sometimes in bewildering succession.

At first, the *Fédération* acted as the militant spokesmen for private office practice, defenders of freedom of doctors to charge as they liked, and opponents of any power of sick funds over doctors. The *Fédération* refused to participate in negotiation of the 1971 convention and refused to sign it. It criticized the *Confédération* for selling-out the doctors, thereby checking the *Confédération's* trend toward less militant language and toward greater collaboration with the sick funds. The *Fédération* eventually signed the convention, but only to ensure its participation in the meetings to draft the next one. Meanwhile, the *Confédération* became far more militant in demands for higher fees, in resisting introduction of a system to control utilization that it had once cosponsored, in defending doctors who were charging patients above price ceilings, and in other matters.

For the *Fédération,* the *Confédération* was as much the adversary as were the sick funds. This enabled the funds and the government to play one off against the other at times. For example, in early 1975, the *Confédération* rejected *tarifs* proposed by the sick funds and organized a nationwide movement of doctors to charge according to a higher schedule, in technical violation of the law. Suddenly the *Fédération* signed an agreement with the sick funds, the government declared that the funds' *tarifs* were official, and the *Confédération* cancelled its plans in disarray.

In late 1975 and early 1976, the *Confédération* and the sick funds deadlocked over a clause in the proposed *convention* that would have allowed CNAMTS to set up new experiments in health delivery (including health centers and groups) without the medical associations' prior approval. The *Confédération* would have held out until the clause was eliminated or amended. The *Fédération* then agreed to sign the *convention*—including the clause—and it would have gone into effect without the participation of the *Confédération* in its implementation. In order not to be excluded, the *Confédération* signed, but with a dissent against the clause.

The negotiating system finally broke down in 1976. The two medical associations compromised with the sick funds over most values to the keyletters but disagreed with the funds about fees for radiologists and travel allowances. The two medical associations then split over tactics: the *Fédération* was willing to sign an agreement and continue pressing for higher radiology and travel payments; the *Confédération* believed that bargaining with the funds would be effective only if nothing were signed. The issues had different meaning for the two associations: Within the *Confédération* are many radiologists and rural doctors, while the *Fédération's* membership is weighted toward the urban clinical specialties. The *Fédération* signed with the sick funds, and the government issued the decree making the *tarifs* official for 1976 and early 1977. The *Confédération* decided that it could not be forced into surrendering for a third time by the *Fédération's* maneuvers with the sick funds, or else the funds would always be able to divide and conquer. So, the *Confédération* refused to sign, argued that no valid agreement was in effect, and advised doctors to charge patients the fees that it recommended (*tarifs syndicaux*). Confusion followed. Some doctors charged the higher fees for radiology and kilometrage, and several *caisses primaires* threatened to strike them from the lists of physicians authorized to treat patients under national health insurance coverage. The *Confédération* called for continued negotiations over fees, but the sick funds refused, on the grounds that a binding agreement had been signed.

When the new round of negotiations began over fees in the spring of 1977, CNAMTS insisted on meeting only with the *Fédération,* on the grounds that the *Confédération* had not signed the previous agreement. (CCSMA and CANAM would have met with the *Confédération* too, on the grounds that it was unrealistic not to negotiate with the principal representative of the doctors. However, CNAMTS invoked the official wording of the *convention*: Only the signatories to an agreement may participate in negotiating the next one.) The *Confédération* tried to influence negotiations by sending letters to and by holding meetings with the Prime Minister and the Minister of Health.

The *Confédération* might have been upstaged by the *Fédération,* if the latter could have obtained a large award. However, the French government's temporary price and wage controls allowed the sick funds to offer only a small increase in fees. The *Fédération* reluctantly signed and the *Confédération* enjoyed the political advantage of accusing it of a sell-out. Eventually the *Confédération* signed too, on the grounds that the award was an accomplished fact and in order to have a seat at the next round of negotiations, when price and wage controls are no longer in effect.

Since France has been ruled by conservatives, the government and the sick funds have not exploited the rivalry within the medical profession to reorganize health care and weaken the doctors. The *Confédération* worries, however, about the fitful increases in government authority as it tries to make health care more organized and more economical. It worries about the future, when the Left may win a national election.

The role of the government

Before 1971, the negotiating system was tripartite and representatives of several Ministries were coequal with the spokesmen for the sick funds and for the medical syndicates.[14] During the 1950s and early 1960s, the government needed to dominate the creation and implementation of decisions, so that doctors agree to price ceilings, so that rules not be evaded, and so that social security be solvent.

The reorganization of social security during the late 1960s and early 1970s was intended to create bilateral relationships between social antagonists turned social partners, with government acting as author of the ground rules, as enforcer of agreements, and as arbitrator of deadlocks.[15] Sick funds and medical syndicates were planned as private parties making private agreements, rather than government agencies performing official actions. In practice, however, government cannot be so inconspicuous in national health insurance, particularly when the sick funds are special creations of government and are not holdovers from the years of private insurance, retaining their staffs, traditions, and corporate personalities.

While CNAMTS and the other sick funds handle day-to-day administration of health insurance, the government (particularly the *Direction de la Sécurité Sociale*) has extensive power to issue regulations and to review operations. The Cabinet is vigilant that the sick funds not make extravagant commitments to providers and not waste money, because the Parliament cannot raise payroll taxes indefinitely, the funds must avoid bankruptcy, and the mandated benefits must continue to flow. The French government is particularly attentive to the workings of social security now, as uneasy feelings spread throughout Europe that open-ended commitments to social benefits will absorb steadily rising proportions of the national income and will unsettle entire economies and national budgets. One of the deep political controversies in France during 1976 was the Cabinet's warning (in the *Plan Barre*) that health insurance must no longer be allowed to cause overruns in costs, lest the sick funds and other social security accounts become bankrupt. The *Plan Barre's* proposal for higher payroll taxes and hints of higher cost-sharing by patients touched off protest strikes by the trade unions: A conservative government was jeopardizing benefits in the program most closely identified with the labor movement. In the end, the government backed down.

The role of government at present varies among different levels in the negotiating system, is ambiguous,[16] and clearly is in flux. Some observers and some officials of the sick funds recommend a completely bilateral system: The Ministries would not participate officially or unofficially except to set statutory ground rules and review the results. The union and employer representatives would have to work out policies and the sick funds officials would negotiate with the doctors, without anyone looking over their shoulder at the Ministries. The medical syndicates would know more clearly with whom they were actually negotiating. On the other hand, some observers—particularly devotees of national health planning and integrated medical services—believe that the sick funds are already too independent and should be supervised more closely. Left alone, they fear, the sick funds will pursue their own policies on remuneration and may construct duplicate facilities.

An indicator of a negotiating system in trouble is the involvement of the Prime Minister. Usually the French arrangements have worked well enough so that the medical associations never needed formal and extended meetings with the Prime Minister to complain to and to learn the government's intentions. (Of course, brief informal chats sometimes occurred on social occasions.) By late 1976, the *Confédération* obtained several appointments with the Prime Minister to discuss improvements in collaboration among the medical profession, the government, and the sick funds in many aspects of health insurance and health care, including how to administer negotiations. Not to be left out, the *Fédération* met with the Prime Minister also, but separately from the *Confédération* and with its own views.

While the sick funds prefer enough autonomy so the Ministries will not overrule them, they find advantages in the present situation. Sometimes they make concessions in the bargaining with doctors in order to get agreements, but the government—usually on the recommendation of the *Direction Générale de la Sécurité Sociale*—cancels the concessions when approving the agreement. This occurred in certain revisions of the *Nomenclature* in 1974; the Ministries are more likely to revise an agreement about the *Nomenclature* than the wording of a *convention*, since the *Nomenclature* is a law. Apparently the Ministry of Finance—concerned about restraining inflation and preventing further deficits in the social security accounts—has been an important influence behind the scheduling of pay awards. Instead of allowing the higher values of the key-letters to go into effect on the starting date of the award, as in the past, a new pattern began in 1975 and was repeated in 1976 and 1977: part of the award takes effect early, and the rest midway through the period of the contract.

Local negotiating procedures

Daily grassroots negotiating machinery exists in the form of *Commissions Médico-Sociales Paritaires Départementales*. Large *départements* have several local committees. Each committee includes eight representatives of the sick funds (the *caisses primaires*) and eight representatives of those medical syndicates that signed the *convention*. The committee is supposed to deal with all relations between sick funds and doctors in the *département,* including discipline, studies of utilization, granting special rights to charge higher fees, and settling disputes. In practice, the committees have been tied up judging which doctors may charge more than the normal fees (i.e., granting the *droit permanent à dépassement*).

Because of the doctors' great suspicion of sick funds, it is uncertain when they will allow the local commissions to undertake controversial programs, such as reviewing and sanctioning the work of doctors who submit too many bills.

OVERVIEW OF THE FRENCH NEGOTIATING SYSTEM

National health insurance in France resembles the prospective American situation in several ways. Although Americans believe that their own doctors are so independent that no organized program can ever be devised, France illustrates how an even more fiercely individualistic medical profession came to terms with national health insurance and profited. The program included many features to appease the doctors: fee-for-service was adopted, a cash benefits rather than service benefits method of payment is customary, the government and official sick funds agree not to tamper with solo office practice, and the profession's leaders can charge higher fees.

Worried about the competing tugs from the needs to negotiate with reformers and from the misgivings of militant traditionalists, the embattled national leadership of the American Medical Association can see its fears vindicated in France. Not even the political virtuosi of the *Confédération* were able to avoid the secession of hard-liners, and the medical profession since then has been weakened by competing negotiating strategies.

Certain details of French fee-for-service are worth examining in greater depth by American health planners. Unlike fee-for-service in much of the world, French medical practice has a tradition of considerable time with each patient, and generous rather than low payment per act. In these respects, France resembles the United States. Therefore, France can demonstrate for Americans how generous global fees can work successfully under national health insurance.

Like the United States under future national health insurance, France has retained a flourishing system of nonprofit and commercial sick funds that supplement the official program. The parts fit together successfully. The *mutuels* have been innovative in ways barred to the official sick funds, such as creating medical groups and supplying special services.

Certain features of the French system indicate problems that the United States will likely experience if national health insurance is enacted (like American Medicare) as part of social security. In both countries, the bills of the aged outrun the contributions of workers and employers. Therefore, France confirms the worries of many Americans about the feasibility of enacting national health insurance as just another part of the tax and social security laws.

In some respects, of course, France's program differs from the program that the United States is likely to adopt. The nonprofit and commercial carriers were replaced by government agencies causing French government Ministries to play a large—if ambiguous—role in negotiations.

French national health insurance is centralized in Paris and is uniform throughout the country, without the federal structure that is likely to be adopted in some fashion in the United States.

STRONG POINTS IN THE FRENCH SYSTEM

The *Confédération* circulates its negotiating position widely within the medical profession and solicits opinions. It can gain new ideas. It is clear to all sides in the negotiations that the *Confédération's* position enjoys widespread support. The leadership is strong enough to be able to adapt the bargaining position in action, but the prior circulation is a check against opportunism. A disadvantage might be limitations on the field of maneuver.

The "common declaration of intentions" is a good way to show that negotiations are progressing and that a complete agreement is eventually possible. Once settled, old issues won't be reopened. Few countries have anything like such binding progress reports, and an entire package of tentative agreements can burst apart because of a few unsettled ones.

The *Nomenclature and* key-letter systems are easy to understand, both by negotiators and by the practicing doctors.

SOME PROBLEMS IN THE FRENCH SYSTEM

Excessive deadlocks

Two issues in bargaining in the medical services are whether negotiations (and the resulting agreements) should be centralized or decentralized, binding on everyone or voluntary. Before 1971, the national negotiators wrote general guidelines that had to be implemented locally. Sick funds and medical syndicates in the *départements* negotiated further, whether to adhere to the national guidelines and whether to add special local arrangements. If the leadership of a medical syndicate in a *département* could not agree and adhere to the national guidelines, doctors could do so as individuals. The doctors who did not practice under social security were those in *départements* with agreements but who had opted out individually, and those in *départements* without agreements who had not joined individually. This system produced more diversity and administrative duplication than is customary in France, which is one of the world's most centralized countries. The scope for individual adherence to a national agreement over the opposition of local syndicate leaders deviated from French syndical traditions. As more doctors in *départements* without agreements between sick funds and medical syndicates adhered individually, the old system seemed unnecessary as a means for protecting their individual rights.

The new system in 1971 attempted to create a centralized government for health insurance. The sick funds and medical syndicates would negotiate a single national agreement for the entire country. (Local variations could be enacted and implemented by committees of medical syndicates and sick funds.) Every doctor in the country would be bound in his treatment and charging of insured patients, unless he formally opted out. Only

4% of France's doctors now refuse to stay in; hospital-affiliated specialists who stayed out during the years of individual adherences are now appeased by formal recognition of their right to charge in excess of the official *tarifs*. The new system at first pleased the sick funds, because the entire country is covered by a single agreement and by standardized procedures. The new system pleased the *Confédération,* who spoke for the entire French medical profession and could sign agreements binding it.

The new centralized system fosters more confrontation and deadlocks than the previous one. Everything depends on the national agreement. Therefore the more intransigent and conservative groups anywhere in the country combat provisions that might be acceptable elsewhere. The *Confédération* leadership must play a double game, exhibiting great militancy in public to convince local intransigents that it is fighting for them on their pet issues, while also trying to work out realistic agreements with the sick funds privately. Experiments and unconventional innovations in health insurance practice are possible, but only if the two sides agree and supervise them at the highest national levels, and only if the ideas can withstand initial barrages of publicity and criticism.

Struggles among the medical trade unions

A serious problem is the split between medical syndicates and their competition for followers and for power. Some observers might think that competition keeps the leaders on their toes, and makes them more responsive to the medical profession. They may, however, compete in demagogy and in forcing higher costs upon health insurance. Their antagonistic tactics during the negotiations produce much uncertainty. Allowing a small association like the *Fédération* to put into effect a contract binding on the entire profession may be a triumph of legalism over the spirit of true negotiation.

Scarcity of information

The negotiators must make crucial economic decisions with less data in France than in most other countries with national health insurance. The sick funds know the total expenditures by broad categories, but little more. The government and negotiators have little accurate data about doctors' total incomes and costs of practice.[17]

The sick funds do not even know the total numbers of acts of each type, to judge whether certain items in the *Nomenclature* are being overused and therefore should be revised. The reason is the French tradition of medical secrecy that is so strong that diagnoses and treatments are not entered on the bills going to sick funds. Rather, the doctor enters the key letter. Since the fees for K vary by the size of act the doctor also enters the numerical coefficient. In late 1976, the basic value of K was 7.20 Francs; as unilateral lymphography (for example) was valued K30, the physician entered "K30" on the bill, he collected 30 × 7.20 F. = 216 F. from the patient, and the patient collected 75% × 216 F. = 162 F. from the sick fund. The words "lymphographie unilaterale" do not appear on the bill. Meanwhile, the sick funds are receiving millions of other bills, with the cryptic notations C, V, K10, K15, K30, K40, etc. No one knows which of the K30s refer to unilateral lymphographies. The negotiators can know only the number of acts performed with the value K30, not the number of unilateral lymphographies. In other countries, negotiators can tell whether some acts are being performed excessively and therefore might either be overpaid or unclearly defined in the fee schedule.

Costs

In France, as in several other countries, a grave problem is how to integrate negotiations over prices of services with a general strategy for controlling costs. Power bargaining determines the prices of individual key letters. The sick funds try to hold fast on certain items that multiply rapidly, such as the key letter for radiology. However, despite the spectre of bankruptcy of the social security accounts during the 1980s, they have not been able to limit other fees so strictly. They cannot limit utilization to their predictions, so the annual spending for physicians' services always exceeds predictions and hastens the crisis.

During 1977, limits were imposed, but only as part of the government's general economic policy. No public or private wage was allowed to increase more than 6.5% during 1977, and the negotiators for medical fees therefore agreed to increase the values of the key letters by that figure. However, no method of linking fees to medical costs or to utilization trends has been devised that will be more durable than the government's general wage controls.

Only in Canada and Germany have the negotiators linked fees and utilization sufficiently to keep the actual costs close to the expectations at the time of the award. Their methods keep fees in line with other medical costs; then the public authorities turn to the next step of limiting all medical costs together.

NOTES

1. Several books describe the past and present organization of the official sick funds (the *caisses*). For earlier history, see Henry Galant, *Histoire politique de la Sécurité sociale française* (Paris: Librairie Armand Colin, 1955). For cur-

rent organization, see Jacques Doublet, *Sécurité sociale* (Paris: Presses Universitaires de France, Fifth edition, 1972), pp. 328-397, 472-486, etc. passim; and the special issue devoted to the twenty-fifth anniversary of social security, *Revue française des affaires sociales,* Number 2, April-June 1971. The *mutuels* are described in Roger Migraine, *Les sociétés mutualistes en France* (Paris: Fédération Nationale de la Mutualité Française, 1968).

2. Described by Galant, *op. cit.,* note 1, supra.

3. The reorganization (the "Jeanneny Reforms") are described in "La réforme de la sécurité sociale," *Notes et études documentaires,* Number 3452, 5 January 1968. How the changes are working out in practice is being studied by Antoinette Catrice-Lorey, Centre de Recherches en Sciences Sociales du Travail, Université de Paris-Sud.

4. For example, Gérard Badou, "La médecine des patrons," *Le médecin de France,* Number 323, 1973, pp. 20-24.

5. Described briefly in Luc Audouin, *L'installation et l'exercice en médecine libérale* (Paris: Maloine S.A., 1975), pp. 91-97, 254-265, and 269-273.

6. The *Confédération's* first decades are described in Paul Cibrie, *Syndicalisme médical* (Paris: Confédération des Syndicats Médicaux Français, 1954).

7. The *Confédération's* and the *Fédération's* complete activities and policies are reported in their monthly magazines, *Le Médecin de France* and *France Médecine.* The divisions among the syndicates and the roles of the two federations in negotiations over medical pay are described in Claude Lortet, *Le corps médical de la convention médicale départementale de 1960 à la convention nationale de 1971* (Paris: Centre d'Etudes Supérieures de Sécurité Sociale, 1973); and Laurence C. Thorsen, *French Medical Syndicates as Political Pressure Groups* (Urbana-Champaign: dissertation for the Ph.D. in Political Science, University of Illinois, 1970). Current negotiations are reported in detail in the weekly newspaper, *Le concours médical informations.*

8. The *Nomenclature,* the key-letters, and the method of calculating the fees are described in William A. Glaser, *Paying the Doctor* (Baltimore: The Johns Hopkins Press, 1970), pp. 39-43.

9. Described in Glaser, *Paying the Doctor* (note 8, supra), pp. 37-45 passim; Lortet, *op cit.* (note 7, supra), and Thorsen, *op. cit.* (note 7, supra).

10. The procedures and documents resulting from the 1970-1971 negotiations appear in Jean-Jacques Dupeyroux et al., "La convention nationale entre la Sécurité sociale et le corps médical," *Droit social,* September-October 1971, Numbers 9-10; and "Engagement National—Convention Nationale," *Le concours médical,* Volume 93, Number 49 (4 December 1971), Supplement.

11. The key wording was "la ou les organisations syndicales nationales les plus répresentatives de médecins."

12. Jean Mignon, "La convention nationale doit être négociée et signée par toutes les organisations nationales les plus représentatives," *Le concours médical,* Volume 97, Number 23 (7 June 1975), pp. 3973-3975.

13. The legal position and force of an accord depend on each country's system of law and the precise definition of the accord. Franck Moderne has written much about the juridical status of the *conventions* in France, such as "La nature

juridique des conventions tarifaires nationales passées entre la Caisse Nationale d'Assurance Maladie et les organisations syndicales . . .", *Droit Social,* Number 5 (May 1975), pp. 335-342; and "Les principes généraux de la médecine libérale et le contentieux de la nomenclature des actes professionnels des professions médicales et paramédicales," *Droit Social,* Number 2 (February 1975), pp. 89-95.

14. Described in part in Glaser, *Paying the Doctor* (note 8, supra), pp. 37-38.

15. Legal aspects of relations between social security funds and the government are described in Doublet, *Sécurité sociale* (note 1, supra), pp. 376-395.

16. During the negotiations for a new convention under the new system in 1971, the Ministries sent observers rather than participants. The sick funds and medical syndicate did all the talking. "Un personnage muet: le gouvernement," *Le médecin de France,* Number 297, March 1971, p. 6. Later in 1971, the Minister of Health and Social Affairs volunteered as a neutral mediator, to bring the two sides together and settle the final outstanding issues. The *Confédération* later grumbled that the Minister was not really a neutral because of the nature of the French system: he must have been in touch with the Ministry's observers at the negotiations; he had been kept informed throughout; and he was biased toward the sick funds.

17. The government has begun to commission special studies to produce such data, such as Philippe Madinier et al., *Les revenus des médicins libéraux conventionnés 1971-1976* (Paris: Centre d'Étude des Revenus et des Coûts, 1977).

CHAPTER IV

Belgium

BELGIUM has a statutory national health insurance that, more than other European countries, resembles the probable situation that will develop in the United States during the coming years. The existing private sick funds have become carriers under the official program and have become quite powerful. The medical profession is fiercely independent, resists all restrictions upon the autonomy of the clinician, and is very militant. There is no single structure in the provision of health services, either through common ownership or through coordinated planning; therefore hospitals, office doctors, and other providers try to do things in their own individual ways. Everyone denounces government as tyrannical, but on close inspection it is weak; the coalition Cabinets are usually so precariously balanced and so preoccupied with survival that they hesitate to legislate over the opposition of powerful interests, such as the sick funds and doctors. Gradually Belgian health insurance may become more standardized and the rules will be observed more faithfully, but only after the constant contention that is a hallmark of Belgian (and American) political culture.

THE SICK FUNDS

As in other Western European countries, social benefits associations (*sociétés mutuelles* or *mutualités*) have existed for centuries. They antedate the independence of Belgium itself. While the government was in the hands of foreigners, the *mutualités* represented the people themselves, and they have always possessed a significance in communal life beyond their mere identity as insurance companies.

Many of the *mutualités* were associated with the local trade unions organized by socialists. Many were associated with the non-Marxist trade unions organized by the Catholic Church. Other *mutualités* were created for white collar workers, craftsmen, and other occupations.

Gradually, *mutualités* of the same persuasion joined together in networks. Each of the 1700 sick funds is small; it can pool its resources for publicity, administration, and bargaining if it joins with others; but the individual sick funds remain distinct. A sick fund joins a federation within one of the nine provinces or within the Brussels metropolitan area. Federations with a similar viewpoint belong to a national association, with headquarters in Brussels. A large association may incorporate several federations from a province.

Almost every Belgian citizen is enrolled with a sick fund under the law. Employees and retired employees were covered by the basic law of 1945. The self-employed and retired self-employed were added in 1963. The employed and such retired persons receive the full range of clinical benefits and disability allowances. The self-employed are covered only for the more expensive risks, giving this group in Belgium the only exclusively catastrophic coverage scheme in any national health insurance program. (In other countries, if someone is covered at all under national health insurance, he is covered for all benefits, and not just for major risks.) As in nearly all other countries, the law levies payroll taxes on both the employee and the employer. The employee sends his money directly to the sick fund, as in private health insurance premiums. Government agencies collect the taxes on employers and eventually route them to each subscriber's sick fund. In addition, the national government subsidizes each sick fund, for administrative and other expenses.[1]

The sick funds and their parent associations are ideological rallying points as well as health financing offices. For example, at a socialist federation's annual meeting, the dais may bear red flags and slogans, the speeches may press for the current political positions of the Socialist Party, and the meeting may end with cries of "Workers of the world, unite!" and with the singing of the "Internationale."[2] The principal associations, their political connections, and their shares of the total membership are:

Name of the association[3]	Political tendency	Proportion of all Belgians
Alliance Nationale de Mutualités Chrétiennes	Social Christian (i.e., Catholic)	47%
Union Nationale des Mutualités Socialistes	Socialist	24
Ligue Nationale des Mutualités Libérales	Liberal	6
Union Nationale des Mutualités Neutres	Nonpartisan	12
Union Nationale des Mutualités Professionnelles	Nonpartisan	9
Caisse Auxiliaire d'Assurance Maladie-Invalidité	Nonpolitical	1
		100%

Each sick fund is small, but all together (and particularly the Christian and Socialist Associations) handle much money, enabling them to hire many administrative employees, erect buildings, and issue publications. The Christians and Socialists build and staff hospitals, ambulatory polyclinics, and rehabilitation centers, a few of them abroad. (Sick funds in most other countries pledge not to build such facilities, as part of the deal buying the cooperation of the doctors.) In some communities, the sick funds are important employers, and everywhere in Belgium they are an important pool of money, not subject to close government control or complete public scrutiny.

The Christian, Socialist and Liberal associations are closely connected to the three principal political parties. Critics grumble that the *mutualités* are the "bankers" of the political parties. The *mutualité* movement as a whole is bipartisan: Regardless of the political complexion of the Cabinet, at least one of its parties is closely associated with at least one of the associations. Often the Minister of Social Affairs—who oversees social security —is an official on leave from a national association of *mutualités*. Several high officials of the *mutualités* sit in the Senate. Therefore, no Cabinet would think of recommending legislation to replace the *mutualités* by an official sick fund (as in France, Canada, or Sweden), to replace national health insurance with a national health service (as in Britain), or to regulate the sick funds very strictly.

A national association usually has a general assembly of several hundred members, meeting once a year. Each individual sick fund sends one or more delegates. Its steering committee meets several times a year to deal with general policy. Usually an association has a council that meets once or twice a month and provides the leadership and managerial direction. It has several dozen members, drawn from the headquarters staff, from several member federations, and (occasionally) from the social and political movements with which the association is affiliated. A smaller executive committee meets at least once a week; it consists of the full-time elected leadership of the association (the President, Vice-Presidents, and General Secretary), several senior executives from the Brussels headquarters, and (in some associations) representatives of a few member federations.[4]

THE MEDICAL PROFESSION

Belgium has had professional associations and scientific societies in medecine, but the customs of localism and the doctors' antipathy to dues have prevented the organizations from acquiring the large nationwide scale and the multiple functions common in other countries. One organization was a kind of trade union, which specialized in economic interests (particularly of Flemish general practitioners) and occasionally negotiated agreements: the *Algemeen Syndikaat der Geneesheren van België*. When a comprehensive national health insurance bill was proposed by a Socialist government during the early 1960s, the medical profession lacked a single, powerful, and combative national spokesman.

While several of the existing medical associations were peacefully discussing the new plans with the government, small groups of doctors in several cities (sometimes supported by local businessmen) declared that direct and strong action was indispensable and urgent, lest the medical profession and their patients become enslaved. They condemned the established medical associations as appeasers. The *Chambre Syndicale de Liège-Luxembourg* was organized in an eastern hotbed of such sentiment. Other such trade unions for doctors were created to fight the government in other provinces, and they joined in a *Fédération Nationale des Chambres Syndicales*, now called the *Fédération Belges des Chambres Syndicales de Médecins*.

During the mid-1960s, the medical trade unions were sustained by struggles and vindicated by triumphs. They led protests against the national health insurance law before and after its passage. They called the first general strike of doctors in any country. Twice the government revised the law after its original passage in order to please the doctors. The *Fédération* survived, but the Cabinet that had written and enacted the law suffered the fate of any Belgian government that stirs up too much controversy: it fell and was replaced by a different coalition.[5]

At present, the *Fédération* is an association of five trade unions (*chambres syndicales*) for the various regions of the country. Each *chambre* holds regular meetings about local affairs and about national questions; each has its own executive committee. The entire *Fédération* is led by a governing board of about forty persons (the *Conseil d'Administration*), elected by the five regional *Chambres*. It meets every month in Brussels and makes all decisions for the *Fédération*. The executive committee of the *Conseil* (the *Bureau*) meets every week, either in Brussels or in the headquarters of the *Fédération,* just south of the capital. The *Bureau* consists of the *Fédération's* president, two vice-presidents, several other officials from headquarters, and two representatives from each of the five regional *Chambres*. The *Fédération's* small office issues a weekly newsletter and gives advice to members concerning financial and legal matters.

Like trade unions, the *chambres syndicales* and the *Fédération* have no functions other than defending the economic interests of their members, influencing legislation about the economics and organization of practice, and negotiating agreements with the sick funds and other public authorities. Usually the *chambres syndicales* and the *Fédération* do not discuss clinical and scientific matters, unless they become questions of public policy, such as abortion. Membership figures are kept secret, since the *Fédération* likes to claim unanimous support from all Belgian doctors. An unknown number of Belgian doctors willingly accept the benefits of the *Fédération's* contracts but do not pay dues to the basic membership units, the *chambres syndicales*. Another unknown is the number of involuntary members, who pay dues to please their more active local colleagues but dislike the *Fédération,* either because it is too vituperative in style or because it is not militant enough in opposing the government and *mutualités.*

To a degree not found in any other country, the Belgian medical trade unions are movements identified with leaders. Each *chambre* is commonly mentioned as the *"chambre* of Dr. _____." In the mass media and in official negotiating situations, the spotlight is on the personal performance of the leaders as much as on their policy stances. A few doctors with the right combination of flamboyant style, taste for medical and national politics, instinct for effective maneuver, and wisdom to avoid dangerous limbs have retained leadership for over a decade.[6] At times, leaders have fallen out personally as well as ideologically, and several *chambres* have broken away to form rival Federations, but these schisms have had limited success for several reasons: their leaders gambled on strikes that failed, they took extreme positions that were unrealistic, and they were less magnetic personally than the leaders of the *Fédération.* The constant danger of such breakaways keeps the *Fédération* at a high pitch, denouncing economic and political threats to the medical profession, and trying to obtain from the sick funds and the government the most money with the fewest controls.

The *Fédération* uses several powerful techniques in dealing with the government and the sick funds. As in other countries, physicians enjoy much social class prestige and a considerable mystique about their power over life and death; if economic disputes disrupt medical services, politicians fear the public will blame *them* for distracting the doctors from their true vocation. In a small country with such a fragile political structure, stubborn pressure groups and forceful leaders can easily dominate the mass media and worry the politicians. The *Fédération* has developed a technique of communicating among all its members and an ability for mobilization unparalleled among other Belgian interest groups. Every doctor is a member of a small cell, linked to higher levels of the *Fédération* by a "telephone pyramid," as in a revolutionary movement fighting an enemy government; a message can be sent from the top down through the network, with each doctor (or his wife) passing the message along to the next group below him; the entire profession throughout the country can be personally alerted within a few hours.[7] Over a thousand Brussels doctors responded to telephone appeals on a few days notice in late August 1976 (despite the vacation season) and attended a rally protesting new government regulations. Nearly half of all Belgian doctors attended a protest rally in the capital in mid-October 1976. If something truly critical had been at stake, the turnouts would have been even higher.

At times, the *Fédération* has been beset by rival medical unions that accused it of being too accommodating in its agreements with the *mutualités,* despite its militant rhetoric. Eventually these rivals made their peace with the *Fédération* and rejoined it. Recently several groups favorable to new ideas in general practice and in health insurance combined in the *Confédération des médecins belges.* Many of its members are Flemish, while French-speaking Walloons are particularly numerous in the *Fédération.* Membership figures for the *Confédération* are secret, since leaders usually claim more strength than they really possess. (Support for secrecy comes from the doctors themselves: Some prudently join both the *Fédération* and the *Confédération.*)

INSTITUTE FOR HEALTH INSURANCE

In the years between its origin in 1945 and 1963, Belgian national health insurance lacked a central management structure. The statutory reform of 1963 created the *Institut National d'Assurance Maladie- Invalidité* (INAMI), an autonomous public agency with numerous functions. It is a structured meeting place among the groups interested in national health insurance, either as taxpayers, providers of services, or consumers. Several committees provide sites for negotiating agreements or for giving advice to the national government. It oversees the conduct of health insurance by interpreting and transmitting the laws of Parliament and the decrees of the Ministry of Social Affairs, and by examining how the *mutualités* and providers carry out their work. It maintains investigators. It collects and publishes information about the operations of the various insurance programs, particularly trends in utilization and costs, so that the public, the government, the *mutualités,* and the providers can make informed decisions. At times the Ministry of Social Affairs orders cost-saving measures in the system, and the mesage passes down through INAMI and thence to the interested parties represented in INAMI's organs.

Dealing with the overall operations and policy of INAMI is a general council (*Conseil Général*) consisting of:

12 representatives from employers' associations
11   from trade unions
12   from *mutualités*
10   from unions and associations of doctors
13   from other health occupations
 4   from government ministries

Including the medical profession in the governing board of a national health insurance system is unusual. Inclusion was intended to eliminate the doctors' complaints about inadequate consultation and unresponsiveness, to involve them in all decisions, and to give them a sense of commitment to national health insurance. However, the *Fédération* and other groups of doctors have shied away from accepting responsibility for a system in which they are only one of many groups, and they consider their representatives to be observers rather than full participants. As a result, the *Conseil Général* has never had the responsibility and authority originally intended, as the meeting ground for the principal interests in Belgian social policy. The full-time general administrator and deputy administrator of INAMI are energetic leaders of the organization, but they are sensitive to the views of the interest groups in the various committees.

The principal division of INAMI deals with health services, and it has a governing committee (the *Comité de Gestion du Service des Soins de Santé*) composed of representatives:

15 from the *mutualités*
12 from the *Fédération* and other organizations of doctors
18 from the other health occupations
 4 from employers
 4 from trade unions
 4 from Ministries of the government

Within this division and reporting to the *Comité de Gestion* are several committees, two of them sites for negotiations between the medical profession and the *mutualités*. The *Commission Nationale Médico-Mutualiste* (colloquially called the *Commission Med-Mut*) negotiates conditions of service and the amount of money for fees. At present it has eleven representatives from the medical trade unions and eleven from the *mutualités*. The *Conseil Technique Médical* revises the fee schedule. Its members include eleven from the medical unions, nine from the *mutualités*, and seven from medical faculties of universities.

Belgium's many official commissions often are created by statutes stating that their membership shall represent a particular segment of the population. In the struggle for power that never ceases in Belgian public life, a favorite tactic by less powerful groups is to overturn the membership of a commission on the grounds that it is not "representative." They file lawsuits with the *Conseil d'Etat,* the judicial body that reviews the work of administrative agencies, to make sure they obey the Constitution and the law. In the jaundiced view of Belgian officials, the *Conseil d'Etat* is a cantankerous and capricious group that can always be counted on to throttle a commission by declaring its membership unrepresentative.[8]

Therefore, the smaller rivals to the *Fédération* regularly harass it by asking the *Conseil d'Etat* to declare various commissions of INAMI improperly constituted, with too many seats for the *Fédération* and not enough for them.[9] In 1975, negotiations for a new contract were held up for months in a struggle over representativity. As the year began, the *Fédération* had eight seats in the *Commission Med-Mut* and the *Algemeen Syndikaat* had two. The new *Confédération* was created, merging the *Algemeen Syndikaat* and several other groups, including a *chambre syndical* that broke away from the *Fédération*. The *Confédération* appealed to the *Conseil d'Etat,* which declared INAMI's committees unrepresentative of the medical profession. The *Confédération* offered to take three seats on the *Commission Med-Mut,* but the *Fédération* refused to give away its eighth; indeed, said the *Fédération,* the *Confédération* should not even be on the committees, since it had hardly any members and was a Trojan Horse for the *mutualités.* The Ministry of Social Affairs was persuaded to write a new decree about representation in the committees, so drafted that the *Confédération* was not eligible. After many months of haggling, the *Commission Med-Mut* was expanded to eleven members on each side, the *Fédération* kept its eight members, and the *Algemeen Syndikaat* was given three. (This might have created problems on the side of the *mutualités.* Rivalries might break out over control of their new eleventh seat, since the numbers had to be kept equal on both sides. It was solved in several committees by giving the seat to a neutral specialist in health insurance who was not currently employed by any sick fund.)

Officially, the seats are not reserved for particular medical unions or for particular *mutualités.* The Minister for Social Affairs legally picks the names. But everyone knows how many seats each union or *mutualité* will have according to the negotiations involving each side's composition. The Minister automatically nominates whoever is suggested by the organization controlling that seat. The representation on the *mutualité* side corresponds to the size and power of the associations: four from the Christian sick funds, and one from each of the others.

Because of the many internal divisions in Belgian society and medicine,[10] the personalized nature of *Fédération* affairs, and the danger of discontent and schisms, the *Fédération* must balance its delegations carefully. The *Conseil d'Administration* picks the *Fédération's* members of INAMI committees in close consultation with the five *chambres syndicales.* Equal numbers of GPs and specialists serve. Approximately equal numbers of negotiators come from the five *chambres syndicales,* in order to avoid the weaknesses of earlier Belgian medical associations, which were dominated by Brussels. The delegations are balanced between Walloons and Flemings, and diverse political viewpoints within the membership are included. An important task of the national leadership is to guide the *chambres syndicales* into naming persons who will provide a balanced delegation and will also be good negotiators. Not many doctors are willing to volunteer for this time-consuming, argumentative, unpaid work, and therefore the same leaders and delegates tend to stay on.

The *mutualités* have an easier time picking their representatives. Each national association sends its leading salaried officials to the *Commission Med-Mut*. Each sends to the *Conseil Technique Médical* one or more of its salaried physicians from the national headquarters.

Each medical faculty in Belgium is asked to send one representative to the *Conseil Technique Médical*. Each faculty picks whomever it prefers by its own procedure, and the Minister always names him.

The Minister of Social Affairs names the chairman. The head of the *Commission Med-Mut* must be a respected and neutral figure, who can persuade the doctors and sick funds to agree.[11] He must also be influential enough in the government to convince the Cabinet to approve *accords* that raise costs. At present the chairman is the highly respected and experienced deputy director of INAMI itself, but he need not be.

The *Conseil Technique Médical* is a more technical and less adversarial body, and its chairman need not be neutral. Recently, he has been one of the representatives of the *Fédération,* with a reputation for fairness.

NEGOTIATIONS OVER CONDITIONS OF SERVICE AND MONEY

The *Commission Med-Mut* writes the *accords* made between the medical trade unions and the *mutualités*. The frequency of its meetings depends on the political climate and on its work. In some years, it might meet twenty times and produce an *accord*. In other years, when mere questions of interpreting a past *accord* arise, it may meet only four times. Occasionally the doctors protest unilateral actions by the government by boycotting all INAMI committees, as the *Fédération* did for much of 1976, and then the *Commission Med-Mut* does not meet.

The *Commission* always convenes in the INAMI building, which is neutral territory. It always meets in the evening, since nearly all the doctors practice. Some meetings last well into the morning. Considerable documentation is prepared for each meeting by the INAMI administrative and statistical staffs. INAMI must prepare each document in both French and Flemish. The secretariat of the INAMI *Service des Soins de Santé* prepares minutes of each meeting that paraphrase the principal statements and summarize the decisions.

When a new *accord* is being negotiated, a paper battle ensues. Two versions of proposed conditions of service and predicted economic facts are submitted on the medical profession's side, from the *Fédération* and *Con-*

fédération; each association of *mutualités* responds with its recommendations and economic reports from its own perspective; and the INAMI staff submits papers about past trends and future probabilities in utilization and costs for all of national health insurance.

The medical profession

The *Fédération* has two commissions representing the general practitioners (the *Commission Fédérale pour les Généralistes*) and specialists (the *Commission Fédérale pour les Spécialisés*). The latter includes two delegates from each of twenty-two working groups of individual specialties. When a new *accord* is being planned and during the negotiations at INAMI, the two *Commissions* meet once a week or once every two weeks, almost always in Brussels. They produce drafts of demands to make of the *mutualités* in the next *accord*. The drafts go to the national leadership and to the governing boards of the five *Chambres syndicales*; the drafts are discussed there and also in the monthly meeting of each *Chambre*. The *Bureau* of the full *Fédération* collects comments and puts together a final draft; two representatives from each *Chambre* serve on the *Bureau* and report their constituents' reactions. A perennial problem is harmonizing the views of GPs and specialists about conditions of service, such as the recent provision of postgraduate training and higher fees to GPs. The document is discussed and approved by consensus in the *Conseil d'Administration*. (It is possible but unusual to call for a majority vote over a contested issue. Three out of the five *Chambres* constitute a majority. However, to avoid schisms, a general agreement is worked out.) Everyone is expected to fight for the official document, even if he dissented during the discussions, since everyone was heard and a solid front is essential for negotiating strength.

The small staff of the *Fédération's* national office prepares the papers for its own internal meetings and prepares the case to be submitted to the INAMI *Commission Med-Mut* for new conditions of service and for higher fees. The *Fédération* staff includes a full-time economist and a lawyer. Occasionally a private consulting firm helps the *Fédération* prepare the calculations about the financial capabilities of the health insurance system, the increasing cost of practice, economic trends in Belgium, the need for increases in fees, or the need for alterations in the structure of the fees.

The *Confédération*—formerly the *Algemeen Syndikaat* by itself—also prepares its case for submission to the *Commission Med-Mut*. The *Fédération* and *Confédération* are hostile, do not coordinate their positions, and submit rival arguments to the *Commission Med-Mut*. Sometimes they oppose each other's recommendations, as in the recent decisions about whether general practitioners with postgraduate training should occupy a higher status and receive higher fees. They submit quite different documentation: where the *Fédération* argues for a single increase in fees, the *Confédération* distinguishes between practice costs and the doctor's net income in its negotiating arguments. Because of its much larger size, vigorous leadership, and ability to mobilize the Belgian medical profession, the *Fédération* dominates the doctors' side of the negotiating table.

The sick funds

The associations of Christian and Socialist sick funds have large numbers of bills and services, they have personnel and equipment for processing claims, and they maintain research staffs for reports about trends in utilization and costs. The reports are produced regularly, and the representatives of the sick funds enter negotiations with a general idea as to what they will be able to afford.

After the doctors present their demands about new conditions of service and higher fees in the *Commission Med-Mut,* the representatives of the sick funds discuss them in their executive committees. The research staffs estimate the costs of the doctors' monetary demands. Because the executive committees meet frequently and are led by the members who serve on the *Commission Med-Mut,* they are constantly involved in the decisions. The large general council hears about the course of the negotiations and gives its opinion during one of its periodic meetings. In the rare instance when negotiations go very quickly and an issue is so important that the general council must be consulted before its next meeting, it can be called into special session. Usually the executive committee and the negotiating team are fully empowered to decide everything. When the negotiators sign an *accord,* that commits the *mutualités.*

The leaderships of the two largest associations—the Christians and Socialists—keep in touch on most issues, in order to work out a common position, and the three smaller associations usually go along. The Christian and Socialist sick funds disagree on some policy goals—the Socialists are more favorable to financing health services out of general revenue—but they agree almost completely when negotiating with the doctors under present conditions.

Agreements

Usually an *accord* runs for five years. In 1975, however, negotiations were so tense that they yielded only a limited *accord,* lasting for one year and devoted to a few topics. The *accord* included a clause continuing in effect all other clauses from the agreement of 1970.

Extending the old *accord* by agreement solves one of the fundamental problems of national health insurance, viz., whether a deadlock will free the doctors to practice and charge whatever they like, or whether the government can then impose its own rules and price controls. If the former is likely, the medical union would be motivated to refuse to agree. If the latter, the sick funds and political parties of the Left would not negotiate conscientiously.[12]

The *Commission Med-Mut* can vote on contested clauses. For that reason, the two sides have equal numbers of seats. However, the chairman avoids showdowns and tries to work out agreements by consensus, an effort requiring great diplomatic skill. The *Fédération* also avoids showdowns within the *Commission,* lest the *Confédération* vote differently and give the *mutualités* a majority. In case of a serious impasse, the *Fédération* tries to meet with the Prime Minister and work out a settlement with him which the *Commission Med-Mut* then adopts. (The occasional meetings between the *Fédération* and Prime Minister deal with the doctors' disputes with the Ministry of Social Affairs more often than with deadlocks in the *Commission.*)

An *accord* is sent by the *Commission* to the next level in INAMI, the *Comité de Gestion du Service des Soins de Santé.* In theory, it can reject an *accord* and ask the *Commission* to negotiate a new one. That never happens: the doctors and *mutualités* who wrote the *accord* have a majority of the seats on the *Comité*; and (up to now) the chairman of the *Commission* is secretary of the *Comité.*

For the first time in the negotiating process, the government is officially involved: four Ministries have representatives on the *Comité,* usually the senior civil servants from the Ministries of Social Affairs, Finance, Health, and Middle Classes. The ministerial delegates often grumble—such as complaining about the increased costs that the government is expected to pay —but never exercise their right of veto at this point. The civil servants say they dare not, since the Cabinet is beholden to the powerful *mutualités* and fears strike threats by the doctors.

The *accord* then goes to the Minister of Social Affairs. In every other country where the agreement requires official enactment or approval, this step is simply *pro forma,* and the Minister automatically issues the decree or announcement of approval, in the name of himself or of the Chief of State. At this stage, the Ministry sometimes belatedly intervenes. It has not been able to participate in the writing of the *accord,* but the medical unions and *mutualités* may have made fundamental changes in the organization of medical care, for which the Ministries of Social Affairs and Health are responsible. Likewise the Ministry was not fully consulted in the financial decisions of the negotiators, but the Ministries of Social Affairs and Finance are expected to pay the shortfalls in health insurance accounts not covered by the payroll taxes. Instead of vetoing the *accord* of 1975 in the *Comité de Gestion,* the Ministries (and the rest of the Cabinet) in early 1976 rejected the higher fees for general practitioners but approved the rest of the *accord.* Personal prestige and personal leadership —always essential to enable the intricate Belgian social system to function—produced a compromise and headed off a crisis in the negotiating machinery. The chairman of the *Commission Med-Mut*—who is also the second ranking executive in INAMI and a man of long experience in social affairs—persuaded the Cabinet, the doctors, and *mutualités* to accept a later starting date for the new rules and fees in general practice.

Because of the frequent bickering, the medical unions and *mutualités* have tried to take money out of contention by indexing the fees, as in other small countries. This assumes stable mutual understandings among the government, medical unions, and sick funds that do not yet exist in Belgium. This also assumes a prosperous economy without excessive inflation, which has not existed either lately. Various procedures have been adopted since 1966. For example, an *accord* of the *Commission Med-Mut* in July 1974 instructed the INAMI staff automatically to increase fees twice a year if Belgium's index of consumer prices had gone up at least 3% since the last round. Each rise in fees would equal the rise in consumer prices. However, because these arrangements have always contributed to inflation and to the government's budget deficit, the Ministry of Social Affairs limited indexation in 1975 and 1976, and the Ministry announced it intended to repeal indexation completely in 1977. The *Fédération* responded angrily that the government had violated its contractual commitments to the medical profession and would agree only if the government granted the doctors something in return for voiding indexation. The *accord* of late 1975 seemed to record such a deal: Indexation would occur once (not twice) in 1976, but the GPs would have a new system of payment. When the Ministry and the *Fédération* fell out over other matters, the *Fédération* said that the *accord* was no longer in effect and the doctors had the right to raise their fees a second time in 1976, according to the index system. (Disparate grievances often become linked in Belgium, making conflict resolution so difficult. At one point the *Fédération* said that it would not urge the medical profession to carry out indexation if the government agreed not to prosecute three doctors recently indicted for performing illegal abortions.)

The health insurance law is passed by the Parliament, and the details of reiations between doctors and the system are spelled out in decrees issued over the King's signature. Because everything is so contentious, all sides have tried to make agreements stick by including so much detail. In the early 1960s, the government had tried to legislate health insurance, as a prerogative of its sovereignty. The *Fédération* successfully paralyzed the country with its strike; the Prime Minister and several Ministers then negotiated extensive amendments to the law directly with the leaders of the *Fédération*. The basic rules about the doctors' work in health insurance and the organization of INAMI and its negotiating apparatus themselves were spelled out in the first *accord*, negotiated by representatives of the *Fédération*, the *mutualités*, the trade unions, the employers, and several Ministries of the government in both official meetings and in much behind-the-scenes discussion.[13] As a result of this precedent, fundamental decision making in health often seems feudal rather than modern: The *Fédération* denies that the government has any right to alter terms of doctors' service without negotiating them with the *Fédération* and without gaining its full approval. Faced with any new decrees unilaterally issued by a Minister (such as several during 1976), the *Fédération* denounces the Minister for violating his legal commitments, threatens strikes, and calls for (and usually gets) a meeting between those two equivalent sovereigns, the President of the *Fédération* and the Prime Minister.

NEGOTIATIONS OVER THE FEE SCHEDULE

France has a fee schedule (*Nomenclature*) of acts with relative values. Each part of the fee schedule has a "key-letter" to distinguish it. The *Nomenclature* remains the same over several years, but each year the monetary values of the key-letters change. The *Nomenclature* is written and revised by a committee of experts; the values of the key-letters are decided by the general negotiating committee.

Belgium has the same system, but it is beset by the contention and deadlocks common throughout its negotiations in health. The *Conseil Technique Médical* works on the *Nomenclature*. The *Commission Med-Mut* fixes the value of the key-letters, often by indexation.

The medical profession

While the *Commission Med-Mut* is organized adversarially and in equal balance, the *Conseil Technique Médical* is not. The medical unions have more seats than the *mutualités*, one of their members is chairman, and they do much of the work.

Most of the initiatives come from the 22 working groups of individual specialties united in the *Commission Fédérale pour les Specalisés*. Each suggests improvements in the wording of items, relative values among items, and addition of new items in their sections of the existing *Nomenclature*. When a new *Nomenclature* was written during the early 1970s, they wrote the first drafts. The *Commission Fédérale pour les Généralistes* contributes to the parts of the fee schedule dealing with the general practitioners.

Because of rivalries among specialties and (particularly) between general practitioners and specialists, the *Fédération* discusses thoroughly the drafts of any new *Nomenclature* and the proposed revisions of any existing one. The views of all groups must be harmonized. The papers follow the same route as the proposed conditions of service that ultimately reach the *Commission Med-Mut*: They are discussed by the governing councils of the five *chambres syndicales,* by the governing board of the full *Fédération,* and by the executive committee of the *Fédération.*

When agreements are negotiated at INAMI—whether *accords* from the *Commission Med-Mut* or revisions of the *Nomenclature* from the *Conseil Technique Médical*—they are approved by the executive committee of the *Fédération.* The negotiators for the national associations of *mutualites* have full power to commit the members. However, the leaders of the *Fédération* are careful to let the representatives of the *Chambres syndicales* share in the decisions. During the early 1970s, separate chapters of the proposed new *Nomenclature* went back to the *Commission Fédérale pour les Spécialisés* for thorough study.

The sick funds

The principal medical officers of the associations of sick funds negotiate the changes. The lay leaderships in headquarters give them extensive discretion, since their work involves technical clinical judgments about the merits and time of procedures. The medical officers from the different associations work together closely, in part to share their clinical knowledge and in part to strengthen their positions relative to the *Fédération,* which tends to dominate the *Conseil Technique.*

The medical officers often introduce their own recommendations for altering parts of an existing *Nomenclature,* instead of allowing the *Fédération* all the initiatives. They produce their own papers within the sick funds, rather than rely on the reports of the statistical staffs, since they deal with clinical procedures.

The negotiating committee

When a new *Nomenclature* is not being written, the *Conseil Technique* meets about every two months. It considers adding new items and clarifying the meaning of existing entries. When a new *Nomenclature* was written in the early 1970s the *Conseil* met more often. Sessions are held during the evening in the INAMI building in Brussels. The INAMI staff provides secretarial services and keeps the minutes.

In theory, relative values of acts are fixed according to their comparative time and difficulty. Money is supposedly not a consideration; fixing the monetary value of the key-letters should be left to the *Commission Med-Mut*. The division of labor is not so neat. The *Commission* may adopt rules about how to allocate the investment costs for practice, which require the *Conseil Technique* to raise the relative values of acts using expensive equipment, thereby enabling a doctor to collect more money. The *Commission Med-Mut* has been trying to raise the incomes, status, and clinical responsibility of general practice in Belgium as in other countries, and it sometimes asks the *Conseil Technique* to add new acts for GPs or redefine existing acts.

In theory, the *Conseil* consists of doctors concerned only with technical matters and not engaged in adversarial conflicts of interest, and therefore it should have no factions and no bloc voting. Such divisions should occur only in the *Commission Med-Mut*. Therefore, the *Conseil* has rules for simple majority voting in case of a division. The medical faculties are represented supposedly as impartial experts. However, the interests of the parent associations impinge. The *Fédération's* representatives present the requests of their specialty subgroups for new acts and for higher relative values for the more complex existing acts. Aware of the additional costs for the sick funds, the representatives of the *mutualités* present clinical arguments in opposition.

The representatives of the clinical faculties have increased in number since the 1960s, as Belgium added more medical schools, and they have unexpectedly become an interest group themselves. They create new techniques and naturally like to see them added to the *Nomenclature,* so that the methods are more widely used. Many run experimental or development programs in outpatient or inpatient services; therefore the higher the relative values for such acts, the greater the earnings of these departments from fees, and the higher the departmental budgets. Many earn fees in addition to their university salaries, and therefore they share the economic interests of the specialty subgroups within the *Fédération*. The representatives of the sick funds grumble about log-rolling: The doctors from the *Fédération* and the medical faculties support each other, and therefore the *Fédération* always has a majority. The chairman usually tries to work out a consensus and avoid a vote, but the results are affected by the knowledge that the *Fédération* can always win a showdown.

The Belgian *Nomenclature* is very long, with separate sections for different specialties. During the late 1960s, as part of a new *accord,* it was agreed to prepare a new and streamlined document. The work took several years and was to be adopted officially in stages, as each was completed. Rewriting a fee schedule requires strong leadership from the medical association, since older specialties lose cherished acts and experience a decline in money and status compared to newer specialties. The delicate political structure of the *Fédération* militated against this; the leaders' fear of rebellions and secessions led it to reject any section of the fee schedule opposed by a specialty speaking through its working group under the *Commission Fédérale pour les Spécialisés,* despite the fact that the *Fédération's* national leadership and leaders of the *Commission* had written it. The *Fédération* would have been more successful if it had delayed introduction of individual chapters until the entire new *Nomenclature* could be presented as a unit. Therefore the fee schedule currently in use is a hybrid: if a specialty liked its chapter, it is in effect; if it did not like its new chapter (such as orthopedics and urology), the old chapter (including old-fashioned procedures and obsolete relative values) is still in effect.[14]

Besides adding new items and altering relative values, the *Conseil Technique* revises the explanatory clauses in the *Nomenclature,* to change the meaning of items or to solve ambiguities.

Approval of the revisions in the fee schedule

The *Conseil Technique* submits its work to the *Commission Med-Mut,* which can reject it. A few such disapprovals occurred during the 1970s, when the *Commission's* representatives from the sick funds believed the changes in relative values or the addition of new acts raised costs. The sick funds are a minority in the *Conseil Technique* but have enough votes to block approval in the *Commission Med-Mut.* The *Conseil* and *Commission* coordinate their work not through interlocking membership or through joint meetings but through messages, attendance by *Conseil* members at *Commission* meetings as technical advisors to the delegates from their parent organizations, and by the work of an INAMI secretariat that services both.

The *Commission* sends the documents to INAMI's *Comité de Gestion.* From there it goes to the Minister of Social Affairs. The *Nomenclature* has stronger legal effect than a mere *accord* between doctors and sick funds. An *accord* is approved by the Minister. The original *Nomenclature* is a decree signed by the King, and so is any revision. The decree is drafted by the INAMI staff.

When the *lettre-clé* system began in Belgium, it resembled that of France. If a long list of acts used the same key-letter, the same unit of money was used throughout. (For example, K = 6 NF in France for every act with a coefficient in the scale for K.) Differences in prices among acts in France are due to differences in their coefficients. (For example, an act with K 50 is worth twice as much as an act with the value K 25.) The committee specializing in the French *Nomenclature* is the only agency that determines the relative values among acts.

The Belgian system soon became more complicated. A specialty complained it was underpaid, and the *Commission Med-Mut* responded. Instead of referring the matter to the *Conseil Technique* with a recommendation to raise that specialty's coefficients and instead of ultimately obtaining a new royal decree, the *Commission* did the job itself. It gave the key-letter for that specialty a higher monetary value than the same key-letter for the other specialties, to compensate for the fact that the aggrieved specialty's coefficients were lower. As usually happens in such situations, other groups followed with similar demands, the *Commission Med-Mut* responded and the result is very complex. For example, in 1976 the key letter N has three values in Belgian francs, viz., 13.2968, 16.0755, or 20.0943; all three values are used for various acts in each of several specialties. Different values were invented recently in order to raise the monetary value of the more demanding acts without having to amend the *Nomenclature* and give them higher coefficients. Within each specialty the range for the key letter N in 1976 was:

Coefficients	Value or key letter
N 1 through N 125	N = 13.2968 BF
N 150 through N 550	N = 16.0755 BF
N 600 and over	N = 20.0943 BF

The result is to eliminate the simplicity of the key-letter system. Instead of announcing a short list of key-letter values as in France, the Belgian negotiators must draft a long memorandum showing the new key-letter and price for each act in the *Nomenclature*.

OVERVIEW OF THE BELGIAN NEGOTIATING SYSTEM

As I said at the outset, Belgium forshadows probable American trends in several respects. Existing nonprofit carriers have become the official sick funds and have prospered under national health insurance. A very militant medical profession has preserved office practice, retained direct billing of the patient, and resisted price control over fees. Government has frequently been unable to enforce its regulations against interest groups and in the courts.

In some respects, Belgium has carried its "American" characteristics to extremes that the United States may never reach. While the nonprofit carriers will become powerful pressure groups in America, they will not become as closely affiliated with the political parties or with organized labor, and they will not become as powerful in national politics. The American Medical Association will remain a professional body and will probably never become as disciplined or as shrill as the Belgian *Fédération*. American doctors are less secretive in their billing.

The social costs of conflict may become so evident that Belgians themselves may try to stabilize their situation. Relations may become more calm, more structured, more like the permanent negotiations among leaders that manage the affairs of other small "consociational democracies."

STRONG POINTS IN THE BELGIAN SYSTEM

Identifying what are "strong" and "weak" points in any arrangement depends on one's values. If Belgium's national health insurance seems less disciplined than that of other countries, some might consider this a weakness. Others might consider excessive structure and controls a threat to liberty and a reduction of consumer choice and therefore might commend Belgium as the last bastion of freedom in Europe.[15]

In a country where health services are beset by so much contention, INAMI has proved essential. It maintains neutral ground and neutral staff work for negotiations. It furnishes a set of spokesmen for the public interest who can influence the combatants and can settle some issues through mediation. These spokesmen acquire enough stature to influence the government too, on behalf of any consensus produced by the negotiations. Its governing boards could become the site of high-level social-policymaking, as they combine representatives of business, labor, carriers, and providers, but this has not yet happened.

SOME PROBLEMS IN THE BELGIAN SYSTEM

The weakness of government

The fragility of Belgian government invites endless contention in health insurance, as in other sectors. Cabinets are precarious coalitions, can easily fall, and are preoccupied with survival. Individual pressure groups, such as the separate *mutualités,* have impregnable influence with individual parties and leaders; and therefore an industry as a whole (such as the health insurance carriers as a group) has great power regardless of government. Well organized and militant associations, such as the doctors, can always frighten the Cabinet. Lower officials can always be bypassed, and the Prime Minister and Ministers can always be drawn into bargaining when the pressure group is determined.

Many of the world's democracies conduct long negotiations before any law or administrative regulation is announced. The interested groups have a chance to comment and offer revisions. Therefore, when the document is revealed, it is certain to be passed, and enactment is *pro forma.* All the interested groups are certain to carry it out.

However, Belgium and the United States follow a regular pattern that is devastating to government authority. An administrative regulation is prepared *in camera* and is announced without warning. It is really a preliminary trial balloon. First, it must sustain challenges in court, and the judge may reinterpret it. Then it will be carried out only if the providers like it. Otherwise, it will become a dead letter in some or all of the country; or, it will be amended one or more times, until everyone accepts it. Because any regulation can be weakened, the system invites constant challenges.[16]

The experiences of Belgium and the United States show that it is fragmented (not strong) democratic governments that have too much "bureaucracy." Both national capitals are run by officials under siege, preoccupied with how to write rules and amendments that will withstand attacks by lawyers and evaders, how to even up scores with pressure groups, and how to make sense out of the melange of regulations, amendments, judicial amendments, and informal accommodations that surround a subject. The societies with greater structure, acceptance of government decisions, and a sense of "rules of the game"—such as Holland, West Germany, Switzerland, and Sweden—seem to have fewer officials, fewer regulations, and far more comprehensible regulations.

Medical trade unions

Belgium demonstrates the dangers of organizing a special union as bargaining agent, instead of making this one of the functions of a professional association. The *Chambres syndicales* have no *raison d'être* other than obtaining more money and better conditions of service, and the insecure leaders are under constant pressure to get more, regardless of the consequences for national health insurance and the health services. Unlike a professional association, the membership is not held together by any bonds other than monetary self-interest; the threat of schism keeps the leaders in a posture of constantly demanding more benefits. Rivalry with other unions intensifies the demands or (in both Belgium and France) produces unexpected deals with the sick funds designed to upstage the other medical union. In the latter cases, the sick funds and government can divide and conquer.

In a medical trade union, an insecure leadership cannot risk offending any group, lest it secede or refuse to join a strike. Therefore, the leadership may not be able to be innovative or sign a general agreement restructuring relations, if one group gains less than others. The Belgian *Fédération* could not persuade all its member specialties to accept their portions of the new *Nomenclature* and therefore it withdrew its agreement.

The role of government

The relationship between the sick funds and the Ministries is always ambiguous in national health insurance. It is often unclear who is the medical profession's true adversary. Often the negotiators for the sick funds seem to express the guidelines from the Ministry. Agreements usually have to be enacted or approved by a Ministry, but customarily this is *pro forma*. In countries where the government negotiates with the medical profession—such as Canada, Sweden, and Britain—its role is not in doubt.

Belgium suffers from a failure to involve government sufficiently at early stages of the negotiations, and a belated exercise of authority in later stages where other governments "let sleeping dogs lie." Because the *mutualités* are private and autonomous, they express their own rather than the government's views during the negotiations and strike the bargain that is best for themselves. They share with the doctors an incentive to raise costs, if the deficits will be paid by the government.[17] The political leaders and civil servants in the Ministries can warn the leaders of the sick funds informally against making expensive or legally novel concessions to the doctors, but the sick funds may consider the government obligated to find the money. The Ministries have a right to enter the process officially only when the completed agreements are reviewed by INAMI's government committees. Then they can only deplore and warn. Effectively shut out of the negotiations, the Ministries recently have tried retroactive action, by cancelling or postponing certain clauses. This however, touches off threats by the doctors and could drive the sick funds into a coalition with the doctors against the government. For these reasons, other governments usually avoid intervening so strongly and so late. Clearly a government—if it wishes to control how its money is spent—must become involved at an earlier point.

Formal agreements and understandings between medical professions and governments usually leave unclear whether the government has the final say and whether it can amend the agreements unilaterally. They are unclear because the medical associations do not wish to push the government into making explicit the obvious fact that a sovereign must have such a right. A problem in the Belgian system is that the *Fédération* claims that the government has waived such rights in agreements with the doctors, including even the right to interpret the agreements. By such logic, the *Fédération* could refuse to make any changes on matters specified in long-standing agreements. When discussions about utilization control, billing, and other questions were deadlocked in 1976, the government issued decrees specifying new procedures. The *Fédération* then called administrative strikes and other sanctions against such breach of contract by the government. After much uproar, the Prime Minister and

Cabinet worked out compromises with the *Fédération,* thereby vindicating the *Fédération's* position in the short run and guaranteeing the same constitutional crisis again in the long run.

Fee schedule

Belgium shares with several other countries a long and detailed fee schedule, rewarding a list of discrete technical procedures. Belgium has had more than the usual difficulty in modernizing and rewriting it, because of the absence of strong and disinterested professional leadership. Giving each specialty a veto proved fatal to reform. The key-letter system —supposed to be more simple than the conventional fee schedule—has been written in a more complex way.

NOTES

1. For the history and present organization of Belgian health insurance, see J. Engels, *L'évolution de l'assurance maladie-invalidité obligatoire 1945-1970* (Brussels: Institut National d'Assurance Maladie-Invalidité, 1970); M. Delhuvenne et al., *Aperçu du Régime Belge d'Assurance obligatoire contre la Maladie et l'Invalidité* (Brussels: Institut National d'Assurance Maladie-Invalidité, 10th edition, 1973); J. Dejardin, *Monograph on the Organisation of Medical Care within the Framework of Social Security: Belgium* (Geneva: International Labour Office, 1968); and J. Petit, *Rapport sur l'assurance maladie présenté par le Commissaire royal* (Brussels: Chambre des Représentants, 26 May 1976).

2. For example, at the general assembly of the Fédération des Mutualités Socialistes du Brabant, reported in the Brussels newspaper *Le Peuple,* 3 June 1976. The President of the Federation said that a *"mutualité* is not only an agency for accounting for receipts and expenses" but is a body for training the cadres for the socialist movement.

3. Every national organization in Belgium has a name in both French and Flemish (i.e., Dutch). For simplicity, I shall usually cite the French name.

4. The past history of Belgian *mutualités* appears in Rudolf Rezsohazy, *Histoire du mouvement mutualiste chrétien en Belgique* (Brussels: Aux Editions Erasme, 1957); and Jos van Roy, *Des caisses de maladie à la mutualité socialiste* (Brussels: Union Nationale des Mutualités Socialistes, n.d.). Their current organization is described in R. Crémer, "Le mouvement mutualiste en Belgique," *Revue belge de la sécurité sociale,* Volume VI, Number 1 (January 1964), pp. 12-132; "Les mutualités en Belgique," *Courrier Hebdomadaire* (Brussels: Centre de Recherche et d'Information Socio-Politiques, 2 October 1964); Yvo Nuyens et al., *De belgische gezondheidszorg in profiel* (Leuven: Sociologisch Onderzoeksinstituut K. U. Leuven, 1975), Ch. IV; and *Votre Mutualité* (Brussels: Alliance Nationale des Mutualités Chrétiennes, 1976), esp. pp. 62-80.

5. The history of the medical unions and their struggles during the 1960's appear in "Corps médical et assurance maladie," *Revue de l'institut de sociologie,* Number 3, 1964; Philippe Pierre Gosseries, "Le syndicalisme belge médical" (Brussels: privately printed, 1967); and John V. Craven, "A Strike of Self-Employed Professionals: Belgian Doctors in 1964," *Industrial and Labor Relations Review,* Volume 21, Number 1 (October 1967), pp. 18-30. The history and current organization of the Federation are described in Suzie Swennen, *Morfologische en ideologische analyse der belgische artsenverenigingen en artsensyndikaten* (Leuven: thesis for the Licentiaat in de Sociologie, Katholieke Universiteit te Leuven, 1974).

6. Particularly the *Fédération's* charismatic, energetic, and skilful President, André Wynen. In no other country is the medical profession so identified with one man. His credo appears in the book, *La médecine sans medecin?* (Brussels: Jean-Luc Vernal, 1972).

7. Described in Swennen, *op. cit.* (note 5, supra), pp. 66-68.

8. Its organization and work are described in *Le Conseil d'Etat* (Brussels: Institut Belge d'Information et de Documentation, 1974).

9. Occasionally a rival union proposes that all nominate candidates for the INAMI committees, and Belgium's doctors can elect them by secret ballot. But the *Fédération* refuses. Guy Spitaels and Marie-Louise Opdenberg, *L'année sociale 1969* (Brussels: Editions de l'Institut de Sociologie, Université Libre de Bruxelles, 1970), p. 69.

10. How Belgian social divisions and combative intergroup relations affect medical services is discussed by Renée C. Fox, "Medical Scientists in a Chateau," *Science,* Volume 136, Number 3515 (11 May 1962), pp. 476-483. The intricate structure of Belgian cabinets is described in *Qui décide en Belgique: Mécanismes et facteurs de la décision politique* (Brussels: Dossiers du CRISP, 1970), pp. 11-12.

11. For example, when the two sides could not converge on one document, the chairman proposed one that became the accord for 1970-1975. Spitaels, *L'année sociale* 1969 (note 9, supra), pp. 75-81.

12. In early 1966, the law gave the government considerable authority to impose fees in the absence of an *accord.* The representatives of the Socialist sick funds voted against an accord and then called on the government (then led by the Socialists) to impose fees. The medical unions threatened to strike, the Cabinet split, a new government came to power, the law was rewritten, and the government's legal power (as well as its political will) to impose fees in the absence of an *accord* was reduced. Guy Spitaels and Simone Lambert, *L'année sociale 1966* (Brussels: Editions de l'Institut de Sociologie, Université Libre de Bruxelles), pp. 13-54 passim; and "Le point de la situation en Belgique, "*Le concours médical,* Volume 89, Number 15 (15 April 1967), pp. 2986-2992. If a national *accord* has been enacted but too few doctors in a region adhere to put it into effect, the government can impose fees. But this has never happened in practice: the *Fédération* persuades the local doctors not to have a showdown, price controls have so many loopholes that adherence is no sacrifice, and the government prudently waits until enough doctors sign up.

13. The terms of an armistice, the government's "memorandum," and the *accord de la Saint-Jean* of 1964 are described in Philippe Pierre Gosseries, "La

collaboration du corps médical a l'assurance maladie-invalidité obligatoire en droit belge," *Revue belge de la sécurité sociale,* Volume IX, Number 3 (March 1967), pp. 369-378. The government's failures either to implement its threats as sovereign or to appease the doctors in bilateral negotiations are described at pages 364-369.

14. H. van Nimmen, "La nouvelle nomenclature des prestations de santé," *Revue belge de sécurité sociale,* Volume XVI, Number 4 (April 1974), pp. 379-397; Marie-Louise Opdenberg, *L'année sociale 1972* (Brussels: Editions de l'Université de Bruxelles, 1973), pp. 52-59; and Marie-Louise Opdenberg, *L'année sociale 1973* (Brussels: Editions de l'Université de Bruxelles, 1974), pp. 73-78.

15. That is the *Fédération's* view, in "Où en sommes-nous?" *Bulletin syndical,* Volume 9, Number 365 (3 January 1975), p. 2.

16. The history and erratic implementation of Belgian health insurance laws are recorded in Petit, *Rapport sur l'assurance maladie présenté par le Commissaire royal* (note 1, supra), pp. 56-77.

17. Besides payment to cover deficits in services, the *mutualités* receive from the government a subsidy for administration that is a constant percentage of their operating costs. Therefore, the *mutualités* have an incentive to increase rather than reduce utilization. Albert Delpérée et al., *Rapport sur l'assurance maladie présenté par le groupe de travail interdépartemental* (Brussels: Ministère de la Prévoyance Sociale, 1976), pp. 67-75. That such incentives actually operate is denied by Andrée Sacrez, "Le problème de l'assurance maladie," *Orientation,* Number 1, 1975, pp. 44-47.

CHAPTER V

The Netherlands

THE SICK FUNDS

AS IN OTHER Western European countries, insurance carriers have existed for many years in Holland. Their past history and current situation differ from those of France in several respects. They originated as private organizations and remain so today, although subject to regulations, support and review by the national government. They have evolved gradually; reorganizations have taken place largely through prolonged discussion and voluntary agreements. In contrast, French health insurance has experienced several sweeping interventions by government, and the carriers are specially created semiofficial organizations (i.e., the *caisses*).

Up to a certain income level all Dutch citizens are required to enroll in a health insurance fund and are required to pay social security taxes. A few others can join voluntarily. The members and their families constitute about 70% of the Dutch population. Others must pay doctors and hospitals privately; most subscribe to health insurance policies sold by insurance companies. A bill currently before the Parliament would extend national health insurance to the entire population, a common trend in all Western countries.

Once over six hundred small sick funds existed throughout Holland. Many were sponsored by doctors, to help their patients prepay their bills. They joined together in an association called the *Federatie van door Verzekerden en Medewerkers bestuurde Ziekenfondsen*. Others were sponsored by trade unions and employers and were grouped in the *Neder-*

landse Unie van Ziekenfondsen. A few Catholic sick funds belonged to a third association; a group that broke away from *Unie* formed a fourth. About 47% of subscribers belonged to the *Federatie* group, about 33% to the *Unie* group, about 12% to the Catholic association, and about 8% to the fourth. At one time, the sick funds in each federation had a definite character. For example, the governing board of the *Federatie* included doctors, *Unie's* included trade union representatives, and the Catholic association was distinctly Catholic. However, all of them steadily became more "secular," more preoccupied with health insurance matters alone. The sick funds within each association merged rapidly during the 1960s and 1970s, in order to save overhead costs, and now there are fewer than 90.[1]

By 1976, secularization and cooperation among the sick funds had reached the point of a merger to form the Confederation of Dutch Sick Funds (the *Vereniging van Nederlandse Ziekenfondsen* or VNZ), which superseded the separate federations. The mergers will take place at the grassroots too: Eventually there will be only one sick fund in each area. Until then, the separate funds will be joined in councils in each of the eight districts into which the country is divided.

The supreme governing power in VNZ is a General Assembly (*Algemene Vergadering*), consisting of representatives from all the sick funds throughout the country. Each representative has a weighted vote, depending on the number of subscribers he represents. Therefore, the number of representatives may diminish as the member sick funds merge and diminish; but each one will represent a larger constituency. Like representative assemblies of associations of sick funds in other countries, it will meet occasionally, perhaps only once a year. It elects the chairman of VNZ for a four-year term.

Leading the Assembly and effectively governing VNZ all year round is a Council (a *Bestuur*). It consists of: the chairman of VNZ; one representative of the health insurance subscribers from each district, presumably drawn from the membership lists of the sick funds; one representative of the doctors and of other health professionals from each district; a director of a sick fund from each district; representatives from each of the four national federations of trade unions; and two independent persons. It meets several times a year and directs the work of the secretariat at headquarters, including setting policy for negotiations with the medical profession.

The organization of the secretariat—as are many other features of VNZ at the time of writing—is in transition. The secretaries of the four original federations act as cosecretaries during the transitional period, until a tighter structure is created. Each secretary heads a principal department, such as specialist services, general practitioner services, and so on. The office is just outside Utrecht, the site of many of Holland's medical organizations. When the four federations were independent, they maintained a special coordinating office to conduct negotiations with the medical profession and to handle public relations, but VNZ now performs all this work.

THE MEDICAL PROFESSION

In all professional negotiations, the doctors are represented by the Royal Netherlands Medical Association (the *Koninklijke Nederlandsche Maatschappij tot Bevordering der Geneeskunst* or KNMG). The Association is a comprehensive system of government for the Dutch medical profession, performing functions that are usually located in other organizations abroad, such as the registration of specialists. It sponsors local and national meetings on clinical and scientific matters, publishes the country's principal medical journals, and gives advice to government and private agencies on clinical matters. The medical association has a large voluntary membership among Dutch doctors: It has enjoyed a good reputation since its founding in 1849, has experienced few schisms and rivalries, and Dutch doctors take it for granted that they should join.[2]

The doctor is automatically assigned to one of three constitutent societies, according to his status: one for the general practitioners (*Landelijke Huisartsen Vereniging* or LHV), one for the specialists (*Landelijke Specialisten Vereniging* or LSV), and one for employed doctors. LSV in turn is made up of twenty-eight sections, corresponding to the twenty-eight specialties. Each of the three societies is governed by an elected committee; LSV's committee is drawn from the member sections. Each has a secretariat at KNMG headquarters in Utrecht.

LHV and LSV organize the negotiations with the sick funds over conditions of service and fees. The negotiating teams are drawn from their governing committees and get their instructions from the committees. Staff work is done by the secretariat for each society and by the statistical personnel of the KNMG.

FORMAL STRUCTURE OF THE NEGOTIATING SYSTEM

The complex social structure of the Netherlands has had a long tradition of calm negotiation. As in Sweden, the success of the negotiating machinery rests on a culture that prizes civility, tolerance, and order.[3] Health services dynamics are typical of this style of intergroup relations. The basic rules are defined by the health insurance law, passed by the two

Houses of Parliament and signed by the Queen. The law is supplemented by decrees and by ministerial directives.[4]

Much effort in France is devoted to reaffirming basic principles, such as rights of private office practice, direct payment of the doctor by the patient, and so on. Often these ideas reappear in several documents during each round of negotiations. These basic themes are not negotiated anew in Holland: the parties trust each other more, agreements once made are taken for granted thereafter, and certain areas of conflict that are constantly renewed in France (such as third party payment v. direct payment of the doctor) were settled irrevocably in Holland long ago.

The health insurance law created a Sick Funds Council (the *Ziekenfondsraad*) in 1949, to govern health insurance and its relation with the health occupations. It was one of a series of laws from 1948 through 1950 that created councils to govern all Dutch economic life. The councils have performed unevenly in other sectors of the Dutch economy—in several fields, they were never created—but the *Ziekensfondsraad* has flourished. (Organized consultation exists in the other sectors, even if the parties do not report to a governing council.) National negotiating commissions draft recommendations concerning medical payment, they forward their agreements to the *Ziekenfondsraad,* and the *Ziekenfondsraad* makes the final decision.[5]

The *Ziekenfondsraad* consists of thirty-five members, selected as follows:

Seven by the Ministry of Public Health. These are not government officials but are distinguished citizens, such as university professors. One is appointed Chairman of the *Ziekenfondsraad* by the Queen.

Seven from the five principal associations of employers.

Seven from the three principal trade union federations.

Seven from the confederation of sick funds (VNZ).

Seven from the principal associations of providers: three from the medical association (including spokesmen for the specialists and general practitioners); one pharmacist; one dentist; and two from the hospital council. (A midwife is included as an alternate representative for the hospitals.)

The Ministry of Public Health is represented by an observer who can participate in all meetings of the council and of the committees, and who can register the Ministry's position by casting an advisory vote. (Occasional statutes add other observers from time to time.)

The *Ziekensfondsraad* has a number of general working commissions (thirteen at the time of writing) concerning medical and pharmaceutical affairs, insurance services, finance, etc. Each commission includes several members of the full *Raad* and persons from outside. (Each of the *Raad's* thirty-five members has a deputy. All seventy persons serve on the working commissions, thereby spreading the considerable work load.) In addition to these working commissions, agreements between the sick funds and providers are reviewed by a set of eight commissions on negotiated settlements, each with five members of the full *Raad*; one reviews agreements about GPs, one is concerned with specialists; one deals with dentists, and so on. Special commissions are appointed at times, such as the group that investigated abuse by providers and control over the medical profession during late 1975. The *Ziekenfondsraad* and its large secretariat are located in Amstelveen, a suburb of Amsterdam.

The bargaining between doctors and sick funds takes place in a set of standing negotiating committees (called *Onderhandelingscommissies Medewerkers-Ziekenfondsen*). Separate bodies exist for the general practitioners who lack the additional power to dispense drugs, the general practitioners who also dispense drugs, the specialists, the physiotherapists, the dentists, the salaried hospital doctors, and others. These committees recommend the increase in average fee that each category of practitioner should get each year. In addition, there exists the Permanent Commission on Tariffs (*Permanente Tarieven Commissie*), which revises the long fee schedule for specialists and performs other duties. Each committee meets about once a month, the one for specialists meets slightly more often.

The staff work is provided by a secretariat located in the General Office of Sick Funds Organizations (*Gemeenschappelijk Bureau van Ziekenfondsorganisaties* or GBZ) in Utrecht. The committees meet there, but occasionally at KNMG headquarters.

Each bargaining committee generates considerable documentation. The governing councils and secretariats of LHV and LSV develop their cases for higher net incomes and higher practice costs and write very detailed justifications; trends in the prices of cars, gasoline, equipment, telephones, etc. are spelled out. These papers from the medical association and the counterdocuments from the sick funds go to the secretariat of the bargaining committees. The papers are reproduced and sent to the other side in advance. In no other country is mutual trust so great that the adversaries allow each other to inspect the basis for their claims before the meetings: in some countries, papers are exchanged after the first bargaining sessions; in others they are never given out but are used only to support one's own oral arguments at the table.

During the negotiations, the two sides develop an agreed set of facts, and the secretariat of the bargaining committees produces these papers. The common secretariat also keeps minutes of meetings; because its work is more complicated, the committee for specialists produces longer and more detailed minutes than the one for GPs.

The recommendations of each negotiating committee and the detailed economic reasoning underlying the decision are forwarded to the *Ziekenfondsraad,* which alone has the official authority to make the decisions about doctors' pay. By custom, the *Raad* cannot amend the bargaining committee's recommendations. It either approves or disapproves, nearly always the former. If it is thinking of a new procedure, such as including a new item in allowable costs, the negotiating committee makes sure that it is acceptable to the *Ziekenfondsraad* by sending a memorandum for its advice. Before the full *Raad* acts on the bargaining committee's proposed award, the recommendations and supporting documentation are evaluated thoroughly by the *Raad's* five-member working commission on agreements that specializes in the affairs of that particular provider. The *Ziekenfondsraad's* decisions are final and may not be overturned by the Government unless they contradict the law, which never happens in practice. The views of the Ministry of Public Health about providers' pay are part of the deliberations of the *Ziekenfondsraad,* through the interventions of the Ministry's observer.

The Government's approval is needed for one of the *Ziekenfondsraad's* judgments, viz., the size of the annual premium charged to insured persons and employers in the form of payroll taxes. The Ministers for Social Affairs and for Health issue this decision as a decree. Even though the government does not tell the negotiators the upper limits on pay awards, they know they must decide within the limited amount of money that the government will allow the sick funds to collect next year.

All agreements about doctors' pay are nationwide, without regional variations.

The Negotiating Committee for Sick Funds and General Practitioners (Onderhandelingscommissie Ziekenfondsen-Huisartsen)

The official membership of the section for nondispensing doctors at the time of writing consists of 10 persons from the sick funds, 10 from the medical association, and three others. The membership of the section for dispensing doctors is almost the same; some of the doctors differ. Unlike other committees, the distribution of numbers is not important for decisions, since the negotiation is a bilateral relation between LHV and VNZ. In other words, LHV and VNZ need not send exactly equal numbers of representatives, since decisions are not made by majority vote. The agreements are signed by a few representatives from LHV (usually its chairman and secretary) and several on behalf of VNZ. During the negotiations, LHV is represented by its permanent secretariat and by several practicing general practitioners who are active in the medical society. The VNZ is represented by its permanent secretariat and by several practicing general practitioners who are active in the medical society.

The VNZ delegation is headed by the secretary who directs the department in VNZ specializing in general practice. At present, he is accompanied by several of the other secretaries. Each side also brings economists and accountants it employs in its secretariat and, at times, part-time consultants from private management consulting firms. Occasionally the two sides bring in outside experts as neutral consultants.

One principal round of negotiating occurs each year to discuss increases in the general practitioners' capitation fee and in a few supplementary charges. (A capitation fee is a fixed annual sum for each subscriber on a GP's list.) During the 1970s, inflation has led to complaints by doctors that their incomes have been falling behind, and the negotiating committee has met more often.

General practitioners' fees have been one of the few cases where the established negotiating system broke down, and special arbitrators had to be appointed. The national health insurance law authorizes the Minister of Public Health to name such a committee of "wise men" and to enact decisions, such as new fees recommended by its report. During the mid-1960s, postwar price and wage controls were relaxed, and Dutch prices and wages rose quickly. Meanwhile, medical administrators were trying to cut costs by encouraging GPs to treat more patients and to refer fewer to hospitals. The GPs in the negotiating committees demanded much higher capitation fees on grounds they deserved annual incomes higher than those of most other occupations, and that they must now perfect their staffing and facilities. The doctors and sick funds deadlocked throughout late 1965 and 1966, and five "wise men" were brought in, viz., a leading professor of economics, a professor who also was chairman of the Central Council on Public Health, a member of the Council of State, a hospital director who once headed the medical association, and a former Minister of Justice.

Their solution was to take general practitioners' payment out of dispute by tying it to an automatic process: The average general practitioner's net income should approximate that of a civil servant of Grade 151. The capitation fee was increased greatly.[6] Thereafter, each year the negotiating committee has distinguished between that part of the capitation fee to cover the costs of practice and that part to provide net income after costs. The latter increases automatically every year, after the secretariat of the negotiating committee learns the size of the salary increase awarded by the Dutch government to civil servants of Grade 151.

The costs of practice for the next year are supposed to be estimated objectively, and the two sides introduce much detailed paper about the equipment, personnel, supplies, and services needed for a good general practice of a particular level of work, and the probable costs during the coming year. The debate is very specific: e.g., the Peugeot 404 had been cited for several years as a typical car for a GP; when it was discontinued in 1975, LHV argued that the equivalent fee for practice costs should increase by that amount. The agreement forwarded to the *Ziekenfondsraad* includes the detailed estimates accepted by both sides for all equipment, personnel, materials, and services needed by an average GP for the coming year.

Besides paying net income and costs, the sick funds deposit a contribution for each GP's pension into a special account they maintain. This fringe benefit is designed to commit the doctor to the success of the system and is now being emulated by other countries. The amount is one of the subjects of negotiation. Therefore the capitation fee for the GP for each subscriber (the *abonnementshonorarium*) consists of three parts: the net income now tied to the annual increases for civil servants (the *nettohonorarium*), the pension contribution (the *pensioenpremie*), and practice costs (*kosten*).

The Negotiating Committee for Sick Funds and Specialists (Onderhandelingscommissie Ziekenfondsen-Specialisten)

The committee at the time of writing has twenty-three members, about half from the sick funds. As in the case of the committee for general practice, the distribution of these numbers is not important, since the negotiations are a bilateral relation between LSV and VNZ. Practicing doctors participate on the LSV side, as well as its permanent full-time secretariat. The VNZ delegation is headed by the secretary who heads the department devoted to specialty practice. He is accompanied by several other secretaries. Both sides use statisticians, and the discussions involve careful comparisons of technical papers about the components and the costs of practice.

The issue is the average increase in level of fees for the entire fee schedule for specialists. The full document is very long, but this committee does not debate individual items. Instead, the award is an annual increase in net income plus an increase in that component of fees designed to cover costs during the next year. Once both were debated, but the negotiators in 1974 decided to take net income out of contention by emulating the procedure for GPs: each year the Dutch government increases the salaries of civil service Grades 152, 153, and 154 by a certain proportion, and the negotiators adopt the same proportion in increasing that part of every specialist's fee designed to provide net income after costs. (The total net income is not expected to equal that of Grades 152, 153, and 154, since the specialists in 1974 were earning more. Rather the annual increase is the same as the proportionate increase for the highest civil servants.)

Relieved of judgments about net income, the negotiators can focus on probable trends in practice costs. This could be very burdensome, since each specialty slightly differs in its facilities and costs. In contrast, the committees for general practitioners can simplify by discussing only two types of practice. The negotiators for specialists' fees try to simplify in the same fashion by guessing that costs for all specialties rise by approximately one average amount.

Determining the pay of senior civil servants

Linking the increase in part of the fees to rises in the pay for civil service Grades 151 through 154 means that the civil servants' machinery becomes part of the decision making apparatus for the doctors. There, too, the Dutch try to make the decisions "objective" and "automatic."

Since 1959, the government has been committed to paying wages equivalent to those for comparable jobs in private employment. Therefore, each year, it raises the pay of civil servants the same amount as the increases for private employees. The data are examined and the new pay rates are ordered by the Directorate General for Civil Service. Staff Management, Ministry of Home Affairs (the *Directoraat-Generaal voor Overheidspersoneelsbeleid, Ministerie van Binnenlandse Zaken*).

New salary scales take effect every January 1. Ideally, the increase should be equal to the rise of private pay during the year just completed. However, the evidence is never available so promptly. Calculations are based on an index of wages paid to all adult employees of enterprises employing 10,000 or more persons, issued by the Central Statistical Office of the government. The definitive figures are never ready until the middle of the next year. Therefore, the Directorate-General for Civil Service Staff Management issues a provisional salary increase on January 1, based on estimates of the movements in the private sector during the previous year supplied by two public economics institutes, the government's Central Planning Office and the autonomous Social-Economic Council. By July 1, the Central Statistical Office's wage index has been issued for the previous year, and the Directorate-General for Civil Service Staff Management can issue the official and final salary scales for the year. Since the scales are retroactive to January 1, the government sends "adjustment payments" to all civil servants, if they were collecting a provisional rate below the final rate.

As the net incomes after costs of GPs and specialists are linked to the increases for the senior civil servants, the doctors experience the same staging in their annual rise in fees. On January 1, they get a provisional rise. Around July 1, they learn the final rates for the year and receive adjustment payments for arrears since January 1. The Directorate-General for Civil Service Staff Management must publish the salary scales in two different versions on January 1 and July 1, and the *Ziekenfondsraad* likewise must print the entire fee schedule for GPs and specialists with two different lists of values in Guilders. The sick funds then send doctors adjustment payments for bills paid at the rates used during the first half of the year.

If the government decides not to raise every civil service grade at the same rate, the fees of doctors therefore will not keep pace with the average increase in private wages. The Left-Center Cabinet of 1973–1977 favored reduction of income differentials in Holland and therefore raised the higher grades of the civil service proportionately less than it increased the lower ranks. Therefore, the specialists and (to a lesser extent) the GPs had smaller increases of fees than would have resulted from a completely automatic across-the-board procedure. While the incomes of the civil servants were limited, some specialists could increase their total incomes beyond the rise in fees, through increased services under national health insurance and through additional private practice.

Permanente Tarieven Commissie

This busy group meets once a month throughout the year. Its ten members—all but one are doctors—include representatives from LSV, VNZ, and the *Ziekenfondsraad* itself. One of the many tasks is constant review of the voluminous fee schedules for specialists: they change relative values, add acts, drop some, and occasionally reorganize the structure of certain parts. The work is routine and can be done by the *Commissie* and the GBZ secretariat; the massive job of rewriting the entire fee schedule has not been attempted for several decades. If a complete review is ever done again—and some critics believe an overhaul is long overdue—then the *Commissie* will need to increase its meetings, expand its membership, and employ subcommittees.

The members of the *Permanente Tarieven Commissie* derive ideas from their own experiences as physicians, from conversations, from medical journals, and from the numerous incoming reports and letters that discuss how the fee schedules work in practice. When discussing the fees of a particular specialty, the commission often hears testimony from members of that specialty, often from the specialty group within KNMG.

Similar to the committee that writes the fee schedule in France, the *Permanente Tarieven Commissie* tries to rate acts by difficulty and by the amount of stress they cause doctors. This is intuitive, since no data exist about comparative difficulty, based either on observations or on surveys of doctors' opinions. If a new act is considered difficult it is given a higher coefficient, comparable to other acts of similar difficulty. An important consequence of this approach is that it can reduce costs: After many years of practice, an act is considered less difficult, and the *Commissie* occasionally reduces its coefficient. In contrast, deriving relative values from prevailing charges may result in a steady widening of differentials and a steady increase in costs.[7]

The *Permanente Tarieven Commissie* often makes clinical judgments about new procedures. The members decide to encourage them by adding them to the fee schedule at higher rates, while reducing the coefficients for the older techniques that they wish abandoned.

Because it is a principal clearing-house for information about the sick fund practice of specialists, the *Permanente Tarieven Commissie* sends information bearing on the economics of practice to the negotiating committee on specialists' fees (i.e., to the *Onderhandelingscommissie Ziekenfondsen-Specialisten*). The two groups coordinate their work closely: All members of the *Tarieven Commissie* belong to the larger bargaining committee.

As it collects information about how the fee schedules work in practice, the *Permanente Tarieven Commissie* hears the complaints about abuses by individual doctors. At present, therefore, it is the group judging professional discipline in national health insurance. (A different and more effective disciplinary structure will be developed during the coming years.)

PRIVATE HEALTH INSURANCE

Thirty per cent of the Dutch population still are not covered by national health insurance but must pay the doctor privately, an unusually large number for a European country. A large proportion of these patients is then reimbursed by private insurance companies. During the late 1960s, the private insurance companies complained that the fees were rising too fast. A negotiating system between private sick funds and medical associations was not created, but instead in 1969 the Dutch government declared that medical fees come under the preexisting Price Control law.[8]

Negotiations of a sort exist between the medical associations and the Ministry of Economic Affairs. The individual specialty groups within LSV and the general practitioners of LHV draft fee schedules each year. They file these with the Central Division for General Price Policy and Services of the Ministry, along with their economic justifications for higher fees. Their representatives present their case in person at hearings. The Ministers of Economic Affairs, Social Affairs, and Health issue decrees each year fixing the price ceiling for specialists and GPs. Usually they reduce the doctors' requests slightly.[9]

In recent years, the private insurance companies and the medical associations have discussed a possible system of bilateral bargaining. This will become moot, if the government presses its bill making national health insurance universal.

OVERVIEW OF THE DUTCH NEGOTIATING SYSTEM

Holland has organized national health insurance in ways that resemble probable future American patterns, and it continues to evolve efficiently. The preexisting nonprofit funds continue as official carriers, including a network resembling America's Blue Shield. National health insurance secularizes and standardizes sick funds, and Holland's are rapidly merging, in order to save administrative costs.

The medical association can be a model for others, because it combines a solicitude for the success of health insurance as well as protection of doctors' self-interest.

Negotiations have long been conducted calmly, with conscientious efforts to develop facts acceptable to all sides. Holland has been a laboratory in demonstrating techniques of linking pay in the public sector to private pay, but it also has inadvertently demonstrated the inflationary dangers. A neutral public agency acts as conciliator and protector of the system, offering a forum for both the providers and the general public.

Holland is one of the few countries where—as in the United States—most hospital doctors earn their incomes by fee-for-service. (In most other European countries, much of their incomes comes from salaries.) Keeping hospital doctors' pay in line with other health care costs and with the incomes of other elites has proved difficult under a fee-for-service system.

Holland is one of the few countries which pays many doctors by capitation. This is possible only for general practitioners. In the light of general practitioners' pressure for higher status, capitation has remained acceptable only through generous increases.

STRONG POINTS IN THE DUTCH SYSTEM

The sick funds and medical association have thorough and efficient methods for working out their negotiating positions. They develop negotiating papers of great sophistication and distribute them in advance of the bargaining meetings.

GBZ and the *Ziekenfondsraad* provide staff support for the bilateral negotiations that is excellent in quality and neutral in viewpoint. The *Ziekenfondsraad* enables other social groups and the government to discuss policy in general and the negotiated agreements in particular before they become final. A good idea is the sending of memoranda by negotiating committees, asking the *Raad's* advice before innovations are included in agreements.

An effective arbitration method—a committee of "wise men"—is available on the rare occasions when the existing machinery breaks down. However, when they include too many doctors, their wisdom may be expensive.

Holland is a good demonstration of how the spirit of negotiation is as important as the institutions. Discussions are calm, polite, and factual.

Holland offers one of the rarest of lessons, viz., how to eliminate organizations that are obsolete and create unnecessary expenses. The federations of sick funds existed separately when Holland had many social, religious, and ideological divisions. When the sick funds became alike in function and lost their ideological identities, the separate organizations were superfluous. So, with a pragmatism rarely found in the world, the Dutch merely merged them. The merger was accomplished like everything else in Dutch life—by painstaking negotiation and by making sure that everyone's interests (and immediate job security) were assured.

SOME PROBLEMS IN THE DUTCH SYSTEM

Having created the most efficient system for negotiating the payment of health providers, Holland can see the inherent weaknesses of the best of adversarial bargaining arrangements. At present, each set of negotiators must follow the law and make their decisions roughly according to a budget, but they need not think much about health policy or about the viability of any larger system. Each bargaining relationship aims to buy peace according to a balance of forces; the different confrontations may result in an incoherent pattern and an expensive total.

In theory the *Ziekenfondsraad* sets a policy for the negotiators, but it is not too effective. Its mandate is limited to administering health insurance and does not extend to interpreting and implementing policy for the country's health delivery. The parties to the bargaining hold many seats on the *Raad* and therefore easily get approval of their agreements. The *Raad* has many other topics on its agenda, and usually accepts the agreements on pay *pro forma*. Therefore, the *Raad* may be too permissive about rises in utilization and in fees.[10]

During the 1970s, Dutch Cabinets moved toward the Left. They favored better organization and planning of health services, and making national health insurance an integral part of a cost-effective structure. In late 1976, the government proposed a Central Agency for Health Services Prices (*Centraal Orgaan Tarieven Gezondheidszorg*). It would consist of independent experts from economics, law, and the health professions. It would advise the government in setting guidelines for all negotiations about pay and prices in the health services. The government by law would require negotiators to follow these guidelines. Bilateral negotiations would continue—perhaps the present arrangements would survive—but the agency would review all agreements. The government's approval would no longer be automatic; it would disapprove any awards out of line from the agency's guidelines.[11]

In nearly every country, the medical association favors bilateral bargaining and opposes government interventions that can overrule the negotiated agreements or that can announce awards in the absence of agreements. So, KNMG strongly opposed the Cabinet's bill. The proposal is one solution to a common dilemma under national health insurance, viz., how to persuade or force the self-interested bargainers to conform to a larger public interest. The pressure politics that the reform intends to control will delay its enactment, since the providers suspect it is a tactic for introducing a national health service.

NOTES

1. For convenient summaries of the past history and recent organization of Dutch national health insurance, see L. V. Ledeboer, *Heden en verleden—van de ziekenfondsverzekering en de verzekering van bijzondere ziektekosten* (Leidschendam: Ministerie van Volksgezondheid en Milieuhygiene, 1973); "Social Security in the Netherlands," *International Social Security Review,* Volume XXIII, Number 1 (1970); and B. M. Teldersstichting, *Het Ziekenfondswezen in Nederland* ('s-Gravenhage: Martinus Nijhoff, 1963). Histories of several sick funds have been written, such as *Geschiedenis van het Algemeen Ziekenfonds voor Amsterdam 1847-1947* (Amsterdam: Algemeen Ziekenfonds, 1947).

2. The history of organized medicine in Holland appears in H. Festen, *125 jaar geneeskunst en mattschappij* (Utrecht, KNMG, 1974). Recent work and policies are described in "Nut en noodzak van een artsenorganisatie," a series of articles from *Medische Contact,* 1974, reprinted by the KNMG.

3. Described in Arend Lijphart, *The Politics of Accommodation: Pluralism and Democracy in the Netherlands* (Berkeley: University of California Press, Second edition, 1975); and Johan Goudsblom, *Dutch Society* (New York: Random House, 1967), esp. pp. 80-82 and 106-109.

4. A convenient compendium is G. A. Sneep (editor), *Ziekenfondswet* (Zwolle: W. E. J. Tjeenk Willink, 1975), especially Chapter IV. A brief overview of the negotiating system appears in Ledeboer, *op. cit.* (note 1, supra), pp. 36-38.

5. Some basic information about the *Ziekenfondsraad* appears in "Social Security in the Netherlands," *op .cit.* (note 1, supra), p. 23. On the Dutch style of negotiations over pay and the stillborn attempt to create complete governing structures in each sector, see John P. Windmuller, *Labor Relations in the Netherlands* (Ithaca: Cornell University Press, 1969), esp. pp. 286-297 and 400-414.

6. The capitation fee was decided after calculations based on certain assumptions concerning the target income of Grade 151 that year, the average size of lists in sick funds practice, the average amount of private practice, and the average costs for such a work load. "Advies Commissie Van der Ven," *Medisch Contact,* Volume 22, Number 1 (6 January 1967), pp. 9-14. A convenient summary of the events is in *Jaarverslag* (Utrecht: Centrale Bond van Onderling Beheerde Ziekenfondsen, 1966), pp. 27-29.

7. For example, William J. Sobaski, "Effects of the 1969 California Relative Values Studies on the Costs of Physician Services under SMI," *Health Insurance Statistics* (published by Office of Research and Statistics, Social Security Administration), 20 June 1975.

8. The statute and its administration are described in Windmuller, *op. cit.* (note 5, supra), pp. 335-336.

9. The rationale for deciding private fees in general practice was set forth by a committee of four "wise men": report of the *Adviescommissie huisartsentarieven voor particuliere patiënten* to the Ministry of Economic Affairs, October 1971; "Minister stemt in met advies van Commissie-Donner over huisartsentarieven voor particuliere patiënten," *Medisch Contact,* Volume 27, Number 6 (11 February 1972), pp. 139-140.

10. For example, a rude awakening was the recent discovery that the *Raad* had been too complacent about the possible submission of fraudulent bills by specialists. *Rapport uitgebracht door de 'Commissie Becht'* (Amstelveen: Ziekenfondsraad, 1976, Report Number 73).

11. The bill is explained in the report by the Ministries of Public Health and Economic Affairs, "Regelen met betrekking tot de tarieven van organen voor gezondheidszorg (Wet tarieven gezondheidszorg)," *Tweede Kamer der Staten-General: Zitting 1976-1977,* 14182, nrs. 1-3.

CHAPTER VI

Federal Republic
of Germany

BOTH France and Holland have unitary governments. Their sick funds differ in legal status—the French are "official" and the Dutch are "private" —but both are centralized and negotiate with the national leadership of the medical profession on all topics.

West Germany, Switzerland, and Canada are federal systems and can provide particularly relevant lessons for the United States.[1] The three countries differ widely in degrees of nationwide unification in the organization of their sick funds, their medical associations, and their negotiations.

THE SICK FUNDS

German social benefits associations have existed for centuries and may be the oldest in Europe.[2] The first national health insurance law—enacted by the *Reichstag* in 1883—required enrollment in funds by all workers in certain occupations and under certain income levels. Instead of being replaced by government departments, the funds became the depositories for money collected by governmental taxation and became the fiscal agent paying out benefits. The basic statute (*Reichsversicherungsordnung* or RVO) and supplementary regulations have expanded coverage, increased benefits, and prescribed the organization and procedures of the funds in successively greater detail since its inception.

By now, nearly ninety percent of the German population has jobs or other statuses that enroll them in the official funds voluntarily. (These are called the *gesetzliche Krankenkassen* or *RVO-Kassen*). White-collar workers and some blue-collar workers may be exempted from the *RVO-Kassen* and enroll instead in alternative funds with different managements and greater benefits (*Ersatzkassen*).[3] Nearly all persons not covered by these programs have private health insurance.

Once 20,000 separate sick funds existed, but the number now is about 1,500. They are consolidated into national associations. The largest number of funds are small ones for workers in individual factories (*Betriebskrankenkassen*). Other official funds are for craftsmen (*Innungskrankenkassen*), farmers (*landwirtschaftliche Krankenkassen*), and miners (*Bundesknappschaft*). The largest number of people belong to the sick funds that enroll everyone not falling into these special funds (viz., the *Ortskrankenkassen*).

Because Germany is federal, the sick funds of each type are united in a provincial association in each of the eleven *länder,* such as the *Verband der Ortskrankenkassen Rheinland.* The 11 state associations of each type are united in a national association, such as the *Bundesverband der Ortskrankenkassen,* the *Bundesverband der Innungskrankenkassen,* and so on. Within each *land,* the *Verbände* are independent of each other. Similarly, at the national level, the *Bundesverbände* are independent of each other; their offices are in different cities. Within each network, there has been a gradual trend of power and functions flowing from the individual sick fund to the *Verband* headquarters, and (more recently) to the *Bundesverband* office.[4]

The sick funds act according to law but are not departments or subordinates of government. The Ministry of Labor merely oversees that health insurance is being conducted consistently with the law; the Ministry recommends statutory amendments and issues new regulations. The funds constantly assert their rights of self-government (*selbstverwaltung*) and the government periodically issues reports reviewing how *selbstverwaltung* is working out in practice.[5] Self-government means that each unit in a network of sick funds (whether an individual fund or a *Verband* at the *land* level or a *Bundesverband*) is ruled by a representative assembly (a *Vertreterversammlung*). Members of the assembly are drawn from subscribers and from employers. Usually the principal trade union association names a single slate of representatives for subscribers, the principal employers association names a single slate of representatives for employers, and the election is automatic. However, occasionally an election is contested in an individual fund or in a *Verband.* Each sick fund or *Verband* or *Bundesverband* has an elected governing board (a *Vorstand*) with members that devote much time to this work and that meets more often than the *Vertreterversammlung.* The full-time management of the sick fund or *Verband* or *Bundesverband* (the *Geschäftsführung*) reports to the *Vorstand* at its frequent meetings and to the *Vertreterversammlung* at its occasional meetings.

THE MEDICAL PROFESSION

The original statute gave the sick funds authority to organize medical care, and not merely pay for it. Therefore, for many years, they hired doctors and managed facilities. Conflicts with the doctors were common: the doctors disliked the terms of their employment and resented domination by laymen, who often were of the political Left; those not in the closed panels employed by the funds resented being shut off from insurance practice. Some groups of doctors organized to fight their employers. Eventually a compromise was struck: The sick funds delegated their authority to organize care to the doctors admitted to sick fund practice, and they paid lump sums to these groups. The arrangement was then spelled out in the *Reichsversicherungsordnung* itself.[6]

The basic unit of the medical profession for health insurance is an association of all doctors in health insurance practice in each *land,* a *Kassenärztliche Vereinigung* or KV. The associations from all *länder* are united in a federation, the *Kassenärztliche Bundesvereinigung* or KBV, with offices in Cologne. Unlike the sick funds and professional medical societies, the KBV and KVs are not "natural" or preexisting organizations, but they are created by clauses of the RVO.

Each KV negotiates over money with each *Verband der Krankenkassen.* The KV then processes claims, receives money from the sick funds, pays the doctors, and reviews utilization. In no other country does such a system exist: it was a solution to the conflict between sick funds and their closed panels; elsewhere the solution was the early elimination of closed panels, allowing every doctor to treat insured patients, and paying the doctors or the patient directly by the sick fund.

The KV is a corporation in public law, operated by *selbstverwaltung.* Like the provincial association of sick funds, it has a representative assembly that meets occasionally (a *Vertreterversammlung*), a governing board that meets regularly (a *Vorstand*), and a full-time staff of administrators and economists. The members of the *Vertreterversammlung* are elected by doctors from different districts. The KVs office staff represents the interests of the members in dealings with the sick funds, with the government of the *land,* and with the KBV. In return for its autonomy, the KV under the RVO is committed to provide adequate medical care throughout the country; many provincial headquarters operate emergency services, locate substitute doctors, and support practitioners in remote areas.

Part of the KV staff processes all the claims (i.e., the *Krankenscheine* filled out by doctors reporting treatments) and pays out money. This function is performed by the sick funds in all other countries. The KV also maintains the investigators and the committees to police abuse.[7]

Only half the doctors of Germany are office practitioners serving insured patients. Some are salaried members on the staffs of hospitals and other organizations; others are office practitioners in completely private practice. These have associations of their own. In addition, there exist associations of various ideological persuasions, and professional societies concerned with clinical matters. The KV and all these other groups in each *land* are united in an *Ärztekammer,* and the eleven provincial associations in turn are united in the *Bundesärztekammer.* The KBV and *Bundesärztekammer* collaborate closely, occupying adjacent buildings in Cologne and publishing jointly German medicine's leading professional news magazine.[8]

FORMAL STRUCTURE OF THE NEGOTIATING SYSTEM

Paragraphs 368f and 368g of the *Reichsversicherungsordnung* passed by the German Parliament provide that payment for doctors' services under health insurance shall be made pursuant to agreements worked out between the associations of doctors and the sick funds.[9] This permits more discretion than in several other countries, where the details are spelled out in the statute. For several decades, overall agreements about the system have been negotiated between the KBV and the *Bundesverbände,* while amounts of money have been settled by the KV and the *Verbände* of sick funds in each *land.* The actual formula for distributing money is left to the decision of the parties too.

In conformity with the RVO, the KBV and the four *Bundesverbände der Ortskrankenkassen, Betriebskrankenkassen, Landwirtschaftlichen Krankenkassen* and *Innungskrankenkassen* together negotiated a general contract for all health insurance practice in Germany (a *Bundesmantelvertrag*) in 1959. The parties meet occasionally to amend the contract. Paragraph 26 of the contract states that the KV shall administer payments, that the rules about payment shall be worked out between the sick funds and the KV or KBV, and whatever payment schedule is adopted by the parties shall be considered an appendix to the *Bundesmantelvertrag.*

For several decades, the provincial *Verband* paid a lump sum (a *Kopfpauschale*) to the KV, and the KV distributed it among the doctors to pay for treatment of the patients from that network of sick funds. Until World War II, some doctors were paid a capitation fee for each patient (a *Fallpauschale*), but gradually fee-for-service became universal. However, as long as the *Kopfpauschale* system was used, the fee schedule was a relative values scale rather than a guarantee of payment in full. Since the *Kopfpauschale* was a fixed sum, a larger number of bills resulted in a lower payment for each act.[10]

A revision of RVO, Para. 368f(3), in 1955 added the possible option of payment in full for each act (*Einzelleistungsvergütung*). A stillborn general revision of the RVO during the early 1960s would have abolished the *Kopfpauschale* system, subsituted payment in full for each act, and given the Minister of Labor power to issue the fee schedule. The bill was never enacted, but parts of the reform have been carried out by regulation or by agreement between doctors and sick funds, because the wording of the 1955 revisions allows it. Since about 1968, all *länder* have a policy of payment in full for each act according to a fee schedule, the method preferred by the doctors.[11]

Any other method could be adopted in negotiations between a KV and a *Verband,* including revival of the *Kopfpauschale,* but the doctors refuse.

As in all countries with fee-for-service, two different procedures are followed to produce the fee schedule and the monetary valuations of each act. Germany's federal system makes the machinery quite separate: The fee schedule is negotiated at the national level and the money is negotiated within each *land,* although recently financial guidelines have been worked out nationally.

The fee schedule

It performs two functions: it guides the distribution of money that the KV's receive from the sick funds; it guides the courts in the award of fees in law suits involving doctors, patients, and sick funds if no contracts are signed between the KV and a *Verband.* As a result of the second official and legal use, it is prepared by the national Ministry of Economics and is issued as a decree of the national Cabinet. The KBV and the *Bundesverbände* of sick funds then adopt it as the appendix to their *Bundesmantelvertrag.*

The health insurance system had long used an ancient fee schedule colloquially called PREUGO, but by the 1950s it was out of date. A general revision of health insurance was being planned during the decade, and the Ministry of Economics invited the *Bundesärztekammer* to submit a proposal for a new fee schedule. The KBV's draft on behalf of the medical profession was long and detailed, in the tradition of PREUGO and corresponding to the German medical profession's technical approach to fee-for-service. The ministry's own economists and medical consultants favored a shorter document, with more broadly defined global acts. The

Ministry opposed the medical profession's fee schedule on the grounds
that it would greatly increase costs and encourage too many technical
acts; the doctors opposed the Ministry's plans as a step toward capitation
and case payments. This was one of the deadlocks that eventually prevented enactment of reform in health insurance.[12]

The changes adopted by the weakened Cabinet during the 1960s included several concessions to the doctors. One was enacting the sort of
fee schedules the doctors wanted. The KBV and the *Ersatzkassen* have
long been able to write their own fee schedules without official approval,
since the *Ersatzkassen* are not governed by the RVO. Therefore, while
PREUGO had become out of date, the KBV and the *Ersatzkassen* had
agreed upon the kind of modern fee schedule favored by the doctors. The
national Cabinet in 1965 issued as the new official fee schedule, the *Ge-
bührenordnung für Ärzte* (colloquially called GOA), a copy of the *Ersatzkassen* fee schedule. For the Ministry of Economics, it had the advantage
of yielding more predictable results than any completely new document.[13]

National negotiations over the fee schedule

The Cabinet's decree adopting GOA authorized the addition of new
acts. An agreement between the KBV and the four principal national
federations of sick funds (local, industrial, agricultural, and crafts) created
a committee to keep GOA up to date. It is called the *Ausschuss nach
Para. 5,* referring to the clause in the agreement creating it and defining
its powers. Many negotiating committees in Germany have precisely equal
numbers of members from each side, but this is a work group of specialists who try to develop a consensus, it rarely calls for votes, and therefore
it has no fixed membership.

Usually meetings are attended by one or two specialists in fee schedules from the KBV headquarters; one of the KV leaders who is particularly
interested in fee schedules; and one or two specialists in fee schedules from
each of the four *Bundesverbände* of sick funds. When special topics are
discussed, the KBV and the *Bundesverbände* may send additional persons
familiar with those fields. The secretarial work is done by the KBV office
that concentrates on fee schedules. Many suggestions and much of the
drafting are made by the KBV's principal specialists in the design of fee
schedules.[14] They collect questions and requests from all over Germany,
via the mail and in frequent personal visits to the KV offices.

The committee often alters the wording of particular acts, to change
their meaning or simply to make them more comprehensible. It can add
new acts, if it considers them appropriate therapies, and it can fix their
rates. (The committee usually matches them with others already in GOA,
so that comparable work earns the same money.) The committee can alter

the relative value of particular acts that it believes are overvalued or undervalued. (In 1971 it raised the value of home visits, in order to discourage their disappearance; and it raised the value of psychiatric examinations, to assuage the psychiatrists' complaint that they could not afford to treat patients under national health insurance.) The committee can alter the relative value of an entire section. (For example, in 1975 it reduced the value of all laboratory tests, to counterbalance the great financial windfalls due to high utilization with automatic equipment.)

In earlier years, the committee met only when a sufficient number of proposals were pending. However, the KBV has been pressing for a general modernization of GOA, and since 1974 the committee has met almost every month. The new section for laboratory fees was the first step in a general revision. Before a change can be implemented in health insurance practice, the committee's recommendations must be adopted by the *Vorstand* of the KBV and by the *Vorstände* of the four principal *Bundesverbände* of sick funds.

GOA has been revised so often by the negotiating committee that it would be hard to understand in its official form: The original GOA must be accompanied by an equally long collection of supplements (called the *Analoge Bewertungen*). So, for convenience, KBV and the principal medical publishing house have issued a consolidated and constantly up to date version called the *Bewertungsmassstab-Ärzte* (or BMA), which the office doctors and sick funds actually use in practice.

GOA in its original form remains in effect as a decree of the Cabinet, for official use in the unlikely event of a breakdown in relations between doctors and sick funds. The KBV and *Bundesärztekammer* favor scrapping the traditional practice of an official schedule issued by the government and revised infrequently, and they recommend constant modernization through the *Ausschuss nach Para. 5*.[15] The Ministry of Economics is unwilling to step out of the picture, since it fears the KBV will dominate the revisions of the fee schedule, with an increasing spread among relative values and a constant rise in total costs. Retention of GOA in its original form may be a restraint.[16]

Provincial negotiations over money

Before World War II and in most areas just after, the payment of money was negotiated each year by the KV and the individual sick fund. However, soon the sick funds for self-protection in bargaining transferred this power to the association office for each *land*. (After the KV and *Verband* agree on a figure, the agreement—called a *Gesamtvertrag*—is still signed between the KV and each individual sick fund.) The KV tries to bargain with each of the four *Verbände* separately within each of the eleven *länder,* since it believes it can thereby get the best results. After getting higher awards from some *Verbände* in some *länder,* it can ask all the others to match them. The proposed reforms of RVO in the early 1960s included a shift in the bargaining to a single national meeting between the KBV and all the *Bundesverbände* of sick funds, and this was an important reason for the doctors' opposition—despite the other concessions they would have received.[17]

Because the doctors prefer striking the best bargain with each provincial network of sick funds, they have rarely (if ever) met with all the *Verbände* together about money. (They meet jointly to write or amend the general agreement governing relations between the KV and all the sick funds in each *land,* called the *Landesmantelvertrag.* The agreement runs for many years and is changed rarely, so the plenary meetings are infrequent.) Although joint negotiations would be in each *Verband's* economic interest, separate action is in its organizational interest. Lest it become a step in a merger under the domination of the large *Ortskrankenkassen* network, the other funds have avoided coordination within the *länder.* However, recently in several *länder,* officials of the different *Verbände* have begun to keep each other informed of their negotiating stances, lest one make excessive and expensive concessions to the KV.

The GOA was written in the *Deutsche Mark* values of 1965, and both GOA and BMA are still printed with such figures. Each year since then, the KV and *Verband* representatives meet to negotiate an increase. By 1976, the actual fees paid to doctors were about 50 per cent higher than the original values in GOA. Once the fees were substantially higher in the richer than in the poorer *länder,* but the differences have steadily narrowed. The *Bundesverband* of each set of sick funds tries to guide the *land* offices to make similar offers; and the national leadership of the KBV itself has been trying to equalize the incomes of doctors throughout Germany by persuading the KVs to file similar requests. By the latter half of 1976, the fees had reached the following levels among the provincial associations of *Ortskrankenkassen.* (100 = the prices in the original GOA.)

Land or bargaining jurisdiction	Per cent
North Wurttemberg	153.09
North Baden	152.88
Lower Saxony	149.68
Bavaria	149.00
Saar	144.00

(The other *länder* stood between 149 and 153.) The fee in 1976 for each act for an *Ortskrankenkasse* patient in Lower Saxony, for example, is 149.68 per cent of the entry in the GOA or BMA.

The KV in each *land* obtains different amounts from the different *Verbände* of sick funds, depending on the network's affluence, the competing demands upon the *Verband's* money, and its bargaining skill. For example, the *Betriebskassen* usually can afford to pay higher fees than the *Ortskrankenkassen* because fewer elderly pensioners belong. The funds for farmers can afford less, because their members' incomes and the insurance premiums are lower. For example, the figures in Lower Saxony for 1976 were.

Association of	Per cent of GOA
Local funds (**Ortskrankenkassen**)	149.68
Industrial funds (**Betriebskrankenkassen**)	155.58
Craft funds (**Innungskrankenkassen**)	152.30
Agricultural funds (**Landwirtschaftliche Krankenkassen**)	149.70

The fee in 1976 for each act for a *Betriebskasse* patient in Lower Saxony was 155.58 per cent of the entry in the GOA or BMA, for an agricultural patient, it was 149.70 per cent. In other *länder,* the range among sick funds has become much narrower. For example, in North Rhine-Westphalia, the figures for 1976 fell between 149 per cent and 151 per cent of the original GOA values. The trend is toward greater uniformity among the funds in each *land*.[18]

The negotiating procedure is nearly the same for all sick funds in all *länder.* At the beginning of each year, the *Vorstand* of the KV formulates its requests. In all *länder* information is collected concerning trends in the costs of practice and in the earnings of doctors; some KV offices develop more detailed papers than others. The KV can calculate earnings from insurance practice and from its own records, but little accurate data about doctors' costs of practice exist in Germany. Some KVs study reports on practice costs from a private accounting firm that helps many private office doctors throughout the country make out their income tax reports.

At the same time, the executives of the *Verband* poll their member funds concerning their financial capacities and whether they can raise premiums next year. The executives also study trends in utilization, and their consequences for costs. (Once the *Verbände* had little detailed knowledge about utilization for individual acts or types of patients, because the KVs processed all claims. Now, many *Verbände* get data tapes from the KVs and run them on their own computers. (Since the KV ultimately must send all the bills back to the *Verband,* some *Verbände* keypunch all the bills for their own purposes and study the results.) [19] The *Vorstand* then meets to formulate an offer.

Small negotiating teams from the KV and *Verband* then meet. Usually it is the chairman, the vice chairman, the business manager, and the assistant business manager from each. If either side adds more from head-quarters, the other usually brings more too. The *Verband* may include managers from a few sick funds. Unlike Holland, detailed documents are not exchanged. Unlike Canada, specialized insurance accountants are not involved. Usually the two sides debate: the doctors tell about the rise in their practice costs, in the difficulty of their work, and in general living costs; the sick funds tell about the rise in utilization, the competing demands on their income from hospitals and from other sources, and the difficulty of raising premiums. After one or a few sessions of several hours apiece, the two sides agree on a compromise figure.[20]

Sending both the chairman and vice–chairman enables the sick funds to include in the negotiating teams representatives from both employers and trade unions. (The two posts are divided between the two social groups.) The organization of this confrontation is an important reason why German businessmen are no longer economic allies of the medical profession and have instead become apprehensive about the mounting costs of medical care.

Once relations between doctors and sick funds were very bitter. Strikes and deadlocks were common. Now the rule is quick agreement every year. On the rare occasions when the two cannot agree, the *Reichsversicherungs-ordnung* and each *Landesmantelvertrag* provide use of a standing arbitration panel (a *Schiedsamt*) that has been created pursuant to regulations issued by the Ministry of Labor. Health insurance does not rely upon a government mediation service but uses its own panels, but they do coordinate with the offices of the *land* governments specializing in arbitration and law. Every four years, two representatives are appointed by the KV and two by the *Verband* to deal with any disputes in their relations. The members elect a neutral chairman, usually a lawyer and often a retired civil servant, who has long specialized in arbitration. If the parties cannot agree on the chairman, a rotating pair of chairman and vice-chairman is assigned by the *land* government. Usually the *Schiedsamt* has no work and no meetings, but it is available in case of trouble. The *Schiedsamt* settles things quickly, and its word is final.[21]

Whether it come from bilateral negotiations or from a *Scheidsamt,* an agreement becomes official only after it is accepted by the *Vorstand* of the KV, the *Vorstand* of the provincial association of sick funds, and the *Vorstand* of each individual sick fund. (If an individual fund balks at a settlement that everyone else accepts, the KV and that fund go to the *Landesschiedsamt*.) The *Gesamtvertrag* is then signed between the KV and each individual fund. If the settlement will exceed the expected revenue of the individual sick fund, its *Vertreterversammlung* must meet to raise premiums. Instead of a standard payroll tax for all citizens, as in most other countries with national health insurance, individual German funds levy slightly different premiums. (Some have more extra cash than others, and they offer benefits in addition to those mandated in the law.)

THE SHIFT TOWARD NATIONAL NEGOTIATIONS

The rapid rise in medical costs in Germany during the 1970s and widespread criticisms by mass media of alleged profiteering by doctors from insurance[22] led the harassed sick funds to take strong action. One result was informal cooperation among the sick funds within each *land* over money offers, and not merely over the wording of the fee schedules. Another result was a shifting of negotiations from the *land* to the national level.

Meetings were held in the early 1970s without upshot: The KBV asked for higher fees than the four principal *Bundesverbände* of sick funds were willing to recommend to their provincial offices. The national discussions to write guidelines were made moot several times when KVs persuaded *Verbände* in the richer *länder* to sign agreements for fees exceeding those discussed in the national sessions. The negotiations gave the associations of sick funds the new experience of coordinating their financial strategies. At these meetings, each *Bundesverband* was represented by representatives from the employer and trade union delegates in the *Vorstand*; by several of the full-time managers; and by experts specializing in finance and in the work of doctors. The KBV was represented by its national chairman, by its vice-chairman, and by several of the full-time managers, including specialists in doctors' fees and contracts.

By 1975, the sick funds were convinced that costs and utilization had become crises, that abandonment of the *Kopfpauschale* system had been a cause, and that they could no longer keep raising premiums. The four *Bundesverbände* met the KBV in January 1975, predicted that utilization would continue to rise and cost them too much, and offered no increase in fees anywhere in Germany in 1975. The doctors were apprehensive about the national mass media campaign against them, were also concerned about the magnitude of the *Kostenexplosion,* and asked for only a 2.75% increase. The negotiators compromised on a recommended increase in fees of 2.35% for the second half of 1975 and all of 1976, in large part because some of the KVs and provincial *Verbände* had already signed new contracts near that figure. The guidelines were followed more or less in *länder* that had not yet signed contracts. Several KVs grumbled about the KBV's attempt to take over negotiation of fees, which had long been their *raison d'être.*

The agreement of 1975 was intended to limit total costs by limiting fees alone; the sick funds hoped that utilization would increase by only

8% over 1974, and therefore they could afford the 2.35% increase in fees. Instead, utilization rose by 10% during 1975, and the sick funds regretted that they had not defended their original position against any increase in fees at all.

In the spring of 1976, the KBV and the four *Bundesverbände* met again and negotiated recommendations for the *land* contracts in 1976 and 1977. For the first time since 1965, utilization and the size of fees were linked. Fees would rise 4% in 1977, provided that the total of fees plus utilization rose no more than about 8% in 1976. If utilization rises more than 6% in 1976—2.35% for fees plus 6% for utilization equals about 8% in the expected increase in costs—the increase in fees is cut correspondingly during 1977, so that the cost of all ambulatory medical services rises no more than about 8% in each year.[23] The KBV agreed, in order to head off resurging interest in the old *Kopfpauschale* system, which remains one of the possibilities under RVO.[24]

The new agreement was a guideline that the KVs and provincial *Verbände* implemented in the binding negotiations. An important reason why it was implemented was the commitment of the provincial associations of sick funds. They had long requested it from their national offices and defended it in their own negotiations in 1977. The national leadership of the KBV negotiated at great length with their KVs, in order to solicit their views, incorporate their desires in the recommendations and persuade them to accede. Nevertheless, some leaders of KVs complained that the concessions were excessive, that other providers (such as dentists) would gain more, and that the KBV lacked such negotiating powers.

So that the power to issue guidelines would no longer be questioned, it was made official in the national government's amendments to RVO in 1977, as part of the package of new laws to control costs. Every year, the federal Minister of Labor will call a conference of national representatives of the *RVO-Kassen, Ersatzkassen,* private health insurance companies, doctors, dentists, hospitals, pharmacists, drug companies, employers, trade unions, *länder,* and communes. The federal Ministries of Labor, Health, and Economics also participate. Data about the performance of the health delivery system are collected from governmental and other sources by the Ministry of Labor and are submitted to the conferees. By March 31, the conferees issue judgments about the economic trends in the system, recommendations about improvements, and recommendations about appropriate payments. Included are suggestions about doctors' fees and predictions about probable utilization. All guidelines are supposed to keep health care costs within increases in GNP. The KV's and the provincial *Verbände* of sick funds are not required to enact these recommendations but take them into account during their negotiations. Therefore, in 1978 Germany had begun to administer the kind of integrated confrontation among all parties to health care cost containment that Holland had been considering.

NEGOTIATIONS BETWEEN DOCTORS AND THE ERSATZKASSEN

Long before 1883, Germany had insurance funds for persons other than the workers for whom RVO was originally designed. Businessmen, white-collar workers, and professionals belonged. As RVO was gradually expanded to the higher income groups, clauses were added allowing these persons to satisfy their statutory obligation by joining the middle class nonprofit sick funds instead of those operating under the detailed provisions of RVO. The former became known as the "substitute sick funds" or *Ersatzkassen,* while the latter (i.e., those described on previous pages) are called the "statutory sick funds" or *RVO-Kassen.* In addition to those required to join some fund by law, the *Ersatzkassen* enroll voluntary members.[25]

Over one-fourth of the German population now belong to *Ersatzkassen.* Most join the funds for white-collar workers, a few are in funds for white-collar workers, a few are in funds for blue-collar workers. Unlike the *RVO-Kassen,* the two networks are not organized federally into a series of provincial divisions: The national office negotiates for each.

Because the *Ersatzkassen* are nonprofit private corporations, they can work out their relations with the doctors directly: The basic contract, the fee schedule, and the annual award of new money are negotiated between the *Kassenärztliche Bundesvereinigung* on the one hand and the two associations (*Verband der Angestellten-Krankenkassen* and the *Verband der Arbeiter-Ersatzkassen*) on the other hand. The government is not involved: one result is greater flexibility; another result is the greater power of the doctors.

The basic contract now in force (the *Arzt/Ersatzkassen-Vertrag*) was written by the two sides in 1963. It created a special working group (the *Arbeitsgemeinschaft Ärzte/Ersatzkassen*), consisting of five members from each side. The KBV's representatives include the head of the office specializing in fees in the KBV secretariat, several members of the Council of the national KBV who are also active in the KVs on the level of the *länder,* and a lawyer. The *Ersatzkassen's* five members include four from the white-collar network (the specialist in contracts and in payment of doctors at headquarters and three from different member funds) and one from the headquarters for workers' funds. The *Arbeitsgemeinschaft* meets three or four times a year. About twice a year, it discusses the terms of the contract itself; it writes amendments and clarifying memoranda. The amendments take effect when the *Vorstand* of each association agrees.

A principal task of the *Arbeitsgemeinschaft* is reviewing and updating the fee schedule. The original *Ersatzkassen-Adgo* was taken over from private practice around 1928. Small changes have been frequent and general revisions—with complete new printings—occurred in 1950, 1963, and 1976. Almost all substantive revisions are proposed by the full-time specialists in fee schedules employed by the KBV, on the initiative of doctors from anywhere in Germany or after consultation with them. The KBV's office specializing in fee schedules does the staff work for this part of the *Arbeitsgemeinschaft's* work. The *Ersatzkassen* have the disadvantage of not employing as staff members or as consultants, specialists in the design of fee schedules, as do the *RVO-Kassen*. They do not repair this omission by asking the advice of the *RVO-Kassen* about their recent experiences with GOA. The KBV representatives have the advantage of working also on GOA with the *RVO-Kassen*. In normal times, changes in fee schedules are merely items on the agenda of the normal meetings of the *Arbeitsgemeinschaft*. During general revisions, such as during 1975 and 1976, the meetings may occur monthly.

Every year the *Arbeitsgemeinschaft* negotiates an increase in the fees. As in negotiations between the KBV and the *RVO-Kassen,* the general level of fees goes up each year, in a compromise between the doctors' claims about practice costs, living costs, and the difficulty of work, and the *Ersatzkassen's* rebuttals about costs. The relative values among acts are modified more often in the *Ersatzkassen-Adgo* than in GOA, because it is not a governmental act and can be revised freely by the negotiators. The representatives of the *Ersatzkassen* often suggest that an act is overpaid and is a financial windfall, and the negotiators may reduce its relative value.

An act under the *Ersatzkassen-Adgo* has always been better paid than the same act under PREUGO and GOA. Until 1965, the *Ersatzkassen* paid all acts in full while the *RVO-Kassen* funds were divided according to the *Kopfpauschale* system. The administrative difference—plus the greater amount of money available from the more affluent members of the *Ersatzkassen*—meant that the *Ersatzkassen* fees were always higher. In 1965, the *RVO-Kassen* adopted payment in full according to a close copy of the *Ersatzkassen-Adgo*. Since then, the *Ersatzkassen* fees went up faster (63% from 1966 through 1976, while the *RVO-Kassen* fees rose by about 50%), and therefore the gap widened even more. In 1976, the basic office visit was 6.25DM under *Ersatzkassen-Adgo* and 4.50DM under GOA. Many other acts showed the same differential, but not all, since a number of specialized technical tasks had been reduced in relative value in *Ersatzkassen-Adgo*. The *Ersatzkassen* negotiators are more generous than the representatives from the *RVO-Kassen* because their subscribers are richer, the subscribers are more willing to pay higher premiums, the subscribers include fewer expensive risks, and the funds do not have to pay so many other expensive benefits (such as disability allowances). Members join the *Ersatzkassen* in the expectation that they will pay higher premiums, bring more money to the doctor, and perhaps get better care.[26]

Elimination of the *Ersatzkassen*—or their conversion into typical *RVO-Kassen*—has long been an article of faith among the official funds, particularly the leadership of the *Ortskrankenkassen*.[27] The critics have many reasons: the *Ersatzkassen's* middle-class character and higher fees allegedly makes the German population regard the *RVO-Kassen* as "second class" medicine; the *Ersatzkassen* take the safest risks away from the *RVO-Kassen* and leave the latter with the greater economic burdens; the doctors supposedly can "divide and conquer" the funds by getting concessions from the malleable *Ersatzkassen* and then press the *RVO-Kassen* to "catch up." One response of the *Ersatzkassen* is a constant reaffirmation of their identity and *selbstverwaltung*.[28] Another is avoidance of any coordination with the *RVO-Kassen* in negotiating with doctors or in anything else.

The *Ersatzkassen* at first during the 1970s did not participate in the national meetings to work out guidelines about fees. They did not seek to keep *Ersatzkassen-Adgo* and GOA identical (as they were in 1965). Instead, the *Ersatzkassen* emphasized that the two documents differed, that *Ersatzkassen-Adgo* was more in tune with modern medicine and enabled them to offer a superior product.[29] The rivalry among the funds worked to the advantage of the doctors during negotiations and may have increased costs. Greater coordination was agreed upon in 1977 and made official in the new national Health Insurance Cost Control Law. The same fee schedule and its relative values would apply to both the *RVO-Kassen* and the *Ersatzkassen,* beginning in mid-1978. Therefore, the rival sick funds would have to participate in the same negotiations to write the fee schedule. As in the financial differentials among the *RVO-Kassen,* the *Ersatzkassen* could continue to pay more for each act.

OVERVIEW OF THE GERMAN NEGOTIATING SYSTEM

Germany's system has many features that the United States might emulate with profit, both as sources for detailed devices for the system that America seems to be developing and as a model for acceptable political compromise. Americans have a stereotyped idea that national health insurance—and any other statutory program—will invite constant regulation by the government. The German experience is a good example of how government can enact the rules and then leave the doctors and sick funds to carry out the program with little government intervention.[30]

As in most other European countries, the preexisting nonprofit carriers continue to exist. To a greater extent than in other countries, they vary in benefits, in administrative services, and in premiums. They can compete by offering subscribers slightly different products. The *RVO-Kassen* unite in those activities requiring a common front, such as writing the fee schedule.

The system is federal but coordinated, as in many other German programs. The sick funds and medical profession are organized into provincial units that manage the details of health insurance. General guidelines are negotiated between the national leaderships of the sick funds and doctors, and regional variations are negotiated by the provincial offices. The result is national uniformity with provincial flexibility. The administrators are provincial notables, not employees of centralized national offices in Bonn-Bad Godesberg and in Cologne: They are attentive to local situations; persons with complaints go to them and not to the more distant national headquarters. The other federal systems of national health insurance—in Canada and Switzerland—have been organized provincially and have had persistent trouble in acquiring enough national uniformity in administration and in reporting. Elsewhere, national health insurance is centralized in its decisions and management.

STRONG POINTS IN THE GERMAN SYSTEM

The KVs have been an ingenious form of organization and have managed to make very stable a system that was once very contentious. The KVs could provide a model for the further development of America's new and still weak counterpart, the medical foundation.[31] As in the KV, the foundation is an association of doctors that administers payments on behalf of insurance carriers. Compared to the KVs, the American foundation handles much less money, includes fewer of the office doctors in its area, and has less power over the doctors. The foundation writes its own fee schedule, while the KV negotiates its fee schedule with the sick funds.

Negotiations over the fee schedule in Germany are calm and thorough. Negotiations over money are conducted with remarkable speed, perhaps as an unexpected dividend of the paucity of statistical evidence. Germany is a good example of a trend in Western democratic societies that America would do well to emulate, viz., settlement of disputes and development of consensus throughout the society by calm and patient negotiations.

Germany demonstrates how a federal system coordinates provincial negotiations when a national policy must be attained. The KBV and the associations of sick funds balance the need for standardization with the need for provincial variations. During the 1970s, they developed a formula for nationwide guidelines that the *länder* implemented voluntarily.

SOME PROBLEMS IN THE GERMAN SYSTEM

Costs

Medical care expenses are mounting in all countries, straining insurance funds that were originally intended to be self-sustaining from payroll taxes alone. It is hard to judge whether financial waste is more serious in one country than in another, but Germany has certainly made the problem a focus of national debate more prominently than others. Spending on health services is particularly troublesome in Germany for several reasons. Its population is unusually health-conscious and seems to go to the doctor more often than in other European countries. Germany is a principal center of modern scientific medicine, and the extensive use of technology, diagnostic methods, and drugs makes its medical services expensive. Doctors earn high incomes, either by performing many tasks under fee-for-service or by collecting high salaries from hospitals; the wages are now high for other hospital employees as well.

The sense of crisis over costs is due to the pressure on accounts. German sick funds are supposed to be self-sustaining without the subsidies that other national governments now fatalistically grant. German employers have always been critical of health insurance because of allegedly generous sick leaves, and they resist further increases in the payroll taxes. Therefore, in its recent national guidelines linking fees and utilization and limiting the annual rise in the combination, Germany is one of the first countries to impose budgetary discipline upon national health insurance. Germany demonstrates how the negotiators from the sick funds and medical association can be budget-conscious as part of the negotiations, without passing the buck to the government. Elsewhere governments have the impossible task of nullifying or reducing an accord over fees, usually choosing instead the slightly less impossible task of finding (or printing) the money to pay the deficit.

Data

In the most sophisticated negotiations, both the medical association and the sick funds have extensive statistics about prices, costs of practice, utilization, and so on. Even if their versions of the facts disagree, the numbers introduce an atmosphere of objectivity and calm. Challenges lead to worried searches in the computer output instead of defensive epithets.

A weakness in the German negotiating system has been the paucity of statistical data about the performance of the system and about the services of the doctors. Germany has never had the tradition of thorough health statistics found in the Anglo-Saxon and Scandinavian countries. In addition, the German sick funds lack the control over the processing of bills that enables their foreign counterparts to generate statistics about how health insurance works in practice. In Germany alone, the doctors themselves in the KVs process the bills and produce the statistics; the sick funds merely get copies. Because of the format of the *Krankenscheine* and the coding and processing decisions of the KVs, it is not possible to link records for the same individual, for family units, and for different quarters throughout the year. The sick funds complain that their bargaining position would be stronger if they had better data. If pay awards are to be coordinated with utilization trends regularly, then the negotiators will need a steady flow of current information.[32]

The fee schedule

Ideally, a fee schedule should be up to date. However, giving PREUGO and GOA the additional status of a law has prevented the health insurance negotiators from revising the fee schedule regularly. By issuing BMA, the medical association manages to circulate an up to date document as if it were the official one. BMA is a compendium of GOA plus the revisions recommended by the negotiators. The history of PREUGO shows that, unless the negotiators can rewrite entire parts from time to time, the fee schedule will become obsolete.

Unity among sick funds

Whether the division between the *RVO-Kassen* and the *Ersatzkassen* is a problem requiring a cure depends on one's viewpoint. The *Ersatzkassen's* admirers say that persons willing to pay higher premiums should be able to enjoy greater benefits. Their critics argue that all sick funds should present a common front so that the medical profession will face stiffer bargaining, costs can be controlled better, and practicing doctors will not find certain patients more profitable than others without sound clinical reasons. The difference in fees and benefits between the two kinds of sick funds was an exception to the trend toward unity and standardization in all countries, but they may become more alike in the future, as a result of the new laws to control costs.

NOTES

1. Comparisons of Germany's more unified federal system and the United States appear in several publications by Christa Altenstetter, such as *Health Policy-Making and Administration in West Germany and the United States* (Beverly Hills: Sage Publications, 1974).

2. The history of the sick funds and legislation from early to modern times is in Horst Peters, *Die Geschichte der Sozialversicherung* (Bad Godesberg: Asgard-Verlag, 1959). The history of the funds associated with the guilds is summarized in Fritz Tervooren, "Eigenständische Krankenfürsorge bis zur Gegenwart," *Lebendiges Fleischerhandwerk* (Frankfurt am Main: Deutsche Fleischer-Verband, 1975), pp. 181-184.

3. Past and recent enrollment figures appear in Dieter Schewe et al., *Ubersicht über die Soziale Sicherung* (Bonn: Bundesministerium fur Arbeit und Sozialordnung, Ninth edition, 1975), Ch. 13.

4. A good overview of the organization and functions of sick funds is Fritz Kastner, *Monograph on the Organisation of Medical Care within the Framework of Social Security in the Federal Republic of Germany* (Geneva: International Labour Office, 1968).

5. Schewe, *op. cit.* (note 3, supra), Ch. 27; *Bericht der Bundesregierung zu Fragen der Selbstverwaltung in der Sozialversicherung* (Bonn: Bundesrat, Drucksache 7/4244, 3 November 1975). The complexities of combining self-government and economic efficiency are described by Theo Thiemeyer, "Soziale 'Selbstverwaltung' unter ökonomischen Aspekt," *Zeitschrift für Sozialreform,* Volume 21, Number 9 (September 1975).

6. The history of the relations between doctors and sick funds appears in Frieder Naschold, *Kassenärzte und Krankenversicherungsreform* (Freiburg im Breisgau: Verlag Rombach, 1967), passim, esp, pp. 56-63, 89-105, and 151-156. Once, in order to limit costs and improve efficiency, the sick funds accepted doctors in a fixed ratio to numbers of subscribers, but such a limitation on rights of practice was declared unconstitutional by the Federal Court in 1960, and now any office doctor may treat any insured person, as in other countries.

7. The organization and work of the KV's are described in J. von Troschke et al., *Arzt in freier Praxis* (Köln: Deutscher Ärzte-Verlag, 1976), Chs. 2 and 3; and Naschold, *Kassenärzte und Krankenversicherungsreform* (note 6, supra), Chs. 6 and 7.

8. The various medical associations are described in William Safran, *Veto-Group Politics: The Case of Health Insurance Reform in West Germany* (San Francisco: Chandler Publishing Company, 1967), Ch. V; and Philipp Herder-Dorneich, *Sozialökonomischer Grundriss der Gesetzlichen Krankenversicherung* (Stuttgart: Verlag W. Kohlhammer, 1966), pp. 59-71.

9. For the text of these parts of RVO and extensive commentary, see Gustav Heinemann et al., *Kassenarztrecht* (Berlin/Wiesbaden: Engel-Verlag, Fourth edition, 1975).

10. For a detailed analysis of how the system worked in practice, see Heinemann, *op. cit.* (note 9, supra), section about Para. 368f and the many sources cited therein. Described also by James Hogarth, *The Payment of the General Practitioner* (Oxford: Pergamon Press, 1963), pp. 231-248.

11. The gradual adoption of payment by the act under the *Kopfpauschale* system and the complete changeover to payment of acts in full are described in *Grundsätze und Forderungen zum Vertragsrecht der Krankenkassen* (Bonn-Bad Godesberg and Essen: Bundesverband der Ortskrankenkassen and Bundesverband der Betriebskrankenkassen, 1974), pp. 36-40; and Philipp Herder-Dorneich,

Die Kostenexpansion und ihre Steuerung im Gesundheitswesen (Köln: Deutscher Ärzte-Verlag, 1976), pp. 135-144.

12. The politics of the proposed reform and its defeat are described in Safran, *op. cit.* (note 8, supra).

13. The controversy during the 1950's and the eventual adoption of GOA are described in Hogarth, *op. cit.* (note 10, supra), pp. 238-239 and 252-254; and in Dietrich Brück, *Kommentar zur Gebührenordung für Ärzte vom 18 März 1965 (GOA)* (Köln: Deutscher Ärzte Verlag, Fourth edition, 1973), pp. v and 1-3.

14. The sick fund's specialists often play important roles too. For example, Dietrich Brück, long the representative on the committee from the *Bundesverband der Ortskrankenkassen,* is author of the principal treatises explaining the use of each item in GOA and in several other fee schedules.

15. *Gesundheits- und sozialpolitische Vorstellungen den deutschen Ärzteschaft* (Köln: Bundesärztekammer, 1974), pp. 76-77. The debate over a statutory or contractual fee schedule is summarized in Gesellschaft für Sozialen Fortschritt, *Der Wandel der Stellung des Arztes im Einkommensgefüge* (Berlin: Duncker & Humblot, 1974), pp. 88-92.

16. For the maneuvering between KBV and the German national government over adopting a new fee schedule and employing a less official method for updating it, see *Tätigkeitsbericht der Bundesärztekammer 1973/74,* pp. 104-105.

17. The competing arguments for nationwide and *land* negotiations over money appear in Gesellschaft für Sozialen Fortschritt, *op. cit.* (note 15, supra), pp. 99-104.

18. Comparisons among all *länder* and sick funds during 1972 and 1973 appear in Gesellschaft für Sozialen Fortschritt, *op. cit.* (note 15, supra), pp. 67-68.

19. An example of the new and more complete statistical reporting is *9. Bericht über Erfahrungen mit der Einzelleistungsvergütung in der kassenärztlichen Versorgung* (Düsseldorf: Verband der Ortskrankenkassen Rheinland, 1975).

20. A condensed paraphrase of the negotiations is "Lohnrunde um sechsstellige Summen," *Der Spiegel,* Volume 29, Number 19 (5 May 1975), pp. 68-73.

21. The arbitration system is described in Heinemann et. al., *op. cit.* (note 9, supra), sections on Para. 368i and sources cited therein.

22. See, for example, Wolfgang Barthel and Jochen Wegener, "Arzthonorare —Die Beutelschneider," *Stern,* Volume 29, Number 7 (5 February 1976), cover and pp. 106-108. A summary and critique of such recent attacks is Friedrich Kolb, "Ist die Existenz des Kassenarztes gefährdet?" *Bayerisches Ärzteblatt,* Volume 31, Number 4 (1976), pp. 289-296. A recent representative sample of the German population said they believed the journalists rather than the doctors: "Journalisten oder Ärzte?" (Allensbach: Institut für Demoskopie, 1976).

23. "Empfehlungsvereinbarung über eine Begrenzung des Wachstums der kassenärztlichen Vergütung," *Die Ortskrankenkasse,* Number 12 (1976), pp. 5-11; Hans Wolf Muschallik et al., "Bewährungsprobe für die gemeinsame Selbstverwaltung," *Deutsches Ärzteblatt,* Volume 73, Number 20 (13 May 1976), pp. 1349-1364; and Heinz Blüthmann, "Deckel auf dem Topf," *Die Zeit,* 14 May 1976 (Overseas edition), pp. 16-17.

24. Recently the sick funds and the Social Democratic Party have issued several monographs saying that the change from the *Kopfpauschale* system to the

Einzelleistungshonorarsystem has made costs and management more difficult for them and that—if an outright return to global budgetting is not possible—far more control is necessary, with planning of utilization and of doctor's income, as well as of fees. For example, *Grundsätze und Forderungen zum Vertragrecht der Krankenkassen* (note 11, supra), pp. 35-48; *Lebendige Kassenversicherung 1975* (Bad Godesberg: Bundesverband der Ortskrankenkassen, 1975), pp. 37-39; *Aktionsprogramm 'Gesundheit 76'* (Bonn: Sozialdemokrate Partei Deutschland, 1976), p. 12. *Grundsätze* . . . . , pp. 37-38, and the *Aktionsprogramm,* p. 12, raise another possibility much feared by the medical profession, viz., replacement of fee-for-service (if it is unworkable) by case payments. Since the SPD now governs Germany, its views are particularly worrisome.

25. They are described in "Die Ersatzkassen—fortschrittliche Alternative gestern, heute und morgen," *Die Ersatzkasse,* Volume 56, Numbers 1-4 (January-April 1976), pp. 18-23, 66-68, 111-115, and 155-158.

26. This has long been the popular belief. Whether different care is actually given is not clear. Gesellschaft für Sozialen Fortschritt, *op. cit.* (note 15, supra), pp. 42-44. *Ersatzkassen* premiums are no longer so much higher than *RVO-Kassen* premiums. Rather, they have more money left over to pay doctors and to offer extra benefits, because their costs for hospitalization and certain other basic benefits are lower. Premiums are compared in Malte Retiet and Hans-Jürgen Materna, "Die Rolle der Ersatzkassen in der gesetzlichen Krankenversicherung," *Betriebs-Berater,* Number 32 (20 November 1975), p. 1487.

27. See, for example, the monographs of the *Bundesverband der Ortskrankenkassen: Grundsätze und Forderungen zum Vertragsrecht der Krankenkassen* (note 11, supra), pp. 43-47; and *Lebendige Krankenversicherung 1975* (note 24, supra), pp. 62-63.

28. For example, the keynote speech by Hans Katzbach at their annual meeting, "Die Ersatzkassen," *Die Ersatzkasse,* Volume 55, Number 12 (December 1975), p. 456. The Minister of Labor's speech on behalf of the government dealt with many topics, but the *Ersatzkassen* journal emphasized in the headline the topic that was most on their mind: Walter Arendt, "Einheitsversicherung nicht sinnvoll," *ibid.,* pp. 458 ff.

29. For example, Katzbach, *op. cit.* (note 28, supra), p. 454; and Retiet, *op. cit.* (note 26, supra), p. 1487.

30. From the perspective of the truly socialist system of East Germany, West Germany remains a citadel of private ownership and individual independence in medical care. West Germany has only national health insurance, while East Germany has a national health service. Kurt Winter, "Health Services in the German Democratic Republic compared to the Federal Republic of Germany," *Inquiry,* Volume XII, Number 2, Supplement (June 1975), pp. 63-68; and Hartmut Rolf, *Sozialversicherung oder Staatlicher Gesundheitsdienst?* (Berlin: Duncker & Humblot, 1975).

31. Described in Carolynn Steinwald, "Foundations for Medical Care," *Blue Cross Reports,* Research Series 7, August 1971; and Richard H. Egdahl, "Foundations for Medical Care," *New England Journal of Medicine,* Volume 288 (8 May 1973), pp. 491-498 and 519-520.

32. *Grundsätze und Forderungen zum Vertragsrecht der Krankenkassen* (note 11, supra), p. 40; "Lohnrunde um sechsstellige Summen," *Der Spiegel,* Volume 29, Number 19 (5 May 1976), p. 72. On the inadequacy of German health statistics generally, see Manfred Pflanz, "German Health Insurance: The Evolution and Current Problems of the Pioneer System," *International Journal of Health Services,* Volume I, Number 1 (November 1971), pp. 319 and 327-328.

CHAPTER VII

Switzerland

In HEALTH and several other matters, Germany maintains high uniformity despite its federal structure. Standardization is achieved through laws and also through extensive negotiations among provincial and local units, before the next round of negotiations with the other side. Switzerland is far more decentralized, since it is a confederation and not a federal system —i.e., an alliance of provinces ("cantons") that retain virtually all power and delegate limited functions to a national government. The United States had a weak confederal government before 1789; once common in Europe, confederations have disappeared almost everywhere. Despite the constitutional differences, Switzerland can be a source of ideas for the United States, because America is an unusually flexible federal system: an American program can be administered as if it were (1) unitary and national through the federal bureaucracy alone; or, (2) truly federal through the state bureaucracies but with high uniformity; or (3) in a highly decentralized fashion giving maximum discretion to the states. Switzerland demonstrates how a national health insurance system can operate, if it is allowed twenty-five different local versions.[1]

THE SICK FUNDS

Switzerland has never had compulsory national health insurance. Several attempts to enact it have been defeated, either within the national Parliament or in national referenda. Instead, the federal law of 1911

117

allows each canton to make its own decision but authorizes the national government to subsidize the sick funds that are recognized carriers. Consequently, twenty-five systems exist, according to the various political pressures in Switzerland's nineteen cantons and six half-cantons. No canton has compulsory insurance for the entire population, but some (such as the City of Basel) come close to full compulsory coverage. Nine cantons pass along the entire decision to their local communes, but in only a few have a majority of the communes made insurance compulsory. All the rest have cantonal laws supporting voluntary insurance. Almost one-third of the Swiss population has compulsory coverage, nearly two-thirds has voluntary coverage, and less than 6% is not covered.[2]

The federal law authorizes participation and offers direct federal subsidies (i.e., the money is not routed through the cantons) to any nonprofit carrier. To be eligible, the carrier must offer certain minimum benefits, not discriminate in acceptance of risks, and follow certain rules. Some are public funds established by cantons or communes. Others are private funds organized as societies, unions or foundations. Some are open to all citizens; some are confined to the employees of a company; others are limited to a particular social group. Some are nationwide. Some have a long history. Their governing councils are picked from the subscribers or from the community by various formulas. Each can function like a private health insurance company by offering additional benefits in return for higher premiums.[3] Because over seven hundred sick funds exist, they must organize together in order to deal with government, negotiate with doctors, and perform other functions. Within each canton, the sick funds belong to an association, a *Kantonalverband der Krankenkassen*. It is governed by a *Vorstand* of representatives elected from the individual funds. Each association has a small secretariat, with an office in the capital city of the canton.

Seventeen cantonal associations in German-speaking Switzerland plus many unaffiliated sick funds unite in the *Konkordat der schweizerischen Krankenkassen,* located in Solothurn. The five cantonal associations in French-speaking Switzerland unite in the *Fédération des Sociétés des secours mutuels de la Suisse romande,* situated in Lausanne. The sick funds in Italian-speaking Ticino form a third federation. The three federations do not negotiate with the doctors but represent the sick funds in dealing with the national government, maintain computing systems that help their cantonal associations process claims, provide tabulations to the cantonal associations for utilization and control, publish statistical reports, and publish newsletters. Besides acting as the spokesman for the German-speaking cantonal associations, the *Konkordat* acts as the leader of all throughout the country and in negotiations with the national government.[4] The *Konkordat* is governed by an annual representative assembly (a *Delegiertenversammlung*) and by a management committee (a *Vorstand*) that holds four ordinary meetings and occasional special meetings each year. The *Konkordat's* full-time secretariat produces statistical data, economic analyses, and publications.

THE MEDICAL PROFESSION

Within each canton, doctors belong to a medical society. It negotiates with the sick funds over fees, lobbies with the cantonal government over legislation and over the administration of medical services, administers professional discipline, organizes a pension fund, advises new practitioners, and occasionally offers postgraduate courses. Only the medical society of Zurich has a full-time secretary.

The cantonal associations unite in the national federation, the *Verbindung der Schweizer Ärzte*. It represents the Swiss medical profession in the legislative activities of the national government, including the passage of national laws concerning health insurance[5] and about medical education. It reviews credentials and recognizes specialists by the granting of a certificate. It publishes the country's medical news magazine. The national association negotiates the fee schedules for the accident insurance program but not for sickness insurance; the former is national but the latter is cantonal.

CANTONAL NEGOTIATIONS OVER HEALTH INSURANCE

Overview

As in other countries with fee-for-service, three things are negotiated, viz., a convention defining relations between the sick funds and the medical profession, the fee schedule itself, and the monetary value of the fees. In Switzerland, all are negotiated within each canton, between the cantonal association of sick funds and the cantonal medical society.

When a new convention is negotiated or an old one revised, the cantonal association of sick funds often asks the advice of the staff at the *Konkordat*. Therefore, it can profit from experiences throughout the country. Sometimes, a *Konkordat* staff member joins a sick fund delegation as a consultant during the final stages. The *Konkordat's* lawyers usually look over the draft of a cantonal convention before it is signed. The cantonal medical society may request information and advice from the *Verbindung der Schweizer Ärzte*. The doctors, however, rely on national leadership less often than the sick funds do, since they do not wish to encourage a trend toward national negotiations.

Germany is a federal country with a single national fee schedule; it is the prices for each act that are negotiated provincially. Switzerland and Canada lack a single national fee schedule. Keeping track of each cantonal document in Switzerland, including all changes, is a task of the *Konkordat's* secretariat. Since medical care is universal, some persons have suggested that the best possible fee schedule be designed and then adopted throughout the country. The monetary values of the fees might still be negotiated within each canton, with differentials reflecting cantonal variations in incomes and costs. This combination of a national fee schedule and a cantonal tariff was recommended by a Commission of Experts that proposed reforms of national health insurance in 1972, and the idea was endorsed by several cantonal governments.[6] It was not adopted because the entire package of reforms was voted down in a referendum by the Swiss population, but support for a national fee schedule is steadily (if slowly) growing.

Vested interests and tradition have preserved the cantonal fee schedules up to now. The doctors prefer to negotiate with the sick funds within each separate canton and not nationally since (as in Germany), their bargaining strength is thereby relatively stronger. However, the medical profession seems gradually to be accepting the possibility of a national schedule: the same acts recur, the single national fee schedule of the accident insurance is a widely admired model, and the cantonal fee schedules are becoming more alike. However, even if clinical science is propelling Swiss health insurance toward a national fee schedule, Swiss tradition holds back. The population (including administrators) hesitates to transfer any power from cantonal to national offices without there being very compelling reasons.

About once a year, the cantonal associations of sick funds and the medical society negotiate an increase in the general financial level of all fees. This has usually been left entirely to cantonal negotiation. The sick funds' financial situation varies so widely—because of differences in the affluence of the population, differences in the subsidies to funds from cantonal governments, and the absence of national equalization machinery —that nationwide settlements have not been possible. Each agreement must be approved for legality and fiscal feasibility by the economic ministry of the canton.

Swiss negotiators do not come with detailed documentation about income, the costs of medical practice, and other economic trends, either for their own guidance or to exchange with the other side. Such detailed data do not exist in Switzerland.[7] The parties quickly fall back on one of the few existing measures of economic trends, viz., the consumer price index of the Statistical Office of the national government.

To combat inflation, Switzerland in December 1972 conferred upon its

Federal Ministry of Economics power to control wages and prices.[8] Awards of higher fees must be approved, and the cantonal government now forwards the agreement to Bern. Because the awards in all cantons usually do not exceed the rise in the national consumer price index, the price control office has never ordered a reduction. (It has cut several increases in industrial prices.)[9] To restrict the rise in living costs, however, it has ordered delays in the effective dates of several cantonal agreements until the next January or July.

Harmonious negotiations in Bern

In most Swiss cantons, relations between sick funds and doctors have been amicable for many decades. Of course, negotiations at times are vigorous and prolonged; but, on most occasions, agreements come quickly. A good example is the canton of Bern.

The organizations have existed for many decades and have a long experience of negotiation. The largest sick fund—the *Krankenkasse für den Kanton Bern* or KKB—originated in 1870.[10] Several smaller funds existed before and others were created later; some are limited to the canton, others are local branches of national networks, such as *Konkordia* or *Helvetia*. These others united in an association called the *Kantonalverband Bernischer Krankenkassen*; at times KKB has belonged, but for over a decade, it has been outside. At present, 99 sick funds belong to the *Kantonalverband*. The *Kantonalverband* and KKB coordinate their policies on doctors, hospitals, and contracts by conferring at least once a month in a work group (the thirty-year-old *Arbeitsgemeinschaft*) with five members from each side. The five members are either senior administrators or members of the *Vorstand* of each side. The executive secretary of the *Kantonalverband* is the secretary for the *Arbeitsgemeinschaft*. To ensure a common front, it is the *Arbeitsgemeinschaft* that negotiates contracts and fees with the doctors and hospitals.

The medical society has an even longer continuous history. Between 1809 and 1911, it was a scientific society called the *Medizinisch-chirurg. Gesellschaft des Kantons Bern*. In 1911 it acquired new powers to negotiate for doctors under the new national health insurance system, it was given a more official representative structure, and it was renamed the *Ärztegesellschaft des Kantons Bern*. As in other cantonal medical societies, it is governed by a representative assembly and a *Vorstand,* although it can also transact business in a plenary session of all members. The society has a part-time secretary and several clerical employees.

The sick funds and medical society meet at least once every two months to transact whatever business has accumulated. The group is formally called a "negotiating meeting" or *Verhandlungsdelegation*. Six members come from the medical society, including a senior member from its *Vorstand* and practitioners from several specialties. Six come from the *Arbeitsgemeinschaft,* including three senior members of the KKB and three from the *Kantonalverband.* The secretaries of the medical society and of the *Arbeitsgemeinschaft* attend, to provide administrative support for the respective sides. At each meeting, one side names its senior member the chairman, and the other side writes the agenda. The chairmanship alternates. To build a friendly atmosphere, the meetings are held in suburban restaurants. Each side is punctilious about the equal treatment of the other side, lest affronts interfere with decisions.

The two sides name *ad hoc* working groups to provide detailed recommendations on new topics, such as new entries in the fee schedule. When specialized topics are discussed at the *Verhandlungsdelegation,* some members of these working groups or other experts attend as advisors to each side.

The basic contract and fee schedule have existed for many years. The last general revision of the contract occurred in 1965, because the national health insurance law had just been amended extensively; the *Verhandlungsdelegation* met several times, just on the contract. In recent years, it has made several amendments in its full sessions. All such changes must be approved by the respective *Vorstände* of the *Kantonalverband,* of the KKB, and of the medical society.

The fee schedule has not undergone a general revision in several decades.[11] Suggestions are frequent for changing relative values, changing the wording of items, and inserting new items. The work is done by special committees of consultants primarily from the medical society, with some from the sick funds. The *Verhandlungsdelegation* can make minor changes on its own authority, but significant changes must be approved by the three *Vorstände.* Such approval comes readily since the *Verhandlungsdelegation* consists of leading members of the three *Vorstände.*

If the national index of consumer prices has risen since the last award by a significant percentage—usually 10%—the medical society requests that higher fees be added to the agenda. The sick funds listen at the first session, confer with their respective *Vorstände,* and then work out a common counter-offer in their *Arbeitsgemeinschaft.* The sick funds must calculate whether the competing demands from other providers will leave enough money for the doctors, whether they can raise the premiums of subscribers, and whether the subsidies from national and cantonal governments will yield enough money. The bargaining over higher fees is not as contentious as in other countries, because the awards usually stay close to the rise in the consumer's price index.

Things are not always perfectly harmonious. Normally control over waste and abuse is administered jointly. During a severe financial pinch in 1975, the sick funds insisted that warnings be sent to many doctors who seemed wasteful. The medical society hesitated. The impatient sick funds then sent the letters themselves, over the protest of the medical society. Cooperation was reestablished during 1976, since both sides fear deterioration in relations. Similar but fewer warning letters went out in 1976, under the joint authorship of the medical society, the KKB, and the *Kantonalverband*.

The government of the canton of Bern is not consulted before or during negotiations. It gives *pro forma* approval to the final agreement.

Functioning without a contract in Zurich

The 113 sick funds in the canton of Zurich belong to the *Verband der Krankenkassen im Kanton Zürich*.[12] Like the other cantonal associations, it is led by an elected *Vorstand* with power to make decisions about contracts and about monetary offers to the doctors. As in several large cantons, it is decentralized into nine communal associations (*Bezirksverbände*), and a representative from each serves on the *Verband* of the cantonal association. Much communication occurs between the cantonal leadership and individual sick funds through the communal associations, and therefore the funds are heard during the negotiations with the doctors. The *Verband* has a full-time secretary and a small staff in the city of Zurich.

Nearly all doctors in the canton belong to the *Gesellschaft der Ärzte des Kantons Zürich*. Like the other cantonal societies it is governed by an elected *Vorstand*, which meets regularly and makes decisions about current business, such as negotiations and agreements with the sick funds. A representative assembly (the *Delegiertenversammlung*) meets at least once a year, hears and discusses reports by the *Vorstand*, and may give the *Vorstand* advice about any topic, such as relations with the sick funds. The full membership meets at least once a year, to elect members of the other organs, decide dues, and hear scientific and professional reports. The plenary meeting is ultimately sovereign and becomes very active during crises with the sick funds, such as during 1964 and 1965. The medical society has a full-time secretary (the only full-timer in any canton) and a clerical staff.

The biggest and richest cities in any country experience conflicts between doctors and sick funds more often than other regions do. These cities have many citizens able to pay high fees, many doctors accustomed to charging what they like, and house the offices of leading practitioners. Therefore, a large faction in the medical profession wishes to be exempt from health insurance and fights inclusion of the biggest city in any national negotiating machinery. Even in Switzerland—whose social system and culture include features for avoiding deadlocks—breakdowns sometimes happen. The most prolonged impasses occurred in Zurich. It was not as critical as it might have been in another country: The national government has legislation to resolve a deadlock, and a roundabout negotiating system developed.

Refusing to sign a contract once was a common tactic used by medical associations against sick funds in many countries. If the doctors refuse to accept payment from the sick funds according to any fee schedule, they hope to charge the patient directly whatever they like. Then the patients must recover whatever they can from the sick funds. Such an expensive result puts pressure upon the sick funds to compromise with the doctors close to the latter's terms.

Eventually governments pass laws providing control in the absence of a contract. On account of its role in international monetary affairs, the national government of Switzerland is concerned that no sector's prices get out of hand. Enough instances had occurred of doctors refusing to sign contracts and charging what they wanted to persuade the national government to fill the vacuum. An amendment to the national health insurance law in 1964 authorizes the cantonal government to impose a "frame fee schedule" (a *Rahmentarif*) if the doctors and sick funds cannot agree. The cantonal government can proclaim it only after consultation with the doctors and sick funds.[13]

The first test occurred in Zurich. Relations had been deteriorating over several matters: doctors thought fees were too low; they did not want to report diagnoses on the bills, lest the sick funds review their clinical decisions; and so on.[14] The medical association believed doctors would be more independent and would gain more money if they no longer were paid directly by sick funds, charged patients directly, and let the patients collect what they could from the sick funds. In other countries, changing from service benefits to cash benefits gives the doctors a free hand. But not in Zurich. The new national statute went into effect as negotiations broke down. The government of the canton stepped in, adopted the fee schedule in the last convention as the *Rahmentarif,* and imposed controls over doctors' charges.

Medical services were not disrupted and health insurance continued to function. The health office of the canton of Zurich (the *Gesundheitsdirektion*) became the intermediary and arbiter in the communications between doctors and sick funds; it kept both at arms length, partly to avoid the danger of bias in favor of one side and partly to avoid the tedium of listening to self-interested appeals. From time to time, the medical society recommended a change in the *Rahmentarif*. It sent a letter to the *Gesundheitsdirektion,* which sent a copy to the *Verband.* If the sick funds agreed and the civil servants in the health office could think of no objection, they recommended the change to their Minister. He in turn reported the change to the executive committee of the cantonal government (the *Regierungsrat*), which issued the regulation altering the fee schedule. However, the schedule did not change as quickly as in cantons with direct negotiations.

About every year and one-half, the medical society sent a letter requesting higher fees. It estimated large increases in the cost of living and in the cost of practice. The *Gesundheitsdirektion* sent the letter to the *Verband,* which usually claimed that general prices and doctors' costs had gone up much less. The *Gesundheitsdirektion* confined the sides to an exchange of paper rather than listen to a debate, and it settled on a bureaucratic solution. Each time, it raised fees by the same percentage as the rise in the national consumers price index since the last award.

The fee schedule became steadily more obsolete under this bureaucratic procedure, and both the sick funds and medical society had an incentive to regain control of the situation.[15] They resumed direct negotiations in 1974, to create a new contract and a new fee schedule. After the new contract went into effect in 1977, the new fee schedule became the *Rahmentarif* of the canton, in case of any new breakdowns. Thereafter, negotiating sessions between the medical society and sick funds settled increases in fees, and the cantonal government reverted to its normal role of giving *pro forma* approval.

The doctors of Zurich came out of the twelve years of deadlock with symbolic rather than real gains. They charge the patients, and the patients are reimbursed by the sick funds; doctors are not paid by the funds directly. Among the concessions was the agreement that doctors must follow the fee schedule and not charge whatever they like. Doctors must enter the patient's diagnosis on the bills going to the sick funds, in the form of a code number.

During the twelve years without a contract, some direct discussions between the medical society and sick funds were inevitable, in order to enable the system to function. For example, the medical society did not want the sick funds and cantonal government to administer by themselves controls over utilization and sanctions against doctors. Therefore, they joined the sick funds in creating a bilateral commission for medical control.

Automatic awards in Basel

In a few cantons, the medical society and the sick funds have tried to carry the Swiss aversion to tempestuous confrontation to its extreme—

i.e., they have searched for ways to eliminate negotiation over fees. In the canton of Basel City, the monetary decisions are handled by a third party using agreed formulas.

In Basel, the spokesman for the over 800 doctors is the medical society (the *Medizinische Gesellschaft Basel*). Thirty-nine sick funds belong to an association (the *Kantonalverband Baselstädtischer Krankenkassen*), while one large fund remains independent (the *Offentliche Krankenkasse des Kantons Basel-Stadt* or OKK). The medical society and *Kantonalverband* have only part-time secretaries; the *Kantonalverband* even lacks an office of its own. Therefore, both have an interest in limiting their own negotiating burdens.

The medical society on the one hand and the *Kantonalverband* and OKK on the other hand have held occasional rounds of negotiation for basic documents, such as the contract and fee schedule. Until the late 1960s, they met annually over money. During the mid-1960s, confrontations were bitter, strike threats were heard, and the cantonal government had to order several payment awards. The solution in the new contract of 1969 was to delegate the decisions permanently to the director of the health insurance office of the cantonal government (the *Krankenversicherungsamt*). According to the contract, that official reads the monthly consumer's price index of the Statistical Office of the national government; whenever he finds that the index has gone up 5% since the last award, he announces a 5% increase in all fees. He has done so regularly since January 1970. The only modification was scheduling the increases in January and July and not during the month when the official noticed that 5% was due; the delay in scheduling was requested by the national office of price control, and the sick funds and medical society amended their contract.

The medical society and sick funds continue to meet occasionally over other aspects of health insurance. Their relationship is no longer infected by a struggle over money.

NATIONAL NEGOTIATIONS OVER ACCIDENT INSURANCE

Even in federal systems as orderly as Switzerland's, inconsistent legislation is sometimes enacted. This is quite common in the United States: A statute may make one program a national-state collaboration in one section, while making another closely related program completely national in another section.[16] While the first part of the Swiss health insurance statute of 1911 retained and subsidized a cantonal system, the second part created a single national sick fund for industrial accidents (the *Schweiz-*

erische Unfallversicherungsanstalt or SUVA).[17] For several decades, SUVA tried to administer medical pay like sickness insurance: It negotiated the fee schedule and the amount of money with the medical society of each canton. However, SUVA found this too cumbersome.

A new procedure was enacted in the amendments to the health insurance law in 1964. Under the confederal constitution of Switzerland, national decisions cannot be imposed upon the canton. Therefore, a distinction is made between negotiating and enacting fees: they are negotiated between the national leadership of the medical profession and of SUVA; but they must be enacted by each cantonal government, before they take effect within that canton. Any doctor may treat a patient for industrial accidents; he is paid not by the patient's regular local sick fund but by SUVA according to the SUVA fee schedule.

Fee schedule

Between 1963 and 1969, a new fee schedule was created in negotiations between the national medical association (the *Verbindung der Schweizer Ärzte*) and SUVA. Large delegations met about once a month. Regularly from the national medical association came the president, vice-president, executive secretary, a member of the *Vorstand,* and a surgeon particularly interested in accidents. Two or three other doctors often came to each meeting, depending on the specialty whose fees were discussed. From SUVA came the chief medical officer, his deputy, and a staff member who specialized in the design of fee schedules. Since the SUVA schedule would be used by three other governmental insurance programs, each sent a representative too. Sections of the fee schedules were drafted by work groups of doctors in those specialties, from the medical association and from SUVA's staff of consultants. Detailed minutes were kept of the plenary meetings, so the rationale for particular entries would be retained.

Up to that time, Swiss fee schedules were successive revisions of documents created decades earlier. Some sounded old fashioned; all were patchworks. The SUVA schedule was a new and streamlined document. Unlike the others, its acts were specified in points and not in francs. It was a true relative values scale, and the designers tried to think in these terms, giving comparable acts the same points and estimating differentials in time and difficulty among acts with different points. The negotiators agreed on the point values by consensus. Most effort was devoted to defining the content of the office visit, since this is the most common act and (in the aggregate) costs the most.

If the negotiators were to do this work now, they would try to base decisions on research about time and work. SUVA's new fee schedules for dentists and physiotherapists have been written with the aid of research about actual practice. So too was the new fee schedule for health insurance in Zurich canton, which resembles the SUVA fee schedule in many ways.

The SUVA fee schedule for doctors was completed in 1969. First, it was approved by the management boards of SUVA and of the other public insurance funds that used it. It was also approved by the legislative meeting of the national medical association (the *Ärztekammer*), i.e., the 150 representatives of the cantonal medical societies. After that it was approved by all the cantonal governments.

Representatives from the medical association and SUVA meet occasionally to discuss revisions. Included in their delegations are specialists in the fields whose fees will be discussed. A special work group is created with consultants from both sides, if an extensive revision is being made in a field, such as the general revision of radiology in recent years. Minor changes can be approved by the *Vorstand* of the national medical association, major changes only by the *Ärztekammer*. All changes must be approved by the management of SUVA and by the government of each canton.

Prices

Each year, the negotiators from the medical association ask for higher fees, SUVA responds with a counter-offer, and the actual award follows the rise in the consumer price index. The agreement involves the value of a single point in francs. It is the same rate for all of Switzerland. Every act in billing is priced as a multiple of its number of points times the current value of the single point, just like the method of multiplying a unit by the coefficient in the *Nomenclature* of France.

In the past, cantonal governments readily approved the awards negotiated by the medical association. In recent years, the craftsmanship of the SUVA schedule has been so widely admired that several cantonal medical societies and sick funds have copied it, and some have linked their financial awards to SUVA's. When the sick funds experienced a financial pinch in 1975 and 1976, those cantons that had linked health insurance to SUVA refused to approve the higher awards to doctors for SUVA patients, since large deficits would have occurred in health insurance accounts from the higher fees that would have followed there. In order to avoid covering these deficits, several cantonal governments (such as Fribourg) refused to approve the SUVA award, therefore invoking their constitutional authority for the first time. SUVA paid doctors the higher award anyway, but eventually the federal courts or the national Parliament will decide the constitutional issue.

OVERVIEW OF THE SWISS NEGOTIATING SYSTEM

Despite the great difference in size, Switzerland's is one of the systems that the United States may be destined to resemble if Congress enacts certain of the pending national health insurance bills. Instead of a single leap from private to official health insurance, Switzerland has evolved gradually, with successive groups enrolled by compulsory or voluntary methods in nonprofit schemes. Voluntary enrollment has been supported by government regulations and by subsidies. Cantons have followed this evolution at different paces, so that the situation across the country at a single time has varied. Eventually Switzerland may arrive at the same benefit structure and the same coverage throughout the country.

Nonprofit sick funds have survived and prospered. They have competed for subscribers by the quality of their service and by offering supplementary policies, For negotiations with doctors, they have united in cantonal associations. The cantonal units have joined nationally when necessary—for policymaking, national political lobbying, and statistical reporting—in the headquarters of nationwide insurance companies and in national associations.

Doctors have continued to practice under fee-for-service in private offices. They have adapted to whatever direct or indirect billing methods were customary in the canton and were provided in formal agreements with the sick funds. A few cantons perpetuated the sliding scales for billing patients according to incomes, but these methods are being abandoned.

STRONG POINTS IN THE SWISS SYSTEM

A great variety of local procedures are permitted in a national system with almost identical benefits. The result is a greater range in payment methods than in any other developed country under national health insurance. Medical care is handicapped by a poverty of national statistics, but apparently there are few other major drawbacks to the system.

Switzerland demonstrates how private carriers can survive under national health insurance and how they can justify their retention by conscientious administration.

Negotiations are conducted in the cantons (with only rare exceptions) very courteously and as thoroughly as the data permit. As in Holland and Sweden, this style of negotiation characterizes relations between groups throughout the entire social structure of the country.[18]

Switzerland illustrates a system working well with very small staffing and low administrative overhead.

Several of the cantonal medical societies and SUVA have developed great expertise in writing modern fee schedules.

SOME PROBLEMS IN THE SWISS SYSTEM

Diversity

Health insurance, like many other features of Swiss official life, reflects the widespread preference for local autonomy and fear of national government. Too much unity and standardization are believed to threaten liberty. Only those activities requiring nationwide uniformity are centrally organized.

Health insurance might profit from greater similarity across cantonal boundaries than exists at present. Not enough data can be calculated about services under health insurance for the country as a whole, because of variations among cantons in recording forms and in research staffing. Each canton knows a little about itself but can compare itself with others and with the country as a whole on only a limited number of indices. Fee schedules are unnecessarily diverse at a time when medical practice and medical education are common throughout the country. Variations in fee schedules and in rules do not create serious trouble for patients and doctors who move from one canton to its neighbor, but the bother is unnecessary when the variations result from nothing more fundamental than local taste.

Greater unity might be possible without central control. Cantons might observe and learn from each other, thereby evolving toward greater voluntary consensus. They don't in practice: In health insurance, cantonal Ministries, medical societies, and insurance associations are usually preoccupied with their own local affairs and do not try to emulate the practices of other cantons. While the great number of local arrangements makes Switzerland a natural laboratory for the study and evaluation of forms of organization, such comparisons are not attempted systematically by anyone. Left to themselves, the cantons would develop increasingly diverse fee schedules and conditions of service.

One solution is greater persuasive leadership by nationwide associations. *Konkordat* has induced the sick funds and the entire health insurance program to function more uniformly, while retaining their autonomy and remaining diverse in many respects. Some of the nationwide business firms in health insurance—such as *Konkordia* and *Helvetia*—could not operate efficiently without greater uniformity, they run their own affairs similarly in all cantons, and they speak up in each cantonal association of sick funds. Harmonization in hospital affairs is encouraged by the work of the national hospital association and its affiliated research institute. These communication channels among cantonal organizations will increase during the coming years but will always have uneven success, because of their voluntary nature, because of diverse participation in a system with twenty-five parts, and because of their limited staffs.

Another force for greater agreement is national organizations. For example, SUVA has been an important counterweight to the tendency of cantons to draw up fee schedules in increasingly unique ways. The national government can be an important unifying force, because it enacts laws, subsidizes all the sick funds, regulates medical education, and performs other acts. However, it exercises influence over the cantonal health insurance very gingerly, because of the country's strong opposition to centralization. Leadership will be needed, but the Swiss prefer it to come out of committees or out of impersonal organizations.

Data

Negotiations between doctors and sick funds require much up to date information about services, incomes of providers, costs of practice, and so on. Swiss negotiators have only a little at present. Economic reporting about health services is still new. It is only the largest nationwide sick funds (such as *Konkordia* and *Helvetia*) that have modern methods of processing bills and generating statistics on the system in action, although the *Konkordat* will develop such capabilities for the others. Processing techniques, though, will still not be able to generate detailed national statistics and permit optimum comparison of each canton with national norms, because of the unique fee schedule of each canton. Because these reports will strengthen the determination of the sick funds to control costs, the cantonal medical associations will slow the evolution toward a national fee schedule.

Staffing

Cantonal medical associations have modest offices, small clerical staffs, and part-time secretaries. A visitor to the substantial national and provincial headquarters of other countries might predict that the Swiss medical profession suffers from this understaffing. If a very large amout of data and legal documentation surrounded health insurance practice, perhaps more people would be needed to assimilate them and prepare position papers. Negotiations are informal and usually harmonious, and much of the burden in developing strategies and in negotiating is borne by practicing physicians as a voluntary service to the profession. Larger staffs and headquarters budgets would enable the cantonal medical associations to perform more services and negotiate in a more eloquent style, but the present arrangements may not seriously impair them. Because so many Swiss dislike large bureaucracies, they predict that larger headquarters would make the negotiations more formal and more combative. Keeping headquarters small might be a good way to reduce problems, they believe.

NOTES

1. A description and critique of federalism in Swiss health services appears in Alfred J. Gebert, "Switzerland," paper in the Proceedings of the Conference on Changing National-Subnational Relations in Health (Bethesda: Fogarty International Center, 1978).

2. The history of the health insurance laws and of the sick funds appears in Paul Biedermann, *Die Entwicklung der Krankenversicherung in der Schweiz* (Zurich: Buchdruckerei Davos, 1955); and *Message du Conseil fédéral à l'Assemblée fédérale à l'appui d'un projet modifiant la constitution fédérale dans le domaine de l'assurance-maladie, accidents et maternité . . . (Du 19 mars 1973)*, Number 11572, pp. 3-9. The current situation is described in Pierre Gygi and Heiner Henny, *Das schweizerische Gesundheitswesen* (Bern: Verlag Hans Huber, 1976), Ch. 7, etc. passim; and Arnold Saxer, *Soziale Versicherung in der Schweiz* (Bern: Paul Haupt Verlag, Fourth edition, 1976.)

3. Basic data about the funds and their benefits appear in *Statistik über die vom Bunde anerkannten Versicherungsträger der Krankenversicherung* (Bern: Bundesamt für Sozialversicherung, annual).

4. The *Konkordat's* role in the amendment of the health insurance law in 1964 is described in Gerhard Kocher, *Verbandseinfluss auf die Gesetzgebung* (Bern: Francke Verlag, Second edition, 1972).

5. As in the activities described by Kocher, *ibid.*

6. *Rapport de la commission fédérale d'experts chargée d'examiner un nouveau régime d'assurance-maladie du 11 février 1972*, pp. 55, 66 and 196-198; and *Message du Conseil fédéral à l'Assemblée fédérale à l'appui d'un projet modifiant la constitution fédérale dans le domaine de l'assurance-maladie, accidents et maternité . . . (Du 19 mars 1973)*, Number 11572, p. 16.

7. Karl Appert, "*Das Ärzte-Einkommen—ein offenes Geheimnis,*" *Schweizerische Ärztezeitung*, Volume 57, Number 14 (7 April 1976), pp. 472-474.

8. M. Zumstein et al., "Probleme der Preis-, Lohn- und Gewinnüberwachung," *Wirtschaft und Recht,* Volume 27, Number 1 (1975), pp. 1-123.

9. In late 1973 and early 1974, as price control was going into effect, doctors in several cantons requested large increases in fees. They said that certain of their costs, such as gasoline, were going up much faster than the cost of living index. Because the cantonal governments would have had to approve the new fees and did not want to be overruled by Bern, they asked the price control office for guidance. Meetings were then held in several cantons, where representatives of the federal price control office could explain their policies to the doctors, sick funds, and cantonal governments. Considerable correspondence then followed.

For example, *Gesellschaft der Ärzte des Kantons Zürich—Jahresbericht 1974,* pp. 20-22; and *Verband der Krankenkassen in Kanton Zürich—99. Jahresbericht . . . 1974,* pp. 8 and 40-47.

10. Its history is reported in *100 Jahre Krankenkasse für den Kanton Bern 1870-1970* (Bern: KKB, 1970).

11. Described in James Hogarth, *The Payment of the General Practitioner* (Oxford: Pergamon Press, 1963), pp. 299-301 and 627-634.

12. The number depends on the way the offices are counted. If each agency of the centralized funds is counted separately, the total exceeds 750. The *verband* deals with about 113 members, which in turn have subdivisions.

13. For a description of the previous situation and a statement of the national government's views, see *Message complémentaire du Conseil fédéral à l'Assemblée fédérale à l'appui du projet de loi modifiant la loi sur l'assurance en cas de maladie et d'accidents (Du 16 novembre 1962),* Number Ad 8251. The situation since the 1964 amendments is described in Fritz Schären, *Die Stellung des Arztes in der sozialen Krankenversicherung (Das 'Arztrecht' des KUVG)* (Zurich: Schulthess Polygraphischer Verlag, 1973), pp. 221-352.

14. The doctors' grievances and their account of the negotiations appear in *Gesellschaft der Ärzte des Kantons Zürich—Jahresbericht 1964,* pp. 11-16, 27-35, 64-72, and 77-124.

15. If they didn't, the government of the canton was prepared to use its legal authority to adopt a completely new *Rahmentarif.* Its proposal to adopt for all health insurance practice the one used in Swiss accident insurance evoked much anxiety among the doctors: they would have been governed by a document imposed upon them involuntarily; the medical specialties would have been underpaid. *Gesellschaft der Ärzte des Kantons Zürich—Jahresbericht 1973,* pp. 22-24. Soon afterward, the medical society and the sick funds reopened direct negotiations to regain control of the situation.

16. William Glaser, "Improving Federalism in American Health Services: Some Ideas from Abroad," paper in the Proceedings of the Conference on Changing National-Subnational Relations in Health (Bethesda: Fogarty International Center, 1978).

17. Described in Gygi and Henny, *Das schweizerische Gesundheitswesen* (note 2, supra), Ch. 8.

18. For example, Serge Grosset and Thomas J. McDermott, "Labor-Management Cooperation in Switzerland," *Labor Law Journal, Volume 14* (March 1963).

CHAPTER VIII

Sweden

SWEDEN has a long tradition of doctors "in the King's service," who gave medical care to the army, the royal Court, and the public, and who offered medical courses at the university. They worked either full-time or part-time and received salaries. A number were "health officers" or "district medical officers" (*distriktsläkare*) who cared for the poor or for rural residents and who also administered public health affairs in a district.

As in other European countries, health insurance developed privately during the nineteenth and twentieth centuries. Subscribers and their employers paid premiums to private sick funds; the patient paid the doctor and was reimbursed by the sick funds. By the end of World War II, two-thirds of the Swedish population was covered voluntarily, an unusually high proportion for a voluntary system.

As in other European countries during the initial postwar years, Sweden sought to expand coverage, standardize benefits, and make finances predictable and substantial. A Royal Commission was appointed to suggest a mechanism. Universal coverage and financing from general taxation in the postwar years implied a national health service as in Great Britain, and the Commission proposed one. All care would be given the Swedish population by salaried health officers, employed by the national government and working out of health centers and hospitals.[1] The Swedish Medical Association opposed the plan: at this time, few of its members were salaried health officers; most members and the leaders were private office practitioners who collected fees from patients. The Commission violated what was rapidly becoming an article of faith in postwar Sweden: no important official recommendation or decision is announced without full consultation with all interested groups, diverse views are woven into a compromise, and nothing is pushed over the determined opposition of an important interest group.[2] The Medical Association retaliated against the government by refusing to deal with the Commission's chairman in his other capacity as director of the chief administrative agency for health services. He was not reappointed when his term expired. National elections weakened the Social Democratic government and strengthened the conservatives; the Social Democrats prudently struck a compromise with the medical association.

The solution under the law of 1953 was to cover the entire population under national health insurance, a method later emulated by other European countries when they reached the stage of universalizing benefits. Payroll taxes on the employed subscribers and on their employers are supplemented by government subsidies, so that everyone can draw benefits. A single network of government sick funds replaced the several private carriers.

During the 1960s, operating control over most of Swedish health services passed to the provinces or "county councils" (landstingen). They took over most of the country's hospitals. They built many health centers and employed increasing numbers of district medical officers. By the mid-1970s, Sweden by quiet evolution had moved very close to the national health service idea that had been rejected in the late 1940s when it had been suggested as a sudden innovation: most care is given by salaried doctors employed by the county councils; only a minority of doctors are private office practitioners, and retirements steadily reduce their number.

This chapter and the next will describe negotiations in the only two Western European countries with national health services, viz., Sweden and Great Britain. The systems and the overall structures for negotiations differ greatly from anything the United States is likely to adopt, but an analysis of the two countries is valuable nevertheless: some details can be emulated in any negotiation system; an understanding of a national health service provides background for better insights into the design of national health insurance; and Americans who blanch at the spectre of government ownership of medical services can learn how it really works. This chapter will describe Sweden's two systems: the negotiations with the salaried doctors employed by local governments, and the vestiges of national health insurance.

THE COUNTY COUNCILS

The councils

Sweden has three tiers of government: nation; province or "county" (läns); and municipality (kommun). Each of the twenty-three counties (plus three big cities which operate the same way) has a miniature parliamentary government. A county council (*landsting*) of at least twenty members is elected by the citizens. The county council levies some taxes, passes the budget, and is specifically responsible for health care. Because so many other government functions are exercised by the national and municipal governments, the county council's principal task is health. Half the county council's budget is covered by the taxes it levies on incomes and other taxable bases; the other half comes from subsidies by the national government, from insurance payments, and from minor sources.

The county council appoints an executive committee that runs the provincial government, similar to a Cabinet in a parliamentary system. The county council also appoints a special committee on health. The county council meets only a few times a year, and the executive committee and health committee run provincial agencies all year round.[3]

Each county has a governor appointed by the national government. He oversees the county government's conformity to the policies of the national government and also acts as a commuication link between the county government and Stockholm.

The association

The county councils are united not through the national government but through their own association, the Federation of Swedish County Councils or *Landstingsförbundet*. Its governing body is a Congress of 137 members, chosen by the county councils in proportion to their size. Each county council sends representatives in proportion to its own internal partisan political divisions. The Congress meets annually. For round-the-calendar leadership, the Congress elects a Board of Governors of fifteen members. It meets about ten times a year. All meetings are held in the *Landstingsförbundet's* headquarters building in Stockholm.

The Congress and its Board of Governors express the collective views of the county councils in dealing with the national government and with the public. They work out national policies to be implemented voluntarily by the county councils concerning their own personnel and health services.

The *Landstingsförbundet* maintains a secretariat of about 150 persons at headquarters. They gather information about the topics of interest to the county councils—particularly health care, health economics, planning methods, and government finance—and supply it to the members, either in the form of regular reports or in answer to questions. They gather information concerning personnel matters, provide advice, and conduct special training courses for old and new employees of the councils. The association supports several autonomous organizations, including Sweden's principal institute for research on health economics and health administration.[4]

The allocation of health manpower is not left to the discretion of county councils, hiring as many doctors as they like, but is planned nationally. A law of the Parliament assigns the work to the Social Board (*Socialstyrelsen*), once called the "National Board of Health and Welfare" and still so named in the English-language literature about Sweden. The Planning Section and the Health and Medical Care Section of the Social Department of the *Landstingsförbundet* collect the requests from the county councils for new positions. The manpower planners learn the number of new doctors who will become available each year and judge where in Sweden they think new staffing will be valuable. Each year the planners in the *Landstingsförbundet,* the planners in the *Socialstyrelsen,* and other interested groups (such as the Swedish Medical Association) chart a roster of salaried medical positions employed by the county councils and by other governments for the entire country, consisting of current positions that are filled, current positions that are still unfilled, and new positions.[5]

Lest they compete for the scarce doctors and bid up pay and facilities, the county councils must follow national guidelines when hiring individuals to fill their new positions. The Personnel Policy Department of the secretariat of the *Landstingsförbundet* develops these principles, with the advice of the Personnel Policy Committee of the Board of Governors. Within the Personnel Policy Department is a Section for Wage and Salary Negotiations, staffed (as is the rest of the secretariat) by full-time employees. The contract governing the pay and working conditions of doctors employed by all county councils is negotiated between this section and the Swedish Medical Association.

THE SICK FUNDS

The funds

Pursuant to the health insurance law of 1953 and beginning in 1955, the many private health insurance funds were merged into single official funds. Local identity was retained, rather than creating a single national agency with local offices. Within each county is one sick fund (now called an *allmänna försäkringskassa* or "general insurance fund") that inherited the personnel, money, and facilities of the earlier private organizations. Besides health insurance, each fund now administers retirement insurance. Each fund has a county office and between eight and thirty local offices.

Each fund has much administrative work. The citizen registers and brings all of his questions and problems there. The office doctor admitted to insurance practice registers there. (These are the physicians who are not full-time salaried employees of governments.) Doctors send their bills to the office, which reviews and processes them, and then sends payment to the doctor. If some billing seems suspicious, it is the county office which investigates.[6]

The association

The sick funds have their own national association, the *Försäkrings-kasseförbundet,* with offices in Stockholm. The association's functions are: meetings to discuss problems and reforms in insurance; writing and printing booklets to train new employees of the sick funds and to explain new procedures; drafting, printing, and distributing forms used by the sick funds and the doctors, including the fee schedule; information to the general public about health insurance; a monthly magazine, informing the officials of sick funds and others about new developments in the national government and in the network of funds; and lobbying in the national government for more favorable policies and more generous subsidies.

The insurance board

Policies are made and some basic administrative tasks are performed in Sweden not by the national association of sick funds (as they might in some countries) but by the national government. While most governments combine policy making and executive administration in the same Ministry, Sweden separates them. A Ministry, such as the *Socialdepartment,* consists of a small number of political appointees and civil servants who perform special studies, plan, write laws, and write decrees that implement laws. The administration of a program is vested in a "board" with a director, a large staff, and one or more headquarters buildings in Stockholm. In practice, the division of labor between Ministry and board is often blurred, particularly in the social services, because both may do a great deal of planning. Because of their size, importance, and influence, the boards are powerful agencies, and many of their Directors General— for example, the head of the *Socialstyrelsen*—overshadow their Ministers.[7]

The National Social Insurance Board (the *Riksförsäkringsverket* or RFV) manages social insurance and oversees the insurance funds on behalf of the *Socialdepartment.* It prepares the budgets for the several insurance programs (including health), manages the flow of money, audits the sick funds, issues and explains regulations, collects data, and publishes reports on the state of the system. Because the RFV is the watchdog of the costs and income of the system, it is their staff that formulates the government's position on any increase in fees that might be offered to doctors and to hospitals. It is their staff that negotiates with the private doctors and with the county councils.

THE MEDICAL PROFESSION

The medical association

The Swedish Medical Association (*Sveriges Läkarförbundet* or SMA) has been the scientific and professional association for all Swedish doctors since its founding in 1903. In recent decades, it has also become the recognized trade union for the Swedish medical profession. At least 90% of Sweden's 16,000 doctors are members, and SMA has no rivals.

Each member belongs to one of thirty local branches that meet regularly to discuss scientific and economic matters. In addition, each specialist belongs to one of thirty constituent associations that sponsor discussions and publications about the scientific work of each specialty. A few other constituent associations exist, for chiefs of services in hospitals, certain doctors in public health, and so on. The local branches send over 130 representatives to the annual Delegates Conference, which sets policies on professional and economic matters. The Conference elects a fourteen-member Central Board, which meets regularly and governs the association throughout the year.

A large secretariat is maintained at the headquarters in Stockholm. It collects and publishes information about both the economic and scientific sides of the medical profession. Its staff prepares the cases for higher pay for both the employed doctors who earn salaries and the office doctors who collect fees. It publishes Sweden's leading medical journal.

During the 1920s, before the SMA took on trade union functions, the junior hospital doctors organized their own trade union, with the acronym SYLF. This militance was finally emulated by junior doctors in other countries—including the United States—during the 1970s. SMA has cooperated with SYLF, which occupies space in the SMA building. SYLF's members belong to SMA, but SYLF is a separate association.

The association of professional persons

Until 1938, Sweden had recurring conflicts between workers and employers. In that year, the national associations of workers and employers signed the "Saltsjöbaden Agreement," resolving to settle all conflicts by negotiation and compromise, in order to avoid the twin spectres of strikes and government arbitration. The national associations of the workers (LO) and of employers (SAF) thereafter determined working conditions and wages, in consultation with the individual trade unions belonging to LO and the individual businessmen's groups belonging to SAF. A few years later, the white-collar workers formed a national association (TCO) patterned after the labor association (LO), and they too developed with their employers an understanding that all disputes would be negotiated and resolved peacefully.[8]

Scientific societies already existed in the professions, and at first sight, they seemed not appropriate bases for a comparable national labor association. However, several trade unions had been formed during the 1930s by younger members of several professions, worried by unemployment, such as SYLF. In 1943 they created the Central Organization of Young Swedish Professional Workers (*Sveriges Yngre Akademikers Centralorganisation* or SYACO).

Working together through something like SYACO was obviously advantageous to the established professional associations, as more professionals became salaried employees of government and of other large organizations. The professionals in government were paid according to a salary scale common to all of them; it would be created unilaterally by the national government, unless some national umbrella organization could confront it on behalf of all professionals. In 1947, several established professional associations copied SYACO and created the Central Organization of Swedish Professional Workers (*Sveriges Akademikers Centralorganisation* or SACO). By 1977, the Swedish Medical Association and twenty-five other professional associations were affiliated with SACO. The large and previously independent national association of civil servants (SR) merged with SACO in a union of equals in 1975, so that organization is now officially known as SACO/SR.

The organization's policies are set by a Congress and a General Assembly. The Congress consists of 200 persons elected by the membership and meets every third year. The General Assembly has 80 members representing the affiliated professional associations and meets once a year. The Congress chooses SACO's fifteen-member executive committee, which meets twice a month and directs the daily work. Some members of the executive committee lead affiliated associations, but most are practicing professionals who volunteer to help their associations. Officials at headquarters also participate in the executive committee. Reporting to the executive committee are several advisory councils and study groups, whose members are drawn from the affiliated associations.

A secretariat is maintained at headquarters in Stockholm. One department deals with the organization of professional associations, in order to strengthen existing members and foster new ones. A second department conducts research about the problems of professionals and managers, such as trends in their labor market, incomes, effects of taxation, social benefits, etc. The negotiations department prepares for SACO's bargaining with all levels of government and with private employers for an improved salary scale and for better working conditions for all professionals and executives. The negotiations department also provides advice and documentation to individual professional associations when they bargain with employers themselves, as the engineers' association does with the industrialists. SACO conducts all negotiations on behalf of some of its members, such as the school teachers, but the members' governing boards must approve. The Swedish Medical Association prefers to bargain for itself on the special affairs of doctors, coordinating its efforts with SACO, particularly in fixing the general salary scale.

Decisions about demands and about acceptance of a contract are made by SACO's executive committee. It is advised by the "large negotiating committee' (*Stora förhandlingsdelegationen*) which in 1976 had one representative from each of ten member associations. The delegate from SMA was chairman. It is called the "large negotiating committee" to distinguish it from the several "small negotiating committees" that actually bargain with employers.

SMA occupies a particularly important position in SACO. The medical profession is respected and well paid. SMA was a founder of SACO. SACO for a decade was a guest at SMA headquarters.

SALARIES

All employees of Swedish governments are paid on salary scales. The scales for the national and county governments differ slightly. Some professionals are employed by the national government, but most doctors are paid by the county councils.

The monthly rates for the county councils' salary scale (*Löneplan K*) fall into 64 steps.[9] The amounts in late 1976 included:

Class	Kronor per month
1	2,295
2	2,527
3	2,683
.	.
.	.
.	.
27	5,092
28	5,209
.	.
.	.
.	.
31	5,576
.	.
.	.
.	.
42	7,343
43	7,537
44	7,737
45	7,943
46	8,153
47	8,370
48	8,593
49	8,839
50	9,091
.	.
.	.
.	.

This is the basic salary scale applying to everyone. Some occupations, such as medicine, obtain supplements.

Negotiation of the basic scale by SACO

The medical profession (like every other) wishes to increase the pay scale applying to everyone and also tries to supplement it. The Swedish Medical Association therefore participates in two negotiations, often simultaneously.

The basic scales for employees of the county councils have existed for several decades. They are never rewritten but are revised from time to time. For example, negotiations during 1976 eliminated the long-standing differentials in pay rates among communities, once based on different living costs. The negotiation usually is limited to the amount of the increase in money for the entire scale.

SACO's committees meet in the autumn, with the aid of documentation from its negotiations department. They consult the consumer price index, issued each month by the Central Statistical Office of Sweden. SACO usually formulates a case that the salary scale should increase at least as much as the rise in the cost-of-living index since the last award. There has never been a clause for an automatic cost-of-living increase in the county council salary scales, but the claim is bargained.

Meanwhile, the leadership and negotiation department of the *Landstingsförbundet* decide how much the county councils will be able to pay during the next year. They decide the amounts they can put into higher rates in the general salary scale and into the extra demands by each profession. From time to time, they meet members of the negotiating department of the national government (the *Statens Avtalsverk*) to make sure that they are offering the same money to comparable occupations.

SACO enters negotiations with the *Landstingsförbundet,* usually during the last months of each year and usually at the latter's building in Stockholm. Leaders of three or four member associations make up the bargaining delegation, assisted by the staff of SACO's negotiations department. The delegation is made up of the principal occupations employed by the county councils: it always includes officials from the Swedish Medical Association, and it also includes engineers, social workers, and (sometimes) dentists. Often the chairman is the head of SMA's negotiating department.

SMA is a prominent part of the SACO negotiating team because of its importance within SACO. Another reason is SACO's concern about retaining the confidence of all doctors: At times rebels within SMA have complained that SACO devotes too little attention to the doctors and fights harder for the lower paid professions, and have proposed that SMA secede.

SACO presses for the same percentage increase for all classes in the pay scales. The result would be to maintain the relative position of the higher groups and widening differentials among classes. The left-wing Social Democrats who controlled the national government and most county councils from the late 1960s until 1976 pressed for greater equality in incomes in Sweden. They favored low increases for the higher grades in the salary scale and also enacted increasingly progressive income taxes. A slowdown occurred in 1971 when SACO negotiated with the national government over its salary scale and over the particular provisions for schoolteachers. When the government only offered unequal increases that narrowed differentials, SACO called a strike of teachers, a tactic that had become obsolete in Swedish industrial relations. A large majority in the Parliament mandated a cooling-off period; even the conservative political parties and mass media condemned a strike to preserve privileges; and SACO surrendered.[10] The militant leader of SACO paid the price for getting his association out on a limb by being "promoted upward and to the left," to quote a favorite Swedish phrase about the fate of mavericks.[11]

The negotiators for SACO and the *Landstingsförbundet* agree on the general pay increase. The *Landstingsförbundet* indicates that additional money is left for the extra provisions for each profession, but they are settled in the separate negotiations involving each association. The general agreement includes matters applying to all professionals employed by the councils, such as vacations.

The new contract usually begins on January 1. Once contracts ran for two years. Inflation has been so strong that SACO and its members have pressed for one-year contracts. Then they can catch up sooner. The county councils pressed for a two-year contract in 1975–1976, and SACO and SMA agreed, provided they could reopen the pay question after the first year. The consumer price index had risen so much after the first year that SACO won a revised scale, but it was not in as strong a bargaining position as it would have been if the old contract had been expiring.[12]

The special negotiations for the doctors: preparations by the medical profession

Before and during the general negotiations between SACO and the *Landstingsförbundet*, SMA prepares its own special case. This is an opportunity to learn the economic and occupational problems of the employed doctors, a chance for the ventilation of their complaints. The governing board of SMA nominates a standing negotiating committee (*Förhandlingsdelegationen*) consisting of: five members of the SMA board; three members from the special sub-association of senior hospital doctors; three from SYLF; two from the district medical officers; one from the organization of medical students; and the head of the negotiating department of the SMA secretariat (*Förhandlingsavdelingen*). The negotiating department of SMA provides the paper work.

The department and the committee start work in the spring, for a contract expiring at the end of the year. They develop a first draft of recommendations on: the position of each category of employed doctor on the standard salary scale of the county councils; rules on seniority; hours of work; overtime work; standby time in the hospital; readiness time at home; free time; vacations; extra pay for various duties; and so on.

The paper is sent to the eighty special organizations of doctors within SMA for their comments. During the summer and fall, members of the negotiating committee and negotiating department hold meetings around the country—e.g., six during August and early September 1976—to hear doctors' problems and recommendations. If doctors have serious suggestions about revising or expanding the SMA's negotiating position, they write formal letters. By November, the negotiating committee drafts the SMA's proposal, and the association's governing board meets to adopt it. The SMA sends the negotiating document to the employers, viz., the *Landstingsförbundet, Kommunförbundet,* and the national government (The *Kommunförbundet* and the national government are included because each owns a few hospitals and employs a few doctors, but the *Landstingsförbundet* is the principal adversary.)

Usually before the detailed negotiating paper is produced, SACO has begun to bargain with the *Landstingsförbundet* over the basic pay scales. The SMA negotiating committee sends several of its members to participate in the SACO negotiating committee. The negotiating departments of the two organizations—i.e., their secretariats—keep in touch.

The county councils

By autumn, the Economic Department of the *Landstingsförbundet* secretariat has worked out the estimates of the money expected during the coming year in the budgets of the county councils. It has provided its governing board and its negotiating department with estimates of the amounts probably available for the basic salary scales and for extra benefits for professionals. Its most important negotiations relate to the doctors, since health is the principal function of the county councils.

The Board of Governors agrees to the general outlines of the additional money and terms of service that might be conceded to the doctors. They are the representatives of the member county councils and have full authority. The staff of the Section for Wage and Salary Negotiation then works out the detailed papers used by the *Landstingsförbundet* representatives during the negotiations.[13]

Meetings to fix special terms for doctors

The secretariats from SMA and the *Landstingsförbundet* face each other, not the doctors from the SMA committees or the county council politicians from their association's committees. The doctors and the politicians instruct their employees and review the agreements. The meetings almost always are in the *Landstingsförbundet* building. Often the association of municipalities accompanies the *Landstingsförbundet* and expresses its views, but the latter speaks for both of them in agreeing upon salary scales for doctors. The national government's negotiation department (the *Statens Avtalsverk*) goes along with these wage awards for the doctors in the two teaching hospitals it controls. Besides larger meetings, the two specialists in the work of salaried doctors from the staffs of SMA and the *Landstingsförbundet* meet to work out details.

The negotiators cannot modify the larger salary scale (*Löneplan K*) that by this time has been settled in the wider negotiations between SACO and the *Landstingsförbundet*. SMA tries to gain financial advantages by obtaining higher rankings for particular groups of doctors (for example, a starting salary of K49 instead of K48 for a grade) or larger supplementary pay. The supplements originated in 1970, to make up the loss of private practice, when Swedish hospital doctors became full-time. Gradually they are being phased out, and the doctors have steadily risen on the scale. SMA's tactic is to raise the higher ranks of doctors first (e.g., from K50 to K54 in the current scales), and then to narrow the resulting differentials in subsequent years by raising the lower ranks of doctors (e.g., from K27 to K32).

The rules of the game in Sweden are negotiation and binding commitments among the peak associations, not dividing and conquering. Therefore, the *Landstingsförbundet* does not try to weaken SMA by encouraging a splinter association. It is aware that the medical association is divided—for example, once the junior doctors were more militant than the senior doctors—but it does not play on the split by catering to one group in order to gain its purposes with the others. Of course, the internal divisions affect the SMA's decisions. For example, in 1970 it reluctantly agreed to a new system of full-time salaried employment in hospitals without rights of private practice in place of the earlier part-time arrangements, in large part because SYLF preferred full-time contracts at high pay.[14]

The final agreement between the *Landstingsförbundet* and SMA is approved by the governing boards of the two organizations. It is a contract and not a law of either the national or county governments. It need not be ratified by SACO. SMA needs SACO's approval only for a strike.

Once many Swedish doctors were full-time private office practitioners who billed their patients by fee-for-service, and the patients were reimbursed by the sick funds. The doctors were supposed to keep close to the fee schedule and many did; the patients were reimbursed exactly three-quarters of the fee schedule. Salaried hospital doctors and salaried district medical officers had part-time private practices, in which they earned fees according to the same schedule.

Since 1970, the volume of fee-for-service practice has diminished. The hospital doctors and district medical officers have full-time salaried arrangements and no longer bill patients. Fewer younger doctors enter private practice, and most seek salaried jobs. The private practitioners are declining in number and are becoming older. Very complex and expensive acts are not included in the fee schedule: they are done by salaried doctors in hospitals. The fee schedule consists of acts that can be done in an ambulatory mode, including minor surgery not requiring overnight hospitalization.

The medical profession

SMA has an economic division concerned with the interests of office practitioners. (For tax purposes, it is legally a company called *Praktikkonsult AB,* but actually it is an integral part of SMA.) In preparation for the negotiations, its staff conducts questionnaire surveys of all office doctors asking about their incomes, practice costs, problems, and requests. They obtain further information about practice costs from a closely allied association of private doctors that operates health centers.

The fee schedule has ten sections, some corresponding to a clinical specialty and others combining several specialties. SMA maintains ten advisory committees for fees, each corresponding to a section of the fee schedule. Each has four to six members, drawn from the doctors in those fields. Each holds four to six meetings a year, usually an evening session in the SMA headquarters in Stockholm.

The advisory committees report demands by the practitioners to raise acts that have become unprofitable, because they consume more time or cost more to perform. Other requests involve problems in the terms of service. An advisory committee may propose addition of new acts.

On the basis of these recommendations from the advisory committees, by autumn the SMA economic staff produces a draft negotiating document proposing some changes in the fee schedule and the terms of service. During the fall, all groups meet together to agree on the final negotiating document and to advise the negotiators.

The aim of all the preparatory work is to enable an office doctor in a forty hour week to earn as much after practice expenses as a senior hospital doctor without the chief of service's managerial responsibilities (i.e., a *biträdande overläkare,* who in 1976 stood at K46 on the salary scale and also collected a supplement). The negotiators need to know the practice costs and the distribution of acts in each field for an average office practitioner. The fees and supplementary practice allowances are calculated in SMA's case to enable the office doctor to net the same as the salaried specialist. An office doctor can earn more by working longer than forty hours.

The sick funds

The bargaining adversary is not the sick funds themselves, but their supervisor, the *Riksförsäkringsverket* (or RFV). The "Principal Supervisory Office" of the RFV (the *Första Tillsynsbyrån*) gathers economic information throughout the year about utilization and costs under fee-for-service. It regularly gets tabulations from RFV's own statistical office, based on regular reports from all sick funds. Also, it learns about trends in the government's consumer price index and in practice costs. It develops an image of the costs of practice and the difficulty of acts from informal information about ambulatory care in the outpatient departments of county council hospitals. The office prepares the government's interpretations of the rules on health insurance and the meaning of the last contract; it hears about complaints and problems from the sick funds and from the public; and therefore it knows which fees and terms of service should be revised or clarified in the next contract.

The RFV staff confers with officials in the *Landstingsförbundet* and in the *Socialstyrelsen,* to work out a government position on the fees and terms of service for the office doctors. They share a desire not to spend too much money. Also they wish not to make private office practice too profitable, lest it reverse the trend toward more salaried employment of doctors by government.

The negotiating committee

Before 1975, the SMA regularly discussed the fee schedule and terms of service with the RFV, but the arrangement was informal. The SMA long argued that Swedish health insurance was a method for the sick funds to pay the patients, the fee schedules were not legally binding on doctors, and therefore the medical profession would not assume contractual responsibility for them. So, the SMA gave "advice" to RFV. This position became less profitable as the bargaining power of the office doctors declined.

In 1975, relations between the office doctors and national health insurance were reorganized in many ways.[15] One change was creation of a standing negotiating committee that would write the fee schedule and terms of service. The *Läkarvårdsdelegation* operates like other standing negotiating bodies throughout the Swedish social structure: It includes representatives of the adversaries and of other interested parties, and its decisions result from consensus rather than from votes.[16] It meets throughout the year to deal with all relations between the office doctors and the health insurance system. The members are:

RFV: the director and deputy director of the "Principal Supervisory Bureau"; and the head of all the control doctors in health insurance

SMA: the managing director and one other, currently the chairman of the special section for office doctors

Landstingsförbundet: two heads of departments, including the head of its department on negotiations

Socialstyrelsen: the head of the department concerned with the economic situation of the medical profession

The chairman is the general manager of the RFV. He tries to work out a consensus but sometimes is handicapped by the SMA's perception of him as part of the RFV delegation. Meetings are usually held at the RFV during an afternoon approximately once a month, except during the summer. Extra meetings are called during periods of negotiation. When a narrow technical point must be settled, often a few persons from the SMA and RFV confer.

The *Läkarvårdsdelegation* is assisted by a working party of specialists in research or in the economics of fees (the *LV-Grupp*). They have four members from the RFV secretariat, four from the SMA secretariat, and one apiece from the *Landstingsförbundet* and the *Socialstyrelsen*. Their task is to produce from time to time reports with facts accepted by all sides concerning numbers and locations of office doctors, trends in age and retirement, numbers of doctors participating and not participating in health insurance, numbers of part-timers, numbers of acts of each type, costs, variations in utilization, numbers and types of doctors earning various supplements, and so on. Therefore, the two sides do not present competing versions of such facts. Recently even practice costs—disputed by negotiators in most other countries—have been settled by consensus in the *LV-Grupp*.

The RFV tends to defer to the SMA on the relative values of the items in the fee schedule, but it may raise some questions about individual items, if it has heard about trouble in the reports from sick funds. Usually the RFV negotiators do not take any position about reducing differentials in the incomes of specialties, or providing the same general increase for everyone. However, the SMA sometimes decides that the GPs or some specialties have been lagging and tries to help them catch up, often by allowing them to perfom acts previously reserved to other specialties. Except for a clinical reason not to let the GP perform such a more specialized act, the RFV usually goes along.

The agreement, including both the revised fee schedule and the terms of service, is issued as a regulation of the national government. Therefore, it goes up to the governing board of the RFV and can be amended. However, this never happens; the RFV's director chairs the *Läkarvårdsdelegation* and nothing would be included in the agreement that the RFV's higher levels would not accept. Since RFV is an administrative board under the Ministry of Social Affairs (the *Socialdepartment*), the latter must agree. The Minister then orders the fee schedule and the terms of service printed in the government's regulations.

OVERVIEW OF THE SWEDISH NEGOTIATING SYSTEM

Once Swedish national health insurance bore some resemblance to possible American trends, but now it is being eclipsed by direct services rendered by government. Sweden has been one of the world's innovators in the social services, and a serious possibility is that direct services similar to the present Swedish trend may replace national health insurance everywhere, either because the insurance mechanism inevitably becomes financially overstrained or because government management is deemed most efficient by legislators. Whether America comes to resemble Sweden during the Twenty-First Century, it will enact nothing like it during the Twentieth.

Sweden is an example of how socialism can work to the benefit of providers and not to their detriment. Because the work of doctors has long been highly prized and because the market under national health insurance placed them on a high level, they have been able to maintain a very prosperous situation under full-time salaried employment. Whether representing office doctors bargaining for fees or employees bargaining for favorable salary scales and supplements, the medical association has been resourceful. Because high pay was granted in the euphoric past, and because increases are always granted at about the rate of the rise in cost of living, government negotiators are generous.

SOME POTENTIAL PROBLEMS (AND THEIR PREVENTION) IN THE SWEDISH SYSTEM

At first sight, Sweden's negotiating system works very efficiently and has no problems. Difficulties that beset other nations seem absent.

For example, in some countries, it is not clear whether the sick funds are fully competent negotiators or whether the medical association really should be bargaining with the government. Sweden resolves this simply. The sick funds are lower administrative agencies, their *Försäkringskasseförbundet* does not make policy and does not speak for them in negotiations. Rather, the negotiator is their supervisor in the government, the RFV.

Coordination can be a problem in the negotiations of some countries. The individual county councils are the principal employers of doctors and could diverge in strategies and offers. They agree, though, to negotiate as a unit, through the *Landstingsförbundet*. The association is careful that all the county councils make known their views and their financial limitations during the preparation for the negotiations.

A problem throughout the world is the absence of an incomes policy for the elite. Incomes policies receive much publicity and evoke great hopes for stabilizing the economy, but usually private managers, investors and the leading professionals can evade them. The medical profession throughout the world is one of the groups most insistent on freedom of action, either the right to fix its own charges or the right to bargain with the public authorities independently for fees and salaries. The competition among these elites for incomes and living standards at least as high as the best paid in their circles is an important reason why income policies fail. SACO in Sweden is one of the few mechanisms in the world whereby the medical profession coordinates its pay demands with other groups and goes to the bargaining table as part of a team. The method does not depress their pay: They still obtain assignments to the higher ranks of the salary scale.

The rules of the game in Sweden provide for agreements among the leaders of the peak associations. They are not supposed to make "end runs" around each other, they should not try to "divide and conquer" by appealing to factions within the other side. While the *Landstingsförbundet* profited from the disagreemeents between the junior and senior doctors, it did not try to play SYLF against the SMA's senior leadership. However, the reliance on established leadership and the dampening of any fragmentation in the peak associations may result in the only significant problem in the Swedish negotiating system, viz., a deepening unease in the population that too many decisions are made by a few leaders, that the individual is dominated by large organizations, and that deviant views are not considered.

All this procedural harmony may have been possible because of social harmony, achieved through generosity in pay awards and in social benefits. Bargaining was calm because providers have always been certain they will get much of their request. By 1978, Sweden was facing a belated accounting for generosity in wages and in the social services: income taxes had reached exceptional levels, governments were running chronic deficits, inflation was very high, several export industries had been priced out of world markets, and individuals' real take-home pay after taxes was limited. If the government had been less generous in the past, negotiations would have been more conflicted and health services would have been strained, but the country's international economic situation might now be less dangerous.

NOTES

1. J. Axel Höjer et al., *Den Öppna Läkarvården i Riket: Utredning och Förslag* (Stockholm: Medicinalstyrelsen, 1948). Summarized in Ann Margaret Lundgren, "Plans for the Reorganization of the Hygiene and Public Health Services in Sweden," *International Health Bulletin of the League of Red Cross Societies,* Volume II, Number 3 (July-September 1950), pp. 11-16.

2. This behavior is deeply rooted in the culture and social structure of modern Sweden, as described in Paul Britten Austin, *On Being Swedish* (London: Secker and Warburg, 1968), esp. pp. 22-39, 45-52, and 85-91.

3. The administration of health services is described in Svenska Landstingsförbundet, *Landstingens Sjukvårdsadministration* (Lund: Studentlitteratur, 1970).

4. The history, organization, and work of the Federation are described in Rolf Ejvegård, *Landstingsförbundet: Organisation, Beslutsfattande, Förhallånde till Staten* (Stockholm: Landstingsförbundet, 1973).

5. Health planning (including a little about manpower allocation) is described in Vicente Navarro, *National and Regional Health Planning in Sweden* (Washington: National Institutes of Health, Department of Health, Education, and Welfare, 1974), Chs. 3-5. Navarro also describes the Ministry of Social Affairs and its boards, *op. cit.,* pp. 20-26.

6. The insurance system and the work of the county offices are described in *Social Security in Sweden* (Stockholm: Försäkringskasseförbundet, 1976); and Rolf Broberg, *Så Formades Tryggheten: Social försäkringens Historia 1946-1972* (Stockholm: Försäkringskasseförbundet, 1973).

7. On the structure and roles of Ministry and boards, see Neil Elder, *Government in Sweden* (Oxford: Pergamon Press, 1970), Ch. 3 and the many sources cited therein.

8. The organization of trade unions and of labor relations is summarized in Lennart Förseback, *Industrial Relations and Employment in Sweden* (Stockholm: The Swedish Institute, 1976); and Nils Elvander, *Interesseorganisationerna i Dagens Sverige* (Lund: Gleerup, 1969). Some highlights of Elvander's book appear in his articles, "Interest Groups in Sweden," *Annals of the American Academy of Political and Social Science,* Volume 413 (May 1974), pp. 27-43; and "In Search of New Relationships: Parties, Unions and Salaried Employees' Associations in Sweden," *Industrial and Labor Relations Review,* Volume 28, Number 1 (October 1974), pp. 60-74.

9. An example from the 1960's is in William A. Glaser, *Paying the Doctor* (Baltimore: The Johns Hopkins Press, 1970), p. 70.

10. SACO and its misadventures of 1971 are described in Arnold J. Heidenheimer, "Professional Unions, Public Sector Growth, and the Swedish Equality Policy," *Comparative Politics,* Volume 8, Number 1 (October 1976), pp. 49-73.

11. It is fundamental to the Swedish system of group relations and decision-making that all leaders of the peak associations behave in moderate and conciliatory ways. Spokesmen for rival groups press competing demands but also must be friends. David Jenkins, *Sweden and the Price of Progress* (New York: Coward McCann, 1968), p. 134.

12. Besides SACO, the *Landstingsförbundet* is also negotiating with LO and TCO, the trade union federations for all its other employees. A complete summary of one year's negotiations over wage scales and terms of service—in this case, primarily for nurses—is in Eric Johansson, "1975 Års Avtalsrörelse en Summering," *Protokoll: Landstingsförbundets Tjugoförsta Ordinarie Kongress 1975* (Stockholm: Landstingsförbundet, 1975), pp. 189-203.

13. The negotiating machinery is described in Ejvegård, *Landstingsförbundet* (note 4, supra), pp. 113-119.

14. The national government's proposal was *Promemoria med Förslag till Ändringar av Sjukvårdsförmanerna inom Sjukförsäkringen M.M.* (Stockholm: Socialdepartmentet, 1969). The prolonged national debate and the adoption of full-time hospital appointments is summarized in Ejvegård, *Landstingsförbundet* (note 4, supra), Ch. XI.

15. The new system and the reasons for the changes are reported in Riksförsäkringsverket och Socialstyrelsen, *Sjukförsäkringens Ersättningsregler vid Privatläkarvård: Utredning och Förslag* (Stockholm: Socialdepartmentet, 1973).

16. The work of the standing committee is described by Claes-Göran Kjellander, "Ingen ro för läkarvårdsdelegationen nu skall den nya taxan revideras," *Läkartidningen,* Volume 72, Numbers 1-2 (January 1975), pp. 8-9.

CHAPTER IX

Great Britain

IN 1948, a governmentally administered structure replaced Britain's national health insurance. The sick funds no longer had a function and disappeared. The United States will not enact anything like this, but for several reasons I shall describe how the National Health Service negotiates with its doctors and dentists. Some methods are worth emulating in national health insurance. Learning how a developed Western country really administers a governmental health service is valuable, particularly when so many Americans fear it.

THE NATIONAL HEALTH SERVICE

The Service is a hierarchy of committees representing lay and medical groups, following guidelines from a Ministry in the national government. The structure was altered most extensively and most recently in 1974. It is supervised in England by the Department of Health and Social Security (the DHSS), and by various offices in the other provinces.[1] (I will refer to "DHSS" when describing England alone and "the Health Departments" when referring to joint action by all of them. Negotiations with doctors usually involve all the Health Departments, led by DHSS.)

The hierarchy of committees in England passes down through 14 Regional Health Authorities (RHA) and then to 90 Area Health Authorities (AHA). The consultants and senior registrars in nonteaching hospitals (i.e., the senior specialists and senior house staff) have contracts with the

Regional Health Authorities: In return for undertaking certain responsibilities they receive a salary. The principal tasks of the Regional Health Authorities are planning, allocating money among the Area Health Authorities, reviewing the plans of the AHA's, managing construction, and providing some services. The Regional Health Authority has a chairman and several unpaid local members, drawn from voluntary associations, universities, the principal local authorities, the health professions, and trade unions. The board meets once a month, to review and approve the work of its chairman and its staff of full-time managers.

The general practitioners, dentists, pharmacists, and opticians in an area have contracts with a Family Practitioner Committee, which acts as agent for the Area Health Authority in administering their affairs. The GPs and dentists are considered independent contractors, who agree to perform certain work for a prescribed payment. It is possible that the Area Health Authorities will administer relationships with all hospital doctors, GPs, and dentists in the future. (Several Area Health Authorities exist specially for the principal teaching hospitals, and they administer affairs of their medical staffs.)

The Area Health Authority is the basic policy and management unit in planning and administering health services. Its governing board— ranging between 15 and 28 members—is drawn from local government, local associations, trade unions, the health professions, and other organizations. Most of the members are named by the Regional Health Authority, and the AHA reports to the RHA. The AHA usually does not administer its own facilities (health centers, hospitals, community health services) but divides them into districts, each headed by a District Management Team, advised by a District Medical Committee. The Team consists of practicing doctors, the nursing officer, and administrators. The Committee is drawn from the practicing general practitioners, hospital doctors, and occasionally dentists in the district. This grassroots organization is designed to involve the typical practitioner in the daily management and economic responsibilities of the National Health Service, a goal not yet achieved in Britain or in any other country.[2]

All English RHAs report to the Secretary of State for Social Services and the Department of Health and Social Security. He appoints members of all RHAs and chairmen of all AHAs. The department combines two previously separate Cabinet-level Ministries, one for health and the other for income maintenance and cash benefits. Assisting the Secretary of State to administer the health side of the Department is a Minister of State (Health) and a Parliamentary Under-Secretary of State; all three sit in the House of Commons. Advice to Ministers on the formation of policy and on the management of the health service is the responsibility of the Department's civil servants, including administrators, doctors, dentists, nurses and other professional advisors. The civil servants are led by the Department's official head, the Permanent Secretary, and by the Chief Medical Officer.

Within the Department is the National Health Service Personnel Group, operated by civil servants. They negotiate conditions of service for all occupations in the NHS. Particular officials specialize in the affairs of hospital consultants, junior hospital doctors, general practitioners, and dentists.[3]

THE MEDICAL PROFESSION

The British Medical Association

The BMA has always performed the usual professional functions of sponsoring scientific meetings, publications, and recreation. In addition, it has been the spokesman for the doctors in working out terms of service with the National Health Service, presenting requests for higher fees and appealing to the general public. Once it was primarily the rallying-point for the general practitioners, but increasingly during the 1960s and 1970s, it has been a vehicle for the senior and junior specialists in hospitals.

The governing agency is the Representative Body, elected by the members. Half are picked from geographical divisions and half from special constituencies, such as the GPs, senior hospital doctors, and junior hospital doctors. It sets policy on all professional matters, including relations with the National Health Service. It meets at least once a year.

The Council runs the BMA throughout the year, implementing the policies of the Representative Body. The Council consists of the leading officials of the BMA (elected by the Representative Body), the chairmen of the principal committees, representatives from particular groups (such as GPs and consultants), and several members of the Representative Body. An Executive Committee leads the Council and manages the work of the BMA Secretariat.

Several committees set policy for the groups within the medical profession and negotiate with the Health Departments for England, Scotland, and Wales. Different viewpoints are argued out within these committees. Sometimes (as in the case of the junior hospital doctors in 1975–1976) one faction overturns its leadership's decisions and changes chairmen. The General Medical Services Committee leads the general practitioners; it has over seventy members, most elected by local committees of GPs. The Central Committee for Hospital Medical Services represents the consultants—i.e., the senior hospital specialists. It has over 80 members, most elected by regional committees of consultants and some named by particular groups of specialists. An increasingly important force in BMA is the Hospital Junior Staffs Committee, consisting of representatives elected by the young doctors in training grades from regions of Great Britain.

The terms of service and payments negotiated at the national level must be translated into the special legal terminology and must be supplemented for Scotland. Therefore, the Scottish members of BMA have their own Scottish office, which deals with the Scottish Home and Health Department. The Scottish doctors participate in all committees and organs of BMA, to fix national policy and negotiate with the Health Departments jointly.

BMA membership is voluntary, but most doctors join. Some militant doctors do not join, because they consider BMA's national leadership too moderate. However, the method of electing the policy committees—from all doctors serving the NHS in a locality and not merely from the local BMA chapter—gives them a voice in negotiations. As a result, the BMA has been pressed to become steadily more militant in its relations with the National Health Service, including the use of strikes.

Because of its scientific and professional functions, the BMA is a limited-liability company. As its negotiators became more militant during the 1960s, some members recommended that it reorganize as a trade union; the older leadership and members resisted successfully on the grounds that the BMA's character should be essentially professional. The Conservative Government's ill-fated Industrial Relations Act of 1971 at first would have required every negotiating body throughout the economy to become a trade union; BMA would have had to become a union, or remain an association and cease representing doctors in labor relations, or organize a parallel trade union for negotiating purposes, as in Germany. The final draft of the Act created a special register for professional associations that acted as negotiating bodies. After the Labour Government replaced the Act with milder conciliation machinery in 1974, BMA was accepted as if it were a trade union in dealing with the National Health Service. However, the more militant doctors, such as many juniors in hospitals, still favor completely converting the BMA into a trade union and joining the Trades Union Congress.[4]

The Royal Colleges

During its first years when the National Health Service was being designed, the terms of service for all doctors and the pay of hospital staffs in particular were strongly influenced by the Royal Colleges. These are scientific and licensing bodies in the specialties, closely allied to the teaching hospitals. Many decisions before and after the introduction of the health service were made without formal negotiating machinery between the profession and the Ministry of Health; the distinguished leaders of the Royal Colleges were able to use the "old boy network" to maximum effect, by informally meeting with civil servants or by "having a word" with the Minister, Prime Minister, or other fellow members of the elite.[5] As labor relations in medicine became more strident in the 1960s, as the BMA became a more inclusive and more representative body, and as eligibility for negotiations seemed to narrow to medical trade unions or to associations willing to be considered as if they were trade unions, the august Royal Colleges became less active in negotiations. Now they participate only by sending representatives to BMA committees.

BILATERAL NEGOTIATIONS FOR CONDITIONS OF SERVICE

A common puzzle in labor relations is how to organize negotiations between the sovereign government and its employees. Can any contract bind the government? In case of a deadlock, who has the final word? Can any arbitrator who is a citizen of that government issue a decision that binds the government? If the government has the right to reject or alter an award made by its representatives or by an arbitrator, will it then take advantage of its employees?

Under national health insurance in most countries, the doctors negotiate with the official sick funds, with government acting as final arbitrator only under exceptional circumstances. The only exceptions in our investigation have been Canada and Sweden. There, the sick funds are really government agencies too, not preexisting private carriers that acquired official status.

At the beginning of the National Health Service, responsibility for negotiation of all terms of service and rates of pay was assigned to standing committees ("Whitley Councils"), consisting of representatives of management and of staff. The management sides are spokesmen of NHS employing authorities and of the Health Departments; the staff side represents employees in the jurisdiction of that particular Whitley Council. The Councils have functioned for other NHS employees, but not for general practitioners, hospital doctors, and dentists. At first, these professions insisted on bilateral bargaining with whomever seemed appropriate in the Ministry of Health. By this method, they could obtain special negotiating arrangements, which might be more advantageous than the more routine Whitley Councils. They could often settle matters with the Minister or Prime Minister, and not be restricted to the civil servants, who customarily represented management on Whitley Councils.[6]

For several decades, terms of service and pay rates for doctors were settled in an *ad hoc* manner, rather than by any standing consultative bodies or procedures. The first terms of employment for GPs were settled during the 1940s in bitter bilateral meetings between the leadership of the Ministry of Health and representatives of the governing committees of the BMA. The first terms of employment for consultants were settled in more harmonious informal conversations between the leadership of the Labour Government (particularly the Minister of Health) and leaders of several Royal Colleges. Once the methods of payment were fixed in these discussions—capitation for general practitioners and salaries for several sessions per week by consultants—two special committees of experts and nonpartisan figures (chaired by Sir Will Spens and therefore called "Spens Committees") fixed the monetary levels of pay.

Terms of service have been settled by bilateral bargaining ever since, with each side sending whatever spokesmen it thinks appropriate. The law specifies that negotiations shall occur but does not spell out the identity of the negotiators, so that the selection can be flexible. The law merely says that "remuneration . . . [and] conditions of service . . . [shall be] the subject of negotiations by a negotiating body and [shall be] approved by the Secretary of State [for Social Services] after considering the result of those negotiations . . ." "Negotiating body" is defined quite tautologically as "any body accepted by the Secretary of State as a proper body for negotiating remuneration and other conditions of service for officers or any class of officers."[7] Discussions on the Department side always begin and often end with the civil servants specializing in the affairs of that group of physicians, although sometimes the doctors demand to see the higher political decision makers with more authority. Even if the Minister of State (Health), the Secretary of State for Social Services, or Prime Minister become involved in settling impasses, the civil servants usually attend the meetings and draft the detailed agreement.

If the BMA believes the Secretary of State or the Minister for Health will be more generous, it may request appointments with them. Civil servants are usually perceived as more cautious about money, more tied to traditional practices. The political heads of British Cabinet Departments are usually thought to be more eager to buy peace and to keep fights out of the newspapers, more responsive to politically influential elites, such as the doctors.[8]

The British Medical Association has always represented the GPs and increasingly has spoken for the senior and junior hospital doctors. At present, the medical profession is represented only by the BMA, and the DHSS cannot "divide and conquer" by negotiating national agreements with a rival, as the public authorities can in France and Belgium. When the Royal Colleges were active and independent on behalf of the consultants, the Minister of Health could split the profession: the structure of the NHS was written in a form pleasing to the Royal Colleges, the

Minister planned to launch the Service with the cooperation of the consultants, and he thereby maneuvered the general practitioners into reluctant acceptance.[9] (Recently a new organization, the British Federation of Hospital Doctors, has claimed substantial membership among senior and junior hospital doctors, but they have not been given places at the negotiations.)

The agreements range from basic long-term regulations to detailed or limited arrangements that expire or are amended within a few years. The more basic regulations are laid before Parliament by the Secretary of State for Social Services and go into effect eight weeks later; the simpler agreements are sent out by the Personnel Division of the DHSS with a letter by a civil servant, after approval by the Department's political heads. The basic regulations cover eligibility to serve in a post in the NHS, professional discipline, relations of the doctors to governing committees, assignment of patients, obligations to patients, times of duty, the general principles of work schedules and of remuneration, and so on. The less formal agreements, issued as circulars by DHSS, include details on pay and conditions that will be effective for a few years, such as: lists of the acts to be paid by fees; the categories of work that will receive different rates of pay (e.g., numbers of patients receiving different capitation fees, or the numbers of hours counted as a session in the hospital); definitions of duty time in hospital service. . . . Both regulations and the circulars issued pursuant to them have force of law.

During the 1950s, bilateral negotiations fixed the monetary levels of pay, supposedly in accordance with the principles in the Spens Reports. These pledged the NHS to correct doctors' pay for inflation but employed certain calculating methods that the general practitioners in particular claimed resulted in underfinancing of their practices and a lag in their relative position in the country's income structure. The British Cabinet then (as now) limited expenditure on the NHS in order to develop other sectors, and it granted pay increases reluctantly. Doctors earned incomes at or near the top of the British income structure but prospered less than their counterparts in Europe and North America. The tension was settled by creation of a standing Review Body of independent and distinguished members of the public, who investigate the facts and recommend pay rates that the government undertakes to accept, unless "clear and compelling" reasons exist for not doing so.

The Health Departments and the general practitioners

From the BMA side, the General Medical Service Committee (GMSC) plans and oversees negotiations about general practitioners' conditions of service. The GMSC sends as negotiators its chairman and four other members. They are supported by a member of the BMA's London staff, who is secretary to the GMSC.

They meet once a month with a team of civil servants from DHSS: the Undersecretary of the Department in charge of the personnel division; his medical counterpart; and the assistant secretaries and civil servants concerned with the subjects under discussion. Civil servants from the Scottish Home and Health Department and from the Welsh Office also attend, to make sure that the agreement negotiated by DHSS is acceptable to their provinces. The group usually meets at the Department, but sometimes at BMA House in London. The paper work before and after the meeting is performed by one of the civil servants.

The two sides have not had a serious dispute since 1965, and therefore the meetings are informal and cordial. In contrast, the contentious sessions between the Health Departments and the hospital doctors have had to adopt more formal procedures.

At times the meetings write a major change or addition to terms and conditions, such as the recent extra fees for contraceptive services or the third and more generous capitation fee for patients older than 75. Often the meetings discuss unexpected or troubling situations in particular health centers or in individual practices, because they may reflect anomalies in the rules that should be corrected. These lead to amendments to a basic contract that remains essentially the same for many years. The consensus on interpreting specific points need not result in new regulations; it enables DHSS to answer questions coming up from its Family Practitioners Committees and enables BMA to answer questions from its individual members and from its local chapters.

Within the BMA, the General Medical Services Committee and the Council routinely receive reports on the meetings with the Department. The agenda of the Annual Representative Meeting includes reports on requests to be made in the future and on agreements recently concluded. Within DHSS, the Undersecretary (who heads the negotiating team) keeps the Permanent Secretary and their political superiors informed and solicits their advice, particularly if important changes or controversial problems are being examined. The minutes routinely go up through departmental channels, for the information of the Secretary of State, the Minister, and the Parliamentary Under-Secretary.

Relations between the general practitioners and the National Health Service have been amicable for a decade, and the BMA has not needed to appeal over the heads of the civil servants to the Secretary of State and to the Minister for Health. The Department has been generous, since it is committed to primary care. In fact, this is a rare case when the political "heads" have thought the civil servants too generous—such as the terms for contraceptive fees—but they have gone along.

The Health Departments and the hospital doctors

Once the Royal Colleges and the BMA collaborated in representing the medical profession in negotiations over conditions of service through the Joint Consultants Committee. Since 1967, the Colleges have become less active in negotiations, but the Joint Consultants Committee survives and now specializes in setting policies about hospital practice, education, and research.

Instead, there now exist within the BMA the Central Committee for Hospital Medical Services (CCHMS) and the Hospital Junior Staffs Committee (HJSC), who send two subcommittees of negotiators to a joint group. The BMA's London secretariat does the staff work for CCHMS and for the entire BMA negotiating group, as well as some of the work for the HJSC. However, the junior doctors have become militant and somewhat independent of BMA House in London during the struggles of the mid-1970s; leadership passed to the junior doctors of the Midlands, and the HJSC does much of its work at BMA House in Birmingham. The joint group from CCHMS and HJSC develops the BMA's position on conditions of service for hospital doctors, and it faces the Health Departments. In the past the consultants have dominated the full BMA negotiating group: Its chairman is a consultant, and the consultants have had a majority of the twelve members. However, the juniors have been rebelling against the excessive power of the consultants, both in the hospital and in the BMA, and they may now favor either the dissolution or the reorganization of the full BMA committee.

The Health Departments' team is headed by the Undersecretary who heads the personnel division and who also directs the negotiations with the general practitioners. With him are one of the chief or senior medical officers, the Assistant Secretary in charge of the hospital doctors, and the two lower ranking civil servants who do the detailed work concerning the pay and service of hospital doctors. Civil servants from the Scottish Home and Health Department and of the Welsh Office also participate alone or with their senior medical officers.

The BMA and the Health Departments normally meet every other month, in an inclusive meeting called the Joint Negotiating Committee (JNC). Each side confers in its own headquarters to prepare its position during the days just before. The doctors must hold two sets of meetings: first, the negotiating subcommittees for senior and junior doctors separately, and then the full BMA group. (The negotiating subcommittees from CCHMS and HJSC constitute the staff side of the JNC.) Both the consultants and the junior doctors have fought with the Health Departments during the 1970s, and JNC procedures have become strained. As if to symbolize the insistence on even-handedness, the meeting places alternate. Summary minutes are kept, but recently the juniors have complained that the DHSS violated the precise wording of the agreements, and they have proposed verbatim recordings.

The JNC has not been able to cope with the recent serious disputes over hours, on-duty obligations, and private practice (for consultants) or over hours, extra duty payments, and the definition of total work schedule (for junior doctors). The BMA has had to keep peace between the consultants and their juniors over rights of private practice, relative pay, and power. Often the subcommittees of consultants and junior doctors have negotiated the controversial matters separately with the Health Departments, instead of in the full Joint Negotiating Committee, but the subcommittees meet back in BMA House to approve the agreements. When things have become too heated and strikes seemed imminent, the doctors have met with the Secretary of State and with the Minister for Health. The subcommittees from BMA were then expanded to involve other leaders from the consultants' or juniors' sides. The government side was joined several times by the influential Secretary of State for Employment, the overseer of British incomes policy. The juniors' tactics were vindicated: The Secretary of State for Social Services was more generous than the civil servants in defining the juniors' work day and overtime hours.

Briefly during 1974, the BMA and the Health Department created an *ad hoc* negotiating structure with bilateral bargaining between the doctors and civil servants, and with the participation of a political appointee. The consultants were demanding a five-day work week and limited off-duty obligations. The DHSS under the new Labour Government wanted to eliminate pay beds, obligate the consultants to do nothing except NHS work during their salaried hours, and offer extra rewards only for difficult work. The drafting of a new contract was given to a Consultants Joint Working Party, consisting of:

Staff side:
A negotiating team from the CCHMS of BMA
A negotiating team from the British Dental Association
Representatives from a small independent association of consultants who
    do not belong to BMA
    Government side:
Civil servants from the DHSS personnel division
Representatives from the Scottish Home and Health Department and the
    Welsh Office
    Minister of State (Health) would be chairman. David Owen seemed an ideal choice for this difficult fusion of two antagonistic viewpoints: He was one of the Labour Party's most promising junior ministers, and he was himself a physician and member of the BMA.

The "Owen Working Party" could not agree upon a new contract and stopped meeting. The three Health Departments (DHSS, the Scottish Department, and the Welsh Office) then announced their own offer of a revised contract, in the light of the discussions in the Working Party. BMA rejected it, and 1975 was a year of strike threats and "working to rule"— i.e., slowing down by exaggerated conformity to regulations.

The consultants were emulating the increasingly militant (and profitable) posture of their juniors. The lower ranking hospital doctors were once considered students with low pay and unlimited hours of work or stand-by duty. However, during the 1970s, they have taken a leaf from industrial workers. During the early 1970s, the miners defied the Conservative Government's wage freeze and won: they struck, the Conservatives called a special election and lost, and the new Labour Government granted the miners' demands. Since then, several other groups in public employment and in the social services—including nurses and other employees of the National Health Service—have struck or "worked to rule" and have forced the government to grant shorter hours and higher pay. Claiming that they were underpaid and overworked by both the NHS and the consultants, the Hospital Junior Staffs Committee selected a succession of steadily more militant leaders and demanded an industrial-type contract with a forty-hour week and overtime for extra duty and stand-by. They dramatized their determination by calling one-day strikes (unprecedented in British medicine), "working to rule," and threatening longer strikes. The Labour Government surrendered, because on principle it favors a fixed salaried work week with overtime provisions for everyone, because it fears blame for disruption of the National Health Service, and because fury pays in collective bargaining. The juniors' success has not been lost on the other employees of the NHS: Many consultants "worked to rule" over the prospective loss of the pay beds for their private patients and might even become so ungentlemanly as to strike in future disputes. (Optimists hope that, instead, the future will bring greater calm and new ideas about how to improve the payment system and the negotiating machinery.)

Even during the new and abrasive labor relations in the NHS, the traditional informal methods were revived. But now they were less effective. In December 1975 and again in mid-1976, when the juniors were occasionally "working to rule" over hours and salaries and while the consultants were complaining over the loss of pay beds and over their own work load, the Presidents of several Royal Colleges conferred with the Prime Minister. However, the old labor relations could no longer settle everything: The conversation paved the way for a compromise bill over the consultants' pay beds, but the junior doctors continued to fight for themselves, until they had been satisfied by the Secretary of State.[10]

Because negotiations and fights spotlight individual leaders and spokesmen, their careers can gain or suffer. If events go badly—either because the interest group fails or because the system suffers expensive trouble—new faces will be installed. Perhaps the old leaders made mistakes; or, perhaps they made the biggest mistake of all, viz., allowing themselves to be maneuvered into the situation of scapegoat by the leadership of the parent organization, when its larger policies went awry. When the full membership of HJSC rejected an agreement that their leaders had negotiated with the Health Departments in 1974–1975, it also voted in a new and more militant governing committee. The Secretary of State for Social Services who battled the hospital doctors on behalf of the Labour Government's policies on pay beds and incomes control in 1974 and 1975 was demoted to the back benches in 1976.

THE REVIEW BODY FOR PAY

Organization

A Royal Commission in 1960 recommended that the government create a "Standing Review Body of eminent persons of experience in various fields of national life to keep medical and dental remuneration under review and to make recommendations concerning that remuneration to the Prime Minister."[11] The structure of the payment system for all GPs, hospital doctors, dentists, community physicians, and other NHS doctors is defined by the bilateral agreements between the Health Departments and the representatives of each group. The Review Body "prices the contract"—i.e., it takes each item of pay specified in the regulations and agreements, and decides its worth during the next year. Likewise, it decides a salary or an average target net income for that class of doctors for the next year under NHS practice.[12]

The first Review Body was a six-member group appointed in 1962. Its staff work was done by civil servants from the Cabinet Office. Deciding the pay of government executives too lofty to submit to the Whitley Council machinery has been troublesome outside medicine, and two similar agencies were created in the early 1970s for them, the Top Salaries Review Body and the Review Body on Armed Forces Pay. Staff services are provided since 1971 by an autonomous secretariat of civil servants, the Office of Manpower Economics.

The British government has long included many commissions with full-time or part-time members of the public. (They are called Quasi-Autonomous National Governmental Organizations or "QUANGO's.") For many years the Prime Minister—on the recommendations of the Ministers and civil servants—appointed members of "The Great and the Good" to these posts. The process was haphazard, mysterious, often suspected of entrenching the Establishment's power over the country, and often suspected of providing political patronage to the governing political party. The system was regularized in 1975. A Public Appointments Unit was established in the Civil Service Department. It keeps *curricula vitae* on all past and current appointees to the country's QUANGO's and constantly looks for new candidates. Each Ministry may also keep a roster of possible appointees, as it did before.[13]

Positions in the Review Body for Doctors' and Dentists' Remuneration have been filled with the help of the pre-1975 methods up to now, but future selections will draw upon the Public Appointments Unit. However, the procedure differs from the method for the other QUANGO's, which are clearly government agencies. The medical profession cannot allow the government to appear to dictate all the members of the Review Body, since the agency is supposed to be neutral between the government and the profession, despite its formal terms of reference as advisors to the Prime Minister.

Therefore, at any time the BMA and Royal Colleges (or anyone else) can recommend to the Prime Minister and Secretary of State for Social Services names of persons for possible appointment to the Review Body, and their dossiers are then added to the files of the Public Appointments Unit. When an opening arises on the Review Body, the Public Appointments Unit suggests a few names from its file, the senior civil servants of DHSS might add more from their files or from their memories, and the BMA might suggest new ones. Officially the selection is done through government channels and the BMA is not sent a formal nomination for approval, but the BMA's leadership has a chance to comment.

Because the Review Body makes many detailed financial and other types of calculations, most of its members have experience in industrial management, economic analysis, or accounting. The chairman is usually a leading business executive. However, lest its perspective be too narrow, it always includes a few persons from outside business and economics. None are practicing or retired doctors. The Civil Service Department and DHSS look for persons who will be "responsible"—i.e., who will not be so generous as to disrupt the government's income policies. The BMA eschews nominees who appear too dependent on government preferment. The BMA prefers persons of great reputation, but they are not easy to recruit to the Review Body, since it requires much work and offers no pay. (The lack of salary supposedly ensures independence of the government.) Since the Review Body's recommendations cover all of Great Britain, its eight members—the current number—include one or two Scots. Members are not picked because of connections with political parties.

The Office of Manpower Economics is independent of the government bureaucracy, although its money comes from the Treasury and its staff is civil servants. Under the control of its Director, it provides all secretarial work for the three standing Review Bodies and supports any special committees of inquiry into the pay and conditions of service of any other occupations in the public service. (There were seven such committees from 1971 through 1976.) Also, it conducts research projects on payment methods. At times, the office has had as many as 70 employees. A senior civil servant is secretary to each Review Body and becomes expert in the pay of that group of occupations.

Submission by the medical profession

At present the Review Body makes awards every spring. Each January, its secretary sends letters containing evidence to all organizations representing doctors and to the Health Departments. The BMA and the Health Departments have already, by this time, been preparing for months.

The initiative in pressing for a new award is taken by the doctors. The separate BMA sections for GPs, consultants, junior hospital doctors, and public health physicians start preparing their cases for higher net incomes and (among the GPs) for higher practice allowances. The economic department in the BMA secretariat supplies the sections with economic data about their members' situations, trends in practice and in living costs, and the general economic situation in Britain. The secretariat of BMA prepares an overall case for more money, with the assistance of outside consultants from an accounting firm and from a university economics faculty.

Representatives of the four sections then meet in the BMA's Joint Evidence Committee. Included are five representatives from the GMSC, three from the CCHMS, two from the HJSC, and three from the section for public health physicians. Each delegation includes the chairman of that section and BMA, and the chairman of the subcommittee that negotiates the conditions of service with DHSS. The chairman of the BMA Council—i.e., the leader of the Association—chairs the Joint Evidence Committee. Several members of the BMA secretariat do the staff work. The Joint Evidence Committee combines the requests of the sections into one coherent document, supported by a general overview of the needs of British medicine.

The Joint Evidence Committee begins meeting each December and continues to meet until just after the Review Body has made its award. It reconvenes occasionally at other times, if a previous award needs to be reinterpreted. The Joint Evidence Committee's final submission document is not circulated within the BMA committees, lest it be leaked, but it is delivered to the Review Body. The Body prefers receiving each side's presentation in confidence, without leaks in the press, without criticisms or commendations by third parties, and without each side knowing the other's claim.

The Review Body can base its decision entirely on written evidence, but usually it invites the Joint Evidence Committee for oral testimony. The Committee is led by the Chairman of the BMA Council. It includes the chairmen of the four sections and the chairmen of the four negotiating subcommittees, accompanied by BMA's economic experts. The hearings are never public, and the other side does not attend. The Review Body fears that public testimony is overstated and repetitious: In private, the witnesses are more factual and more likely to concede weaknesses in their claims. To answer the Review Body's questions or to repair defects in its original submission, the BMA often prepares and sends supplementary evidence.

A similar procedure is followed by the British Dental Association. First, the Association prepares and submits written claims for the dentists in office practice and in public health. Then its spokesmen testify before the Review Body.

Sometimes the Review Body invites the doctors or dentists back for a discussion of one point, such as the expenses of general practitioners. At that time the BMA or BDA sends only members of its evidence committee specializing in that subject.

Any other organization claiming to represent doctors can submit evidence to the Review Body. Several new groups, hoping to expand their influence by means of extreme or original proposals, leap at this opportunity for recognition in a public forum. In 1976, the Review Body received documents from two militant associations representing consultants and junior doctors (they recently joined in an association hoping to rival the BMA), a trade union for doctors, and a small but aspiring association of dentists. The Review Body and its secretariat dutifully but wearily study all these documents. (Ideologically excited splinter groups are often eager to write at great length and publish their documents in their magazines, while the BMA is careful not to try the Review Body's patience.) The Review Body has never invited the smaller associations to testify.

Submission by the DHSS

Even though the Health Departments do not know the precise request filed by BMA, they can guess the principal themes and the general magnitude from the complaints and recommendations in the *British Medical*

Journal and *The BMA News Review.* Throughout the year, the statistical services of DHSS collect data and prepare standard tables about payments to doctors and their work.

During the final months of each year, the civil servants in DHSS prepare papers on what each category of doctors can be or ought to be paid during the next year; the Treasury prepares estimates of the costs and future resources of the National Health Service; and the Department of Employment writes statements on incomes policies. The political appointees, civil servants, and economists at the head of DHSS receive the guidelines from the Treasury and the Department of Employment, decide what DHSS can afford during the next year and outline a general wage plan for the Personnel Division. The civil servants in the Personnel Division then produce a coherent submission, combining its positions on the various categories of doctors and dentists. The separate sections of the report—an overview and the situation for each group of doctors and dentists—are short and moderate in tone. The Secretary of State submits this volume to the Review Body. When they have been completed, the latest statistical tables are sent over as a second volume.

Several members of the Department then testify before the Review Body. The main evidence is given by the highest civil servants (except for the Permanent Secretary himself). They are the deputy secretary, the two undersecretaries, the four assistant secretaries heading the personnel sections concerned with the pay awards, and a statistician from the Department's Statistics and Research Division. If the Review Body invites the Department back for additional evidence on one topic, the delegation may consist of only the deputy secretary and the undersecretary and assistant secretary specializing in that topic. After the meetings, the Department may send additional information to the Review Body. Sometimes the Review Body invites oral testimony from the Treasury and Department of Employment, concerning the government's budget plans and income policies.

If they insisted, the BMA and the Health Departments could present a joint proposal to the Review Body and testify together. However, that degree of harmony has never been attained in the past and is unlikely in the future. One of the few joint presentations arose out of mutual suspicion: After they had produced a contract in 1976 and had then argued over its meaning, DHSS and the junior hospital doctors came to the Review Body together, to make sure that everyone described the contract in the same way.

The Review Body once encouraged the BMA and DHSS to work out agreed estimates of practice expenses for general practitioners in a joint subcommittee, similar to the one that performs this work regularly in Holland. The data would come from doctors' tax returns, filed with the

Board of Inland Revenue. However, the two sides do not try to agree on the facts and interpretations, and the Review Body makes its own neutral estimates.

Sometimes the Review Body hears oral testimony from other persons involved in the payment of doctors, such as the chairman of the independent committee that gives extra merit awards to some consultants.

Work of the Review Body

During the spring, the Review Body meets at least once every two weeks to discuss documents, hear testimony, and comment on the reports drafted by its secretary. Sessions are held in the conference room of the Office of Manpower Economics. Usually each meeting lasts all day. The appointed members of the Review Body do not have private offices and rarely turn up to study files. Occasionally the Chairman comes to discuss matters with the Director of the Office or with the Secretary.

The descriptions of current facts and the projections of future economic trends in the BMA's and Health Departments' evidence are self-serving, and the Secretary—assisted by the statistical section of the Office of Manpower Economics—develops a neutral version. Often the Secretary of the Review Body asks government agencies or private research institutes for facts. The Board of Inland Revenue supplies the important data about expenses in general practice; the annual New Earnings Survey of the Department of Employment provides comparisons with income movements in the other professions and elite groups.

During its early years, the Review Body tried to complete its work in three-year cycles with an award that would endure for three years. It did not try to take account of price movements by predicting the levels for each year and then announcing the award as three ascending steps. Instead, it tried to predict the total rise in costs and in British incomes for the period and make an average award that the doctors would get throughout the entire time: that pay would be excessive during the first year, correct during the second year, and low during the third year. The method worked badly during the early and middle 1960s: prices in suddenly prosperous Britain rose faster than expected, and the average awards were always too low; even if they had been overpaid during the first year, the doctors always protested that they were unjustly underpaid in the third year, and they demanded extra money in the next award to compensate for losses suffered from the previous one.

During the late 1960s the Review Body changed to two-year awards (and biennial meetings) but still tried to predict the rate of price increases for the entire period: The award would be too high for the first year and too low for the second year but correct on average. In the light of their experience during the three-year awards, the doctors always predicted very large price rises and pressed for large awards. By this time, Britain was entering its now chronic international financial crises, and the government had to impose controls over income. A payment system that predicted rapid inflation and gave an occupation an extra payment for the first of two years seemed to feed inflation. In 1970, the Review Body made a very large award. The Prime Minister allowed only half of it for senior hospital doctors and asked the office administering the income policy to advise about the rest.

Since then, the Review Body has made awards for only one year instead of predicting long-term price movements. Therefore, it works every year, as do committees fixing doctors' pay in other countries. Because different factions of the medical profession have been disputing with DHSS on several matters during the 1970s, a series of bilateral agreements have been delivered to the Review Body for pricing, thereby increasing its work during normally quiet months. In 1973, it issued its regular report and two later supplements on special topics; the regular report for 1974 was followed by one supplement; 1975 yielded the comprehensive report plus three supplements.

The reports of the Review Body include extensive summaries of how fees, salaries, practice expenses, and other payments have been working out during recent years. Aspects of medical practice that may be affected by pay are described, such as recruitment, emigration, distribution among areas of the country, and distribution among specialties. Statistical appendices are included. The Review Body often points out that certain fees or payment devices are not working out as intended, or the system is encountering certain anomalies (such as lower differentials among ranks than were intended). These are recommendations that the BMA and the Health Departments negotiate changes in the regulations, and usually the parties do so.

The Review Body during its first years was expected to base its awards primarily on "changes in the cost of living, the movement of earnings in other professions, and the quality and quantity of recruitment in all professions."[14] Since 1970, the Review Body has been authorized to base its awards on whatever criteria it chooses, but comparisons with other professions and discouraging excessive emigration are emphasized.[15] At times the Review Body reminds everyone of another criterion not often publicized in struggles over pay, viz., "to avoid a situation in which the taxpayer has to pay more than he or she should toward the remuneration of doctors and dentists."[16]

The criteria have different implications, and the Review Body must choose among them. Usually it has tried to keep the medical profession in line with other high ranking professionals in Britain but not give it more money. This has required large increases when the British economy boomed (particularly substantial improvements for the general practitioners in the 1960s), but no more than enough to enable the doctors to catch up. If British doctors suddenly threatened to emigrate in large numbers, the Review Body might then have to award much more money. The BMA and conservative newspapers claim such losses are occurring or are imminent. The Review Body now regularly examines the evidence about emigration, concludes that losses have not yet increased beyond a limited (but not insignificant) number of junior hospital doctors with doubtful career prospects in Britain, and only occasionally adds money to an award that would have been decided according to relativities alone.

Recently the BMA has tried to persuade the Review Body to adopt a new standard for comparison, viz., the incomes of the doctors of Europe, who collect fees and (unlike the British) earn far more than the other professionals in their countries. The BMA claims that, when doctors can move freely throughout the Common Market, too many British doctors will emigrate to the Continent. So far, the Review Body has responded with characteristic caution: "We propose to keep the matter under review" and will increase pay for this reason only if emigration actually increases and only if higher pay clearly can restrain it.[17]

When no incomes policy is complicating its calculations, the Review Body first agrees on a target income for the average member of that category of doctors. From data about health services in recent years, the secretariat knows average work loads, such as the numbers of sessions for hospital doctors and the numbers of patients on G.P. lists. After considerable calculation by the secretariat, the Review Body then fixes the prices for each unit of service so that the average workload attains the target income, such as the salary rates for each rank and level of seniority in hospital care, the capitation and other fees for general practice. If programs associated with certain pay rates have not been going well, those rates are raised or lowered, instead of remaining in the same relationship to prices. Dentistry is the only part of the National Health Service paid by fee-for-service; instead of revising and pricing the entire fee schedule every year, the Review Body announces the target income for the average dentist and lets a special committee administer the details.

Conformity to government policies

The Review Body takes into account the budget plans of the government. DHSS and the Treasury tell how much money they intend to make available for the National Health Service and for its various activities during the coming year. However, since the Review Body can select its own criteria, it need not fit its award into these ceilings. Occasionally it has granted the doctors substantially more than the DHSS and Treasury expected, and they (and Parliament) have felt obligated to find the money.

A new criterion since 1969—and possibly a permanent one—has been the incomes policy of the British government. Annual pay increases are limited for all occupations and may occasionally be forbidden for the most affluent. Must the Review Body automatically conform to these limits? If so, the government thereby decides the pay of the doctors and its other employees; it does not negotiate and a Review Body is not an independent arbiter. Should there be any dependence by the Review Body on the government during periods of an income policy?

These relationships between the Review Body and the government have precipitated two organizational crises. In 1970, the Review Body defied the government and eventually won a Pyrrhic victory. The Labour Cabinet had been following an incomes policy and appealed to the Review Body to make any award within it. The Review Body explicitly refused: It declared that its first duty was to the maintenance of the National Health Service, and that a large pay increase (particularly in the hospitals) was necessary to head off widespread emigration. It denigrated the incomes policy by pointing out that the Labour government had not enforced it well.[18]

The Cabinet took up the gauntlet: It reluctantly accepted all the increases for junior doctors but only half for consultants. It referred the rest of the consultants' award to the National Board for Prices and Incomes, ostensibly for advice but actually for burial. The entire Review Body resigned at once in protest over this restraint on its independence and authority, and the BMA advised the doctors to reduce their administrative work for the NHS. These events were part of a general mobilization of the Conservative Party and the upper classes against Labour for the forthcoming general election. The Conservatives defeated Labour in the election, scrapped Labour's incomes policy, reconstituted the Review Body with new members and its own staff, and pledged that the Review Body's powers included applying at its own discretion all government policies, including any future limits on pay. The new Review Body gave the consultants the rest of their award.

Must the Review Body implement the government's incomes policies literally, or can it breach them for the sake of effective medical services? The BMA welcomes a Review Body that will fight the government (as in 1970) but is vigilant for any signs of excessive docility. In 1974, the new chairman of the Review Body imprudently told a newspaper that the BMA's current pay claim was unrealistic, since it would exceed the government's new incomes guidelines, and no government could be expected to accept serious breaches. The doctors protested the chairman's views (and his indiscreet method of revealing them) quietly through BMA channels[19] and noisily in the columns of the magazine *World Medicine,* and he soon resigned.

Implementing the award

The Review Body reports to the Prime Minister and makes no announcement to the negotiating parties. The Prime Minister refers the pay award and its supporting report to a Cabinet committee, consisting of those Ministers concerned with pay in the public service. The committee has affected the awards only twice. A decade ago it recommended scheduling an increase differently from the Review Body's timetable, and in 1970, it precipitated a politically expensive uproar by recommending that part of the award be reexamined. The committee completes its review within two weeks, so that the award can be announced by April 1, the usual starting date. A back-bench MP from the government party is asked to pose a question to the Prime Minister, during the latter's twice-weekly "Question Time" in the House of Commons. His written response is the first news for the doctors about their pay for the year.

Acceptance by the Cabinet binds the Health Departments. Political realities bind BMA. They go along with the Review Body for several reasons: the BMA suggested the Review Body system in the first place, in order to avoid the deadlocks in bilateral negotiation over money; the Review Body is often generous, so the BMA perceives it as "fair"; the awards depend only on acceptance by the Cabinet and not on acceptance by the BMA, and therefore it would go into effect anyway; if the BMA tried to boycott the Review Body's deliberations, the Review Body would get its evidence from one of the BMA's small rival associations. The BMA can block or delay only the fees that are so small that the DHSS is willing to suspend their introduction too. For example, the BMA believed that the new fee for general practitioners' contraceptive work in 1974 was too low. DHSS and BMA agreed on a higher fee in bilateral negotiations, and the new rate that was endorsed by the Review Body permitted the program to go into effect in 1975.

A new payment formula may evolve in unexpected ways. For example, the fee schedule for dentists in 1949 proved high and dentists' incomes increased greatly; the overtime allowances for junior hospital doctors were used more than expected in 1975 and 1976, and some earned more than starting consultants. Therefore, the Review Body secretariat tries to keep in touch with the current operations of a new payment system by getting reports from DHSS and BMA, or by asking questions. In this way the Review Body might correct anomalies during the next round. Sometimes the staffs at DHSS and BMA ask the Review Body's staff for a full explanation of the reasoning behind a part of the last award. The communications are usually by letter, because the Review Body's staff does not wish to appear unduly close to either side.

Fee schedules in dentistry

British doctors are paid by flat rate systems, as are almost all physicians under national health services in the world. American doctors under national health insurance will be paid primarily by fee-for-service. Therefore, while Britain is an interesting case study of how doctors negotiate with a government, the payment devices themselves cannot provide lessons for the United States. However, dentistry follows fee schedules and offers a model of how the doctors and government work out fees.

Conditions of service in dentistry under the National Health Service result from negotiations between representatives of the British Dental Association and the Health Departments, just as in medicine. Pricing of the contract is done by the Review Body, after evidence from both the Association and the Health Departments. The Review Body each year awards an average net target income for the average dentist working an average numbers of hours. The money is paid out by fee-for-service.

Dentists in British private practice have always used fee-for-service, and the National Health Service continues to pay them in this way. A list of acts and of relative values was agreed upon in discussions between the Dental Association and the Ministry of Health, and the Ministry set the prices. When utilization and costs proved unexpectedly high during the first years of the NHS, the Ministry cut the prices, over the protests of the dentists. The Royal Commission in the late 1950s sought a more calm procedure for deciding incomes and writing the fee schedule: the new Review Body would fix dentists' as well as doctors' incomes and would propose an average net target income for the year; a Dental Rates Study Group would write the fee schedule to achieve the target income.

The Study Group includes equal numbers of representatives from the British Dental Association and from the government. In its organization and work, it resembles the committees that write fee schedules under national health insurance in other countries, except that the public representatives are civil servants and not officials of sick funds. From the British Dental Association come seven persons, primarily dentists who lead the Association but also a few administrators from the secretariat. From the government come: three civil servants from the part of the Personnel Division of DHSS specializing in dentistry; a dental officer of DHSS; a statistician from the Statistics and Research Division of DHSS; a civil servant specializing in dentistry at the Scottish Home and Health Department; and a civil servant from the Welsh Office.

The chairman is expected to settle disagreements and shape decisions, since the two sides are self-interested. He is usually an accountant, conversant with the affairs of small businessmen like dentists. To ensure his independence of the government, he collects expenses but no salary. He is the point of contact for the Review Body and sometimes testifies at their annual reviews.

The Study Group conducts mail questionnaire surveys to learn dentists' hours of work, the time spent on individual procedures, and other facts about dental practice. From the Board of Inland Revenue, it obtains tabulations of the costs of dental practice during the last few years. To estimate the latest developments in practice costs, a subcommittee of the Study Group studies a sample of the catalogues from dental workshops and laboratories. To learn the relative frequency of each act, the Study Group gets tabulations from the Dental Estimates Board, which processes all dental bills under the National Health Service. The Study Group transmits some of this information, such as the length of the work week, to the Review Body to help in the latter's calculations. To conduct this research and its other work, the Study Group has two secretaries—one from the British Dental Association and one from DHSS—backed up by the research staffs of the two organizations.

Fees are intended to cover both the expenses for each act and the net income after expenses recommended by the Review Body. The Study Group's staff learns the expenses of the average practice from Inland Revenue, adds the average net income from the Review Body and prorates them over the fee schedule according to the number of acts of each kind performed by the average dentist during the year and the average length of time for each act. Ideally, all the acts in the average combination should cover practice costs and yield the average net income. As in all such calculations, some dentists will earn more and some less, depending on their productivity and work week. As in all such calculations, decisions are not as precise as hoped, therefore the fee schedule does not yield the exact incomes as expected. A chronic difficulty is getting accurate information about the time for each act and the number of acts of each type in a work year.

The Study Group's goal is to make each item equally remunerative. Selection of treatment is left to the dentist, guided by clinical need rather than profit. Therefore, the Study Group does not overpay any acts to encourage their use or underpay others to discourage them. If new equipment is adopted by enough dentists to make an act much more profitable for many, the fee is reduced. It is reduced for all, including those still employing the less efficient methods, because the fees are set for the average dentist. A fee is raised relative to others in the fee schedule, if the materials for that act are going up.

The Study Group must work quickly: the Review Body's award is announced just before April 1, when it goes into effect; the Study Group holds three daylong meetings and usually the new dental fee schedule is ready by July 1. It is issued as a "Determination" by the Secretary of State for Social Services. It takes effect retroactively from April 1, the date of the Review Body's award. The Dental Estimates Board orders payment of all bills for work done since April 1 according to prices in the new fee schedule. If the bill lists some work performed before April 1, it is paid according to last year's fee schedule.[20]

OVERVIEW OF THE BRITISH NEGOTIATING SYSTEM

Until the early 1960s, Britain struggled with the common problem of how to make the sovereign government a genuine bargainer, with neither the proclivity to decide everything at its convenience nor the political motivation to make expensive concessions. The Review Body was an ingenious and successful invention, evolving out of the tradition of British Royal Commissions that report to the sovereign but stand above the government. The chairmen and personnel of the Review Body have been selected with the mystery necessary to blur their commitments to anyone but the Queen. They have acted almost always with the neutrality, unanimity, and confidentiality necessary for such a delicate position.

The United States has increasingly turned to arbitration to decide deadlocks between unions of public employees and government agencies. But, in a republic, the arbitrator is appointed by the head of the government itself and not by a monarch. Unless he has a reputation for great independence, the employees are apprehensive. If he really is independent, government officials challenge whether decisions should be made by anyone who is not responsible to the electorate.

The Review Body has had to resolve the problem of whether its pay policy is independent of the government's, and it has experienced its handful of crises over this. At present the precarious formula commits the Review Body to the Parliament's incomes policy, but the Review Body has full power to interpret the policy in its own way. Presumably the Cabinet's explanation of its policies and the Review Body's prudence will keep them consistent, but a split and a confrontation are possible.

Terms of service are negotiated bilaterally between the doctors and the government; these discussions are held in a manner similar to direct public-sector bargaining in most countries. Such discussions—in Britain as well as in several other countries—seem to become deadlocked and em-bittered more often than do direct negotiations between doctors and autonomous sick funds. As in all public-sector bargaining by doctors, the profession often thinks that the government is "taking advantage" of a monopolistic situation and that government fails to understand the "special problems" of medicine. The British medical profession has learned that brinkmanship and passion pay off: Governments make con-cessions to avoid strikes and buy peace. Therefore, periods of conflict alter-nate with long periods of peace, when a category of doctors enjoys a favor-able contract, as the general practitioners do now.

STRONG POINTS OF THE BRITISH NEGOTIATING SYSTEM

The Review Body's criteria, its prestige, and the self-restraint of the British medical profession have persuaded the doctors to accept a financial position with limits unique among developed countries. The consultants are among the highest paid groups in Britain, but are not as far ahead of the rest of the elite as they are on the Continent and in North America. The GPs are well off but are not near the top of the British income struc-ture. Doctors might consider this a "problem," since they would prefer even higher pay. Advocates of budgetary discipline over health care costs might consider this a good model.

The negotiators on both sides are always aware that the National Health Service will have to function close to a predicted budget during the coming year. Therefore, both are conscious of the total costs of new conditions of service and of higher pay. The government negotiators, of course, know they are bound by the Departments' budget, but the same awareness of how the system works usually restrains the BMA's demands. (In countries with national health insurance and a tradition of Treasury subsidy of the sick funds, such restraints were once much less evident, but Treasury warnings now produce discipline even there.) The knowledge that doctors' conditions of service and pay awards must fit into an annual budget is one reason why Great Britain delivers good medical care with a lower-than-average expenditure from its gross national product.[21]

SOME PROBLEMS IN THE BRITISH SYSTEM

During its first years, the National Health Service had several mech-anisms for negotiating conditions of service and pay: formal meetings between the BMA and the Ministry; informal conversations among the leaders of the Royal College, the Cabinet, and (sometimes) the BMA. At times the customary machinery has failed to prevent deadlocks and bitter outcries, and it has been replaced, first for the GPs and later for the hospital doctors. The "old boy network" has been less active in settling the consultants' affairs as the Royal Colleges have transferred responsibility to the BMA, and the formal machinery has been revised. During certain periods when the machinery has been revised or conditions of service rewritten, recriminations have been very noisy and strikes have been threatened. Usually that group eventually gets what it wants in negotiating institutions, in terms of service, and in pay, and the situation quiets down.

One of the problems from this habit of noisy controversy is the effect on the public consciousness. Many Britons—and the Americans who read their selective newspaper coverage of British affairs—assume that the entire medical profession is desperate and that "socialized medicine" is about to collapse. However, it is always a particular group at a particular time that experiences that "desperation", such as the GPs in the late 1950s and early 1960s, the junior hospital doctors throughout the 1970s, and the consultants occasionally during the 1970s. The press and public seem not to notice when the revised negotiating machinery has proved efficient and a group is satisfied with its situation, e.g., lately the once indignant GPs.

A problem in negotiating with the government is that, if the standing committee is limited to civil servants, the medical profession at times will try to make "end runs" around them and deal with the Minister. In the "hey-day" of the "old boy network," this was easy, but in the present age of bureaucratic negotiating machinery, the Minister can be drawn in only if it seems the established machinery has failed. This gives the medical profession an incentive to make more than the usual noise and threaten a strike, in Britain as well as in Belgium. If the aim is involvement of the Prime Minister, nothing less than the imminent collapse of the National Health Service must be threatened, also as in Belgium. The tactic always succeeds: The Minister grants more than the civil servants (sometimes much more), and the doctors learn again that "end runs" are always worth trying.

One solution is to integrate the political appointees and the civil servants together more visibly in the negotiating process. This would require expanding the modest staffs of the political appointees and adding them to the DHSS negotiating teams. This could be part of a larger reform, long discussed in British public administration, to expand the authority of the political appointees in the Ministries and to improve the communication in both directions between them and the civil servants. Then all details of the department's negotiating positions would be the full product of both and would be changed only by both together.

1. Even before the official "devolution" of powers from the national government in London to provincial authorities in Scotland, Wales and Northern Ireland, the reorganization of the National Health Service enabled the provinces to adopt different administrative structures. Therefore the following paragraphs about Regional and Area Health Authorities describe England more precisely than the others. Ministerial responsibility for the health service lies in Scotland with the Secretary of State for Scotland and the Scottish Home and Health Department; in Wales with the Secretary of State for Wales and the Welsh Office; and in Northern Ireland the Secretary of State for Northern Ireland and the Northern Ireland Office. The National Health Service functions alike throughout the country, since everything is ultimately decided by the Parliament of the United Kingdom.

2. The medical profession long complained that it was not consulted in the conduct of the National Health Service. Now its problem is too much time in committee meetings. Rudolf Klein, "A Policy for Change," *British Medical Journal,* 7 February 1976, p. 353. This new problem can arise only in a public service, not in the less structured and less participative national health insurance.

3. The foregoing paragraphs are brief and oversimplified. A thorough description is Ruth Levitt, *The Reorganised National Health Service* (London: Croom Helm, 1976).

4. The early history and organization of the BMA appear in Harry Eckstein, *Pressure Group Politics* (London: George Allen & Unwin Ltd., 1960). Current organization is described in the annual *BMA Calendar,* published by the Association. The issues in changing to a trade union status are summarized in the editorial in *BMA New Review* Volume I, Number 13 (May 1976), p. 199. Most British doctors think of the B.M.A. as primarily an energetic negotiator to promote their interests, according to the sample survey summarized in P. R. Jones, "Why Doctors Join the British Medical Association," *Social and Economic Administration,* Volume 7, Number 3 (September 1973), p. 203.

5. The role and power of the Royal Colleges during their earlier years are described in Rosemary Stevens, *Medical Practice in Modern England* (New Haven: Yale University Press, 1966), passim.

6. The Whitley Council machinery is described in H. A. Clegg and T. E. Chester, *Wage Policy and the Health Service* (Oxford: Basil Blackwell, 1957): and Levitt, *The Reorganised National Health Service* (note 3, supra), pp. 160-166.

7. .National Health Service (Remuneration and Conditions of Service) Regulations 1974 No. 296.

8. On relations between the Ministers and their civil servants generally, see Hugh Heclo and Aaron Wildavsky, *The Private Government of Public Money: Community and Policy Inside British Political Administration* (Berkeley: University of California Press, 1974). The experiences of the first Secretary of State for Social Services with his civil servants are recorded in Richard Crossman, *Diaries of a Cabinet Minister* (London: Hamish Hamilton and Jonathan Cape, 1977), Volume 3.

9. Stevens, *Medical Practice in Modern England* (note 5, supra), pp. 76-94; and Arthur J. Willcocks, *The Creation of the National Health Service* (London: Routledge and Kegan Paul, 1967), pp. 69-72 and 106.

10. A complete history of the disputes of 1974-1976 has not yet been published. A good account through the winter of 1976 is "Médecins britanniques en grève," *Schweizerische Ärztezeitung,* Volume 27, Number 14 (7 April 1976), pp. 478-481.

11. *Royal Commission on Doctors' and Dentists' Remuneration 1957-1960: Report* (London: H. M. Stationery Office, Cmnd. 939, 1960), p. 145.

12. On the history of the methods of determining doctors' pay, before and since creation of the Review Body, see Gordon Forsyth, *Doctors and State Medicine* (London: Pitman Medical Publishing Company, 1966), Ch. 3; and Levitt, *The Reorganised National Health Service* (note 3, supra), pp. 103-107 and 110-112.

13. Since modern investigative journalism relishes unveiling traditionally mysterious processes, such as the appointment of The Great and the Good to their high stations, several London newspapers have recently described the selection. See *The Observer,* 2 May 1976, and *The Times,* 4 through 7 October 1976.

14. Royal Commission, *op. cit.* (note 11, supra), p. 145.

15. The current criteria are summarized in Review Body on Doctors' and Dentists' Remuneration, *Fifth Report: 1975* (London: H. M. Stationary Office, Cmnd. 6032, 1975), p. 35.

16. Review Body on Doctors' and Dentists' Remuneration, *Sixth Report: 1976* (London: H. M. Stationery Office, 1976), p. 4.

17. *Ibid.,* p. 7. In preparation for this new argument, the BMA had commissioned a thorough study of doctors' incomes in the nine European Community countries and had submitted it to the Review Body: Denise Deliège-Rott, *Medical Doctors of the Nine Countries of the Common Market: Systems of Payment and Levels of Remuneration* (Brussels: Department of Medical Demography and Health Economics, Ecole de Santé Publique, Université Catholique de Louvain, 1975).

18. Review Body on Doctors' and Dentists' Remuneration, *Twelfth Report* (London: H. M. Stationery Office, Cmnd. 4532, 1970), pp. 5-6.

19. The chairman violated the Review Body's customs of neutrality and discretion in many ways. John Stevenson, "Halsbury: No to Pay," *Pulse,* Volume 29, Number 10 (21 September 1974), page 1. The BMA's reaction appears in *British Medical Journal,* 5 October 1974, pp. 6 and 56; 12 October 1974, pp. 119-120; and 23 November 1974, p. 432.

20. Some of the work of the Dental Rates Study Group is summarized in *Handbook for General Dental Practitioners* (London: Department of Health and Social Security, 1976, Appendix 2).

21. Comparisons of Great Britain and other developed countries appear in Robert Maxwell, *Health Care: The Growing Dilemma* (New York: McKinsey & Company, Second edition, 1975), Ch. 2.

CHAPTER X

National Health Insurance
for the United States

IF THE United States decides to make Medicare more predictable and more financially ordered or if it adopts an organized national health insurance program, it can profit from a variety of devices that work well overseas. It should avoid other methods that work badly. It should certainly avoid the attitude that it has nothing to learn from anyone else's experience. American policy makers do not yet know the answers. They cannot, because they are still hazy about the questions.

AMERICAN EXPERIENCE IN NEGOTIATIONS

When other countries enact national health insurance, usually it is a logical next step in the evolution of a definite structure. However, America has had little recent experience in prospective payment of providers and in the negotiation of such pay. Although collective bargaining in the private economy and now even in public employment is taken for granted, and though the United States has been an innovator in techniques of collective bargaining, this country has been late to realize that advanced societies require a mode and methodology of negotiation in all sectors. The United States has had persistent trouble with its fledgling programs in official health insurance because it has depended either on unilateral government regulation, on "market forces", or on provider discretion rather than on some system of negotiations.[1]

The difference between America and Europe today results from their different histories, although that does not make it inevitable that national health insurance in the United States must be organized altogether differently. For a long time, the United States and Europe seemed to be evolving in the same direction. During the nineteenth and early twentieth centuries, many American trade unions organized local sick funds that bargained with doctors in the United States, as in Europe. Many were wiped out by the Depression. In order to salvage these efforts, some reformers considered including national health insurance in the Social Security legislation during the 1930s. (It was omitted because—among other reasons—adding a novel and controversial section might have led a hostile Supreme Court to declare the entire statute unconstitutional.)

After 1941, the United States unexpectedly developed health insurance for workers different from the European pattern. During the war, employers offered health insurance and health services as fringe benefits, in lieu of the wage increases forbidden by wartime incomes policy. During the late 1940s, unions added such fringe benefits to their bargaining demands, and money for health insurance was included in contracts. In only a few industries was the money deposited in sick funds controlled by the unions. Usually the employer—with more or less advice from the union—turned it over to Blue Cross, Blue Shield, or a commercial carrier, according to a plan. Vigorous bargaining occurred between union and employer and (often, but not always) between employer and carrier. The carrier's negotiations with medical societies and with practicing doctors were the next step but were not defined by the contracts that had been negotiated earlier in the sequence.[2]

FEES AND FEE SCHEDULES

Fee schedules of medical societies

Lists of prices for acts have been issued in several American professions, including medicine. Usually they are published by state or county medical societies. The professional societies describe the lists as "advisory" or "informational," but some customers and governments attack the fee schedules as attempts to fix minimum prices and eliminate competition, in violation of the antitrust laws.[3] It is not fee schedules *per se* that are illegal but the methods of writing and using them. They are not negotiated but are written unilaterally by the professional society. They make no reference to protecting the public by setting maximum fees but, complain the government's prosecutors, are signals to members of the profession concerning minimums.

A few state medical societies have prepared sophisticated relative values scales, based on existing patterns of charges and on expert judgments about the nature of acts. They are prepared entirely by the research departments and committees of the societies and are not negotiated with Blue Shield or with the private carriers. For fear of arousing antitrust suits and public criticism, the California Medical Association stresses that its widely used California Relative Values Studies are merely research reports about differentials among doctors' charges in past years and are not intended to control doctors' fees during the next years.[4] Whether the medical society is writing a fee schedule or a retrospective research report about past charges, the experience in Canadian Medicare and in Dutch private health insurance shows that it cannot retain a free hand very long. Eventually such schedules or relative values scales are included in negotiations or are reviewed by government agencies.[5]

Blue Shield and Medicare

Blue Shield Plans long used fee schedules for a double purpose: if the patient fell below a particular income level, some doctors (not all) accepted the fee schedule in full payment; for other patients, the fee schedule was the carrier's reimbursement to the patient, after the latter paid the doctor. Private insurance carriers have used fee schedules also, but only to define their obligations to the patient. The schedules of payment are not negotiated between Blue Shield or the private carrier and the medical society. Rather, they are written by the Blue Shield Plan's or private carrier's own actuaries and medical advisors. Some Blue Shield Plans have had informal and roundabout consultations with the state or local medical society through interlocking directors: A few doctors active in the society have served on Blue Shield governing boards.

While most countries follow a trend toward prospective payment schedules for providers, such as fee schedules, the United States has steadily abandoned them. Once Blue Shield had many service benefits plans with fee schedules for lower income groups, but these have disappeared as more people have exceeded the income threshold.[6] By the mid-1960s, the National Association of Blue Shield Plans was trying to work out what seems at first sight to be a contradiction, viz., a service benefits scheme without a fee schedule. Doctors would bill Blue Shield according to their usual and their peers' customary fees and would accept such fees as payment in full without additional cost-sharing by the patient. At the same time, Congress wrote the legislation for Medicare. The medical profession had moved so far away from the principle of fee schedules—whether or not negotiated— that it successfully pressed Congress to abjure any obligations to bargain collectively over charges or to use fee schedules. Instead, in statutory language resembling Blue Shield's, the federal government's social security funds are obligated to pay "reasonable cost" or "customary charges." [7]

Neither Blue Shield nor the Social Security Administration (recently succeeded by the Health Care Financing Administration or HCFA) developed systematic methods of negotiating the meaning of these ambiguous standards with the doctors. Each state or local Blue Shield Plan has been free to adopt such a payment-in-full option; those who did were free to work out their own definitions of the "usual, customary, and reasonable" criteria. The staff of the National Association of Blue Shield Plans in Chicago originated the payment method and developed statistical formulas, and most members have followed its guidelines.[8]

At some stage, each Blue Shield Plan discusses the administration of the reasonable-charge payment-in-full option with the state medical society, since the Plan must gain the cooperation of enough doctors, in order to market it. The doctors press the Plan's staff to make the program more profitable, but the staff must balance the probable costs against the income it can expect from premiums. The discussions vary among states in style and outcome; they are not as formal as the negotiations described throughout this book. Several antitrust suits filed against Blue Shield and against state medical associations allege that these discussions are collusive.

In a similar fashion the Social Security Administration (now HCFA) did not create any negotiating system under Medicare. The program has been supervised but never administered by the national government. Rather, a Blue Shield Plan or a private insurance company in each state processes bills and pays doctors, under contract from the Social Security Administration. The private firm has been a "fiscal intermediary" administering the government's rules and paying out its money, not an "underwriter" with discretion and risk. From the start of Medicare until 1972, each carrier interpreted the "customary, prevailing and reasonable charge" wording in the statute in its own way, helped (or confused) by regulations, memoranda, and phone calls from the Bureau of Health Insurance of SSA. After 1972, Congress expanded the Bureau's authority to define "customary, prevailing and reasonable charges" and require implementation by the fiscal intermediaries. Neither the Bureau nor the carriers have negotiated or consulted with the medical profession by any regular procedures. Rather, payment decisions have been made from a legal standpoint unilaterally by the United States Government according to a law. Actually, payment decisions usually are made by computers, programmed ingeniously according to the national government's regulations and supplied with data on past billings by each doctor and by his peers. Although neither the Social Security Administration (now HCFA) nor the fiscal intermediaries have faced the doctors across the negotiating table, they have faced (or heard) them everywhere else, in an intermittent barrage of complaints and public protests, testimony and "end runs" to Congress, "end runs" to higher-ups in the Department of Health, Education, and Welfare, and lawsuits against enforcement of regulations.[9]

The United States Government, as the biggest purchaser of health services on the nation's market, might have set a pattern in the determination of fees through bargaining. But the health insurance programs for civil servants and for military dependents resemble the plans arising out of private employment. Both use the Blues or commercial carriers as underwriters. Neither provides government bargaining with the medical profession nor prescribes how the carriers shall determine fees. The carriers follow their usual practices.[10]

Workmen's compensation

One of the few extensive uses of prospective payment for medical care in the United States is in workmen's compensation. In 1972, eighteen states used fee schedules. (The others used some form of retrospective reasonable-charge methodology.) In theory, the fee schedule is written and issued by officials of the state agency, but they rely upon the drafts proposed by advisory committees drawn from the state medical association, insurance carriers, the state agency itself, and (often) other consultants.[11]

The discussions have some features of negotiation between the medical association and other groups, but they differ in other respects. The medical association lacks the numerical parity that it possesses in the negotiating bodies under national health insurance abroad. The fee schedule follows the customs in the rest of medical practice and is not an original piece of work. Not so much is at stake, since only a few doctors take workmen's compensation cases, chiefly in surgery and orthopedics. Therefore, the medical association is not as extensively involved as it would be under national health insurance.

Antitrust policies in medicine

In the present unsettled situation, different government agencies try to enforce their own and somewhat contradictory images of medical practice. In the absence of statutory collective bargaining, the Federal Trade Commission has recently filed suits and conducted investigations to enforce the only organization it finds sanctioned in the law: doctors, patients, and carriers would compete and bargain individually in a "marketplace," and the price of each act should be a temporary figure according to that moment's equilibrium of supply and demand.[12] As an alternative to the current provider-dominated regulation, some persons favor much less organized control and much more competitive behavior by all parties in medical care.[13]

SALARIES OF HOSPITAL DOCTORS

The one sector of medical practice with an increasing amount of bargaining has been the one with a grievance. As in other countries, America's junior hospital doctors complain about very long hours of work, additional hours on call, and insufficient pay. They grumble about exploitation by the senior doctors, who work shorter hours, transfer their duties to the house staffs, and earn high incomes. In several American cities, junior doctors have organized trade unions and have negotiated with individual hospitals or with associations of hospitals for shorter hours and for higher pay. Sometimes with the help of experienced labor organizers, they have learned how to mobilize their membership, how to bargain with their employers, and (in New York City in 1975) how to strike.[14] Probably militant unionism by junior doctors will become a permanent feature of medicine in America, as in Germany, Sweden, and Britain. However, the union movement must thread its way through legal obstacles: for many years, hospitals were exempt from coverage under the National Labor Relations Act; they are no longer exempt but need not bargain with junior doctors under federal law, according to a ruling of the National Labor Relations Board in March 1976, classifying the junior doctors as students and not as employees.

Several medical trade unions have been organized with wider memberships to fight for established doctors on other fronts, such as getting higher fees from workmen's compensation boards, higher fees from state Medicaid programs, and higher salaries from state governments. They are rivals of the AMA and state medical societies at present but hope for a division of labor in the future, whereby the unions represent the medical professions on economic issues while the professional associations concentrate on scientific and clinical matters. The unions have small memberships and an ambiguous mission: Collective bargaining cannot develop in medicine until the identity of the bargaining adversaries becomes clear. At present, they act as mobilizers and as political lobbies, with few opportunities to bargain, although some are more successful than others.[15]

Sensing the importance of the movement on behalf of interns and residents, the AMA House of Delegates in 1977 endorsed their rights to bargain. Eventually the Association itself may create a special department to represent them in negotiations with hospitals and governments. If the AMA can organize itself accordingly—as British and Swedish experiences suggest—it would become transformed by a forceful new element in its internal affairs. The AMA would increase its membership and power, by preempting the field of the doctors' unions. The AMA will probably be more successful than the doctors' unions in obtaining bargaining rights for the interns and residents under the National Labor Relations Act. Or, it may develop relationships with employers in health that do not require recognition under the Act.

RETROSPECTIVE V. PROSPECTIVE PAYMENT METHODS

Is the American situation good enough now? Why have an organized negotiation system at all? If payment rates are fixed in advance, are the results the same or any better than if consumers or carriers pay according to the providers' own judgments or according to some definition of "reasonable costs"?

Savings in money

One possible criterion is waste. At present, every country tries to gain control over rising costs of medical care. Can any foreign national health insurance systems offer evidence whether prospective payment methods are more or less costly than retrospective methods? Can any suggest economical ways of administering retrospective methods? This is not possible, because no country uses retrospective methods of paying providers under national health insurance. Rates are bargained or set in advance, even when it is one government agency paying for medical services supplied by another. My European and Canadian informants took it for granted that, unless rates are set in advance, prices rise unexpectedly and suspiciously, and arguments result. They found it hard to believe that Amercians were writing national health insurance bills without definite procedures for negotiating or fixing rates in advance but were hoping that a commitment to reimburse all costs will somehow not be abused.[16]

The closest one can get to a controlled test of possible savings from prospective payment systems are comparisons of American programs. Despite the weak administration of prospective payment systems in the United States, state Medicaid programs spent less money if they used fee schedules than if they used some form of reasonable-charge methodology.[17] The research uses a statistical comparison among states and could not explain the differences. (Several experiments in prospective reimbursement among American hospitals show no results or weak results, but they are inconclusive because of faulty design and ineffective administration.)[18]

When one compares entire countries, doctors' fees as a general rule may have gone up faster in the United States than abroad *relative to the consumer price index in each country,* except during periods of a total wage freeze, because America lacks a prospective payment system and negotiations. Table 1 shows the ratios between physicians' fees and the general indexes of consumer prices in France, West Germany and the United States during the 1960s and 1970s.[19] America nearly froze fees under its Economic Stabilization Program from 1972 to 1974; its fees resumed their rapid upward movement thereafter.

In contrast to American experiences under Medicare and private practice, the fees actually charged under national health insurance abroad usually rise at about the same rate as the consumer price index. As I said in previous chapters, this is often intentional: The price index is a floor, and fees are linked to it, although some countries are exceptions. During periods of inflation, fees abroad lag behind general prices for short periods, although doctors' incomes often (not always) keep pace through rising utilization. At times, the negotiators intentionally raise fees faster than the price index, as in the French efforts to raise the position of general practitioners.

Table 1

Ratio of annual rise in physicians' fees and
annual rise in general consumer price index

	France		West Germany	United States
	General Practitioners (Value of C)	Specialists (Value of K)		
1966	0.3	1.3	0.0	2.0
1967	2.1	1.3	0.0	2.4
1968	2.2	0.7	1.5	1.3
1969	2.2	1.0	1.0	1.3
1970	0.8	0.8	2.1	1.3
1971	1.5	0.8	1.3	1.6
1972	2.5	0.3	1.1	0.9
1973	1.0	0.7	0.5	0.5
1974	0.5	0.4	1.1	0.8
1975	2.0	0.8	0.6	1.4
1976	1.2	0.9	0.5	1.9

If a number exceeds 1, the fees rose at a faster rate than the CPI. If it is less than 1, the fees rose more slowly. German data are based on movements of fees of the *Ortskrankenkassen* in North Rhine-Westphalia. Annual shifts in fees vary among *länder* and among sick funds, but all maintain the same pace in the long run.

Parenthetically, comparisons between the United States and other countries by figures like those in Table 1 should be treated cautiously. I suspect that all underestimate American health prices and health spending. Doctors' fees are reported on standard and official forms in Europe and Canada; charging extra is usually illegal; where extra charges are permitted, they are regulated, and a very large proportion of each country's bills pass through a single accounting and payment system. Such standardized processing and central reporting do not exist in the United States. Estimates of American doctors' fees are one of many items in the regular sample surveys that yield the consumer price index. Therefore, reporting of doctors' fees is subject to more omissions, greater errors, and more deliberate understatement in the United States than in Europe and Canada. Therefore in Table 1, I suspect that the United States exceeds France and Germany even more often and more widely.

Savings from conflict

An important reason for a prospective payment system, such as a fee schedule, is that everyone knows the price in advance. Almost every economic transaction in the world occurs only after the provider has exhibited his price list or has negotiated a unique price with the customer. American medicine is one of the few situations where the customer rarely knows or understands his obligations in advance.

When the individual pays his doctor personally in the United States, he is sometimes surprised by the number of separate items or by the size of certain charges. (Where the services have been simple and when doctor and patient are old friends, of course, such problems are fewer.) The "usual, customary and reasonable" charge (UCR) payment method of Blue Shield and the reasonable-charge methodology of American Medicare are supposed to be predictable without imposing standard fees. Charges are supposed to be calculated from percentiles of the average fees charged all patients in one or more previous years; the individual doctor is not required to conform to an average, but he (or his patient) is reimbursed at a rate within bounds fixed by his own customary pattern of bills and by the entire set of bills rendered by his colleagues. Each doctor has a unique charging pattern. Some can charge customarily much more than their colleagues; the system of profiles is supposed to restrain only sudden increases of fees by individuals. The method requires a complete data base for calculating community averages for each act and the individual doctor's profile of customary charges. All these calculations are made by the carrier's computer, and the machine's decision whether to pay the doctor's bill in whole or in part is supposed to be final.

In practice, the system is full of contention, with the details and degree of conflict varying among the many Blue Shield and Medicare state plans with such arrangements. Physicians often ask for their profiles (i.e., the computer printout showing their average charge for several acts during the recent past), and often apply for amendments. Many individual bills are submitted in excess of the doctor's own profile and of the community average; the Blue Shield Plan may deem it prudent to pay in full, or (often but not always) the Plan and doctor haggle over the amount of payment. Because of widespread dissatisfaction with these arrangements under Medicare, most American doctors refuse to participate; they bill the patients directly and at rates of their own choice—i.e., they refuse to "accept assignment."

The invitation to conflict under present American procedures was illustrated by recent experiences of the Aetna Life and Casualty Company. Aetna reimburses the patient but does not pay the doctor directly. It does not use a fee schedule but calculates each doctor's customary charges and the community averages from bills, as in Blue Shield's UCR. Aetna tried to restrain fees without the clarity of a fee schedule, without any direct relationship with the doctor, and without any procedures agreed with local medical societies. It did not tell patients to refuse to pay higher fees to doctors but conveyed the implication: Aetna would reimburse the patient at the doctor's customary level; if the patient refused to pay the doctor more and was sued, Aetna would pay his legal expenses. The result was much conflict and inconsistent local court decisions, some in favor of the doctors.[20]

An argument for a prospective payment system is that all such uncertainties are eliminated. Prices are known in advance. If certain doctors can extra-bill over the fee schedule, as in France, their identities are known in advance. An argument for organized negotiations is that the haggling occurs among the specialists in economic decisions and does not involve the individual doctor and the ordinary patient.

Much uncertainty and dispute over payment in the United States is due to the diversity among carriers. The patients during an average day's practice have several different insurance carriers and—even when the carriers are the same—their contracts provide different benefits. At the time of treatment and initial billing, few patients and doctors understand exactly what benefits are covered and how much will be paid by the carrier and by the patient. The good or bad news comes to the patient and doctor later, when the carrier's computer looks up the patient's contract and writes the check. Since each case is billed individually and since each bill requires several forms and mailings, many bills are lost or filled out erroneously. The many disputes aggravate the administrative problems.

Prospective payment under national health insurance standardizes the situation. Unless a substantial number of citizens remains uncovered—a steadily disappearing situation among developed countries and found today only in Holland—nearly every medical bill in the country is processed and paid according to the same procedure. Except when sick funds have slightly different fees schedules—true only in Germany today—all payments

and rules are the same for all patients and doctors. Besides avoiding uncertainty and disputes, the doctor saves paper work: He can submit his
bills to the sick funds in batches.

HOW TO ORGANIZE NATIONAL HEALTH INSURANCE

National health insurance is a method of organizing a country's spending for doctors, hospitals, and other providers. Extensive organization has
accompanied its introduction in every other country. In the few cases
where legislation was enacted with little structure, such as nineteenth-
century Germany and modern Belgium, the financial waste and disorder
led subsequently to more stable organization. Many Americans are
tempted to enact expanded health insurance legislation and pray that
"market forces" or "incentives" will bring about better services at moderate costs. But such proposals are merely new examples of the loose spending efforts that have been the bane of American government during the
last decade. They often become perverted.[21] Other countries do not
assume that social programs will be accomplished by merely offering providers and consumers money upon vague conditions.

The completely self-regulating market with many individual buyers
and many individual sellers is a Utopia that has never existed in any
economic sector. "Real life" markets are struggles for advantage; elements
on each side employ restrictions and collaboration; participants on each
side vary in knowledge and in management and bargaining skills. Present
(or absent) to varying degrees in all other markets, competitive and "ra-
tional" situations are particularly unlikely in the transactions between
health care providers and patients. The problem in health delivery in
general and in national health insurance in particular is how to organize
the struggling forces, in order to provide good care at the right times and
places, make the services cost-effective, and prevent domination by one
group. One problem is how to redress inequalities in power between providers and consumers. Instead of relying on the unlikely ability of individual consumers to drive hard bargains with competing providers, a
more realistic solution is to organize consumers into a countervailing force.

Doctors and patients

Organization means neither total standardization nor socialistic tyr-
anny. A national health insurance system can pay whatever practice
arrangement doctors and patients like. It can pay several different ones
at the same time. For example, the sick funds in Sweden pay fees to office

practitioners, to private medical groups that pay variable salaries to the doctors, and to county councils that pay fixed salaries to district medical officers. Britain's National Health Service pays capitation fees to both office doctors and to GPs located in health centers. Patients in all Western countries can choose their doctors and their preferred types of practice.

National health insurance standardizes certain features of doctors' work—often to their advantage—but considerable diversity and competition can remain. Doctors continue to differ in clinical skill and in relations with patients; they continue to differ and compete in attracting patients and the respect of their peers. Some are more successful in winning professional honors and in gaining leadership posts. As the examples of France and Britain show, professional recognition can lead to official designation for higher fees, higher patient cost-sharing, or higher salaries.

Medical associations

No matter how negotiations are set up between the medical profession and the public authorities, the participants need certain organizational capabilities. Medical societies continue to exist, but in a new and more powerful form. They need an apparatus to make decisions: representative assemblies and governing councils set goals for terms of service and pay of individual doctors, and they approve agreements. The societies need economic and clinical research departments to produce information and develop position papers. The societies train their officials and several leading members in methods of persuading meetings of doctors and in methods of negotiating with adversaries. National and state medical societies need to cooperate closely.

To create policies and implement decisions, the medical associations must develop effective self-government to resolve priorities among groups. In order to write fee schedules, the different specialties must agree on a single document and (possibly) on the assignment of acts. The GPs and specialists must decide whether to maintain or narrow their income differences and whether GPs can perform advanced acts normally done by specialists. The association may decide to reduce differences among specialists.

One might think such "political" activities quite foreign to a professional association. But the American Medical Association—like any professional society—has been doing all this for some time. It will merely need to strengthen its existing internal apparatus for polling the membership, making decisions, balancing priorities, relating regional and national viewpoints, and negotiating with outsiders. The difference will not be so much in the structure of the medical association as in the objects that are negotiated.

Health insurance funds

As foreign experience shows, the carriers can be organized in several ways: one government agency for the entire program; one private or semi-official carrier; many private (usually nonprofit) sick funds. If many carriers operate under American national health insurance, they can compete for subscribers, as German, Belgian, and Swiss programs show. The sick funds with greater administrative efficiency or with younger memberships can offer slightly lower premiums. Or, they can use the same amount of money to offer extra benefits, such as dentistry, checkups, physiotherapy, convalescent care, and programs in health education. The more efficient funds can offer better administrative service to their members. Carriers can compete in ideology and in image.

If there are several (rather than one) health insurance carriers, they will need to combine into associations to deal with common problems and (if government does not do the negotiating) to bargain with the medical association. They will need to develop negotiators to face medical associations.

American carriers are presently ahead of the medical associations in developing such personnel: they have more researchers to develop plans, indemnity schedules, and a case for higher premiums; they have more negotiators who argue before state insurance departments. But this is political lobbying of a technical sort; bargaining with the doctors is another matter, requiring different skills.

Rate regulation does not disappear under national health insurance; the sick funds bargain on two fronts, no longer only on one. Rate regulation of carriers will change somewhat in the United States, since the state or national[22] government no longer will try to perform the entire task of controlling the carriers' costs through negative comments concerning their applications for higher premiums.[23] The complete record of the negotiations between carriers and doctors will be evidence in applications to the rate regulators, who can then judge whether doctors' practice costs really have risen greatly, whether the carriers have diligently controlled utilization and bargained effectively with the doctors, and so on.

Under national health insurance the carriers—and particularly Blue Shield and Blue Cross—would clearly become watchdogs over the money and would develop a more consistently adversarial orientation than has been their custom. At present, the government and orientation of American nonprofit carriers are in transition. Blue Shield and Blue Cross were created by medical associations and by the hospital industry, as mechanisms to help patients prepay their bills. They have been liaisons between the providers and the public ever since. Like other provider-initiated private sick funds abroad, the Blues have long had doctors, hospital directors, hospital trustees, and other persons involved in health on their governing boards. Antitrust suits have been filed by American national and state governments, complaining that such boards are favorable to providers, grant high fees, and raise health care costs.[24] Blue Shield and Blue Cross Plans gradually have been changing their boards and will become even more consumer-minded in the future.

At present, a state Blue Shield Plan has a complicated task as intermediary and educator. It must persuade the state's medical profession to accept some form of paid-in-full scheme, using either a relative values scale or a reasonable-charge (UCR) system. Persuading the leaders of the state medical association often is easy; both the Plan and the association then must persuade the membership. Bargaining and explaining continue for years over the original terms and over changes. Blue Shield must balance the demands of the profession against the probable premium structure that results. If the Plan concedes too much to the doctors, its premiums will price it out of the competitive health insurance market; or, the state insurance commission will not allow increases in premiums for current subscribers or for employee-paid contracts, and the Plan will go bankrupt.[25] This complex juggling will disappear among the more standardized forms of national health insurance; limited versions remain under the more flexible systems, such as Germany's. But the American carriers will become less of an intermediary trying to persuade doctors to cooperate and more of an adversary, bargaining to make a mandated system cost-effective.

National health insurance in America will doubtless accelerate the present trend for mergers between Blue Shield and Blue Cross. This division in health insurance between hospital costs and doctors' fees arose from historical accident, and no other country has anything like it. National health insurance requires a unified strategy in finance, combining both hospital affairs and ambulatory care, and only unified sick funds can carry out this point of view.

For-profit insurance companies usually are banned from national health insurance abroad, either because of ideological preference for nonprofit administration or because much of the money comes from Treasury grants. Even if permitted to act as carriers in American national health insurance, they might become too squeezed financially: the law will mandate a minimum list of benefits; carriers must pay doctors and other providers at the same rates as the nonprofits; their premiums cannot exceed those of the nonprofits by much; and, by law or by competitive pressure, they cannot pass higher cost-sharing to the patient. Even at present, health insurance is a "loss leader" for several companies, enabling them to attract subscribers into more profitable lines. If they cannot be "fiscal intermediaries"—i.e., pure financial administrators, with the government paying for all cost over-runs—the private carriers might decide that underwriting national health insurance is too risky. As in other countries, their role might be reduced to insuring for extra benefits.

A regular negotiating situation

The negotiators on each side will go through annual cycles of preparing and then meeting each other. The same people will confer regularly, instead of occasional confrontations of strangers. As in American industrial relations, they will have to become friendly adversaries, fighting for their constituents, but also making the negotiating process more productive through deeper mutual understanding and respect. The most successful negotiating systems abroad—Holland, Sweden, West Germany, and Switzerland—depend on strong bonds across the table. But even if relations are often passionate—i.e., if the United States resembles Belgium more closely than Holland—much business can still be transacted and order can be restored, if the adversaries know each other well.

It is not only the leading negotiators who become an important bridge. The staffs of the opposite sides, such as the statisticians, must learn to respect each other and work out common solutions.

Attitude toward government

National health insurance will work more successfully in the United States if the country follows the rest of the democratic world and abandons the antiquated mental dichotomy between an evil "government" and a virtuous "private" sector. If one actually looks at social services in other developed countries, it is not clear what is governmental and what is private. All are activities in a merged public sector: some persons seem to be employed by organizations belonging to something called a "government"; others are affiliated with organizations that are not part of "government"; a rapidly increasing number work for semiautonomous and semiofficial organizations that do not fit the customary classifications. The people on the government payroll do not give orders to the others, but the health and social services function by interaction and negotiation. It is not merely the medical profession and the sick funds that negotiate pursuant to laws and regulations, but the laws themselves are the products of prolonged negotiations. Health insurance and other social programs are governed by a mixture of governmental and nongovernmental rules and are supported by mixed money.

The problem is not to fight and ridicule government but to manage it effectively. Perception of one's own government as "we" or as an enemy is one of the fundamental differences between the United States and several other developed countries, rooted in quite different economic histories.[26] A willingness to use "our" government pragmatically is one reason why social programs operate more harmoniously and with less venality elsewhere. Hostility toward government does not limit it or keep it "on its toes" efficiently, as Belgian and American experiences show. Rather it sows confusion and even more bureaucracy: regulations are accompanied by confusing conditions and exceptions; a decision is fought and its implementation is altered by complaints and lawsuits; officials work under siege; since old programs work badly, new programs are added, often without adequately fitting them together.

Cost controls

Greater financial discipline will be needed under national health insurance than at present, both among the sick funds and doctors. Neither can continue to count on passing cost over-runs easily onto the national Treasury or onto the patient. If the patient is expected to share costs by paying some money to the doctor, the amount should be fixed. Every foreign country recognizes this, some earlier than others.

Financial discipline will be necessary in the United States, even if national health insurance is not enacted. An argument for national health insurance in the United States is that so much of American medical care will be financed through a single set of accounts and will be described according to standard reporting that effective control of costs could not continue to be postponed.

Information

Accurate data will be needed about utilization and costs. The information will be needed in forms comprehensible to the negotiators and relevant to their decisions. Information will be needed that will enable legislators and administrators to monitor the system's operations. A data system will be needed that incorporates all bills, written and coded according to a common format.

At present the United States leads the world in computing power in claims processing, but different carriers do not cooperate in coding and merging data, and the same carrier may not merge bills from its several plans. A problem in Medicare is the reluctance of the fiscal intermediary to allow comparisons with the bills from its normal business.

STRUCTURE OF HEALTH INSURANCE

The United States has an unusual federal system. Programs enacted by the national Congress can be either national or federal—i.e., executed either through the national bureaucracy or through state governments. In other federal systems in the world at present, constitutional law or governmental practice assigns a subject either to the national or provincial governments. If certain conditions for a program are controlled by the national government (such as revenues) while others are controlled by the provinces (such as jurisdiction over health), a common practice abroad is a joint national-provincial program. A federal program in the United States can be highly standardized among all states, or the state governments can be allowed wide discretion and autonomy, or the state governments can be allowed not even to participate. Therefore, any of the systems described in this book can become a model for American national health insurance, although each would have certain problems in the American setting. But whatever structure is adopted should be coherent.

Decentralized

One possible arrangement can emulate Canada, with some features from Switzerland. The national government would provide fixed subsidies to state programs that offer minimum benefits. National laws set basic rules, including some limits on the patient's cost-sharing. This ensures financial discipline within each state: the state legislature and administrators cannot allow the sick funds to run excessive deficits and then pass the buck to the national or state Treasuries.

Under this arrangement, the state legislature can decide how to organize its health insurance program and how much money should be spent. No two states need be alike, and they would vary on: type of carrier (whether a governmental sick fund, a single private one, several private ones, nonprofit or for-profit carriers); whether a cash benefits or service benefits arrangement; structure and content of the fee schedule; amount of cost-sharing by patients within limits; encouragement of special forms of practice (such as HMOs or organizations with salaried doctors). A state could decide not even to have an official health insurance program, and it could retain the present situation, but its citizens probably will press for inclusion, as they have in all Canadian provinces.

There would have to be organized negotiations over terms of service and pay between the state medical society and (on the other side of the table) either the state government, a single state-wide sick fund, or a state association of sick funds. The current regulatory arrangement would have to change or disappear; state insurance departments set forth rules and approve increases in premiums at present but do not participate in decisions about benefits and their rates.

A decentralized federal system would be complicated to administer:

Switzerland's twenty-five programs may be too many, and a decentralized America would have fifty. The medical society would have more bargaining power in a decentralized than in a centralized system, because doctors are more respected and politically resourceful on the local level than insurance carriers, and because the state medical societies can compare notes through the national AMA. Several states might lack enough administrators to manage or oversee health insurance, in addition to their other customary health functions.

Perhaps the number of units can be reduced below fifty by merging several states into regional planning and bargaining units in national health insurance. That would be a novelty in the administration of American federalism and American health services, but it should be explored in an attempt to make federalism a more usable structural principle in American government.[27] Such agencies would be created and staffed by the states and not merely be yet another health jurisdiction created by laws of the national government. Several other regional programs should be administered by the same interstate agency, such as health planning. National health insurance is a method of paying for service, and must be integrated with the development of these other services. Self-evident in any other country, the creation of consistent jurisdictions among related programs would be a novelty in American health.

A scenario of decentralization will satisfy the peculiar American belief that this highly standardized society is really diverse and full of unique local needs.[28] Also it will permit differentials in pay and costs. In a centralized national system, the doctors in the lower paid areas will demand equality with the New Yorkers and make the system far more expensive. In any decentralized program, an important policy problem is the allowable range among states or regions. At present, the differences in fees are wider than would be predicted by costs or by the skills of the doctors.[29] Such differentials exist in every country on the eve of national health insurance and diminish thereafter, but America's range may be wider than others. Should the American differentials be reduced under national health insurance by forcing the expensive states to freeze fees for a while, forcing the states with lower fees to bring them up, and by using national subsidies to increase spending in the less affluent states? Disparity formulas can be included in national grants-in-aid but, as the Canadian experience shows, working them out involves complicated political log-rolling among the provinces. The medical societies would probably prefer a free hand: If they can raise the fees in the best paid states, they can keep raising them in the other states, in the familiar tactic of eternal catch-up.

If stagflation is the normal condition in the coming years, the United States—like other countries—will need to formulate and administer policies on incomes and on prices in the public sector. A decentralized method of negotiating the pay of doctors under national health insurance will be very difficult to integrate into an incomes policy. Also, coordination will be difficult with any national policy on the prices and spending of providers in the health services.

Centralized

The opposite arrangement would copy France and Holland. The states would play no administrative or decision making role, but they might be geographical boundaries in setting up administrative units of the national structure. The laws of Congress would spell out everything.

The carriers throughout the country would be united in one national association or in several national associations. Each would have a powerful headquarters, including negotiating departments. A network of consultations and of meetings would ensure a flow of information and advice between the local funds and headquarters. This is not as novel as it sounds: in the form of the national offices of Blue Cross and Blue Shield, the United States has more national organization among nonprofit carriers than did other countries on the eve of national health insurance; the private insurance companies are national in structure.

The American Medical Association would have to be organized as a decision making body that learns the needs and opinions of all its members throughout the country, develops positions, and sends a negotiating staff to confront the national association(s) of carriers. The national headquarters would have to become more powerful than it is at present; like medical associations in other federal countries, the AMA now is a federation of autonomous state societies. The negotiating department would include experts on the writing and revision of fee schedules, as well as experts on the economics of practice.

The negotiators would agree on terms of service and sign a national contract. They would also write a single national fee schedule, perhaps in the form of a relative values scale. Prices of the unit values or of the "key-letters" might vary among parts of the country according to practice costs or according to some public policy, such as giving doctors an incentive to go to underdoctored areas. The trend in America—if it follows the pattern of other developed countries—will be eliminating regional differentials in fees, on the grounds that practice costs become more alike and that tiny differences in fees are ineffective incentives in achieving a public policy.

The fee schedule and fees should be written by bilateral negotiating sessions or in standing committees that include (but are not necessarily confined to) the medical association and sick funds. They should not be written by independent regulatory commissions after testimony by the doctors and sick funds, in view of the lack of independence and disappointing history of such national regulatory mechanisms in the United States.[30]

Regulation of health insurance carriers could no longer be left to the states but would have to be assumed by the national government, so results would be uniform. Management or oversight would be handled by regional or local units of the Department of Health, Education, and Welfare. One set of units that already exists is the Health Systems Agencies (the HSAs) created under the National Health Planning and Resources Development Act of 1974. If the HSAs become effective planners and managers, they would be appropriate for supervision of national health insurance. But so far, their activities are barely understood by Washington, and their future functions and effectiveness are unknown.[31] Obviously, a unitary program should not be enacted if the national government can never learn how it is executed in the field, and if the administrative subdivisions are so numerous and so uninformative that the program is carried out in excessively and eccentrically diverse ways.

Mixed

Why should the United States organize a national program in a federal manner, when it has the option of enacting everything through Washington? Federal-provincial collaborations are tense and unstable in most federal countries,[32] and several of my weary Canadian informants thought the United States lucky, if its health insurance system could be organized under a single national agency.

However, substantial participation by the American states or by regional groupings of states may be politically inevitable and administratively desirable. Excessive government control is one of the more frightening spectres in the rhetoric about American health policy, and probably only a decentralized program will be enacted by Congress. The nation has been rebelling against Washington and the Eastern seaboard, and a federal arrangement will give all parts of the country a sense of participation.

Unlike other federal countries, where the Constitution or political balances require that all programs follow a standard format, the United States is free to decide pragmatically how best to organize each program. Such an administrative judgment about the merits of centralized or state organization rarely enters legislative decisions, but it should, in the case of national health insurance. Because the Social Security Administration and the Health Care Financing Administration have had so much trouble with Medicare, delegating the management to the states or to specially created state-level agencies would bring in more talent and eliminate many headaches. National health insurance in the United States could be one of a set of social programs jointly designed and managed by the national government and states, in place of the past custom of haphazard design by Congress and the ambiguous division of administrative responsibilities between Washington and the states.[33]

A good solution for the United States might resemble West Germany's. Laws of Congress would set forth the general frame of national health insurance and mandate minimum benefits everywhere. Nationwide bargaining over terms of service and over the fee schedule would take place between the AMA and the national association(s) of carriers. A standing committee of the AMA and carriers would keep the fee schedule up to date.

Financing of health insurance would take place at the level of states or of regions combining groups of states. The state or regional sick funds would collect the premiums from the national Treasury or directly from the subscribers and employers, with the rates defined by national law. State governments might supplement this money. Differentials among states or regions would be reduced (but not eliminated) by national grants-in-aid. The state medical society and state association(s) of sick funds—or perhaps regional groupings of both—would negotiate each year to set the financial values of the items in the fee schedule. In any state where the carrier has been "nationalized" by the state government or replaced by a state agency, the state government would negotiate with the doctors. State (or regional) negotiators could amend the fee schedule for extraordinary reasons. They could add items, if they wished.

National guidelines about money would be written by the AMA and the national association(s) of sick funds. Such guidelines would be particularly important if the country had an incomes policy, a large budget deficit, and serious over-runs of medical costs. Important decisions in the design of national health insurance are, how binding these guidelines should be and whether the state agreements should be reviewed by a national commission.

The United States in several recent laws has developed a state option, found in no other federal system. A program created by Act of Congress can be administered by a state, if the state meets or exceeds the law's standards; otherwise, the program is administered by the national government. National health insurance might be organized in this way: where state governments are committed, they would administer it; if a state government thought health insurance politically difficult or administratively burdensome, the program within its boundaries would be managed by an agency of the national government. Once a state assumed responsibility, it might be unable to hand it back to Washington. Therefore, the number of state programs would steadily (if slowly) increase. (The state option has been included in only a few statutes so far, and it is still too early to judge whether it will become common or successful.)

Following are many detailed ideas suggested by foreign experiences concerning the structure and conduct of negotiations. Others are mentioned at the conclusion of each chapter earlier in this book.

The following techniques might be adopted either in national, state, or regional bargaining, depending on how national health insurance is organized in the United States.

Health insurance funds

Usually a country tries out the pre-existing private carriers as official fiscal intermediaries before replacing them with governmental sick funds. The three countries with official funds—Canada, France, and Sweden— had practical reasons for abandoning the private carriers: better utilization control, more complete statistics, less party politics, and lower administrative costs due to merger of separate offices. Where the private nonprofit carriers have been able to do this themselves, as in Holland and Switzerland, they have survived. American carriers will probably be retained at first under national health insurance and can survive, provided they can meet the foregoing requirements.

As I have said, providers serve on the boards of the nonprofit American carriers, but their presence is being challenged. Blue Shield and Blue Cross believe they need to include providers on their boards in order to gain their confidence and to persuade them to cooperate with paid-in-full direct-payment schemes. But this is not done abroad: the sick funds need not persuade providers to accept a payment method, since it is mandated by law; the statute may specify the membership of the boards; and the adversarial position of the carriers precludes participation by the providers. Providers may have founded certain carriers abroad but, as the Dutch and Canadian experiences show, eventually they disappear from the management. More homogeneous boards are more decisive.

One European pattern appropriate for the United States is to draw the boards from the two groups that provide the money, viz., employers and subscribers. The European method is to recruit them from employers and from trade unions, and the same method could be used in American national health insurance. Many able persons in such organizations have become interested in health lately. They would provide original viewpoints, vigilance about costs and a tempered enthusiasm about broadening benefits. Employers would have to develop a health policy more sophisticated than their present hybrid of containing costs for the bulk of employees while devising generous benefits for management. Subscriber representatives might be drawn from consumer groups as well as from trade unions, although their occasionally uneasy relations might give the employers effective control.

The European model cannot be emulated exactly because its presuppositions are not duplicated completely in the United States. The European system of representation assumes not only that the peak associations speak for their social constituencies but that the followers belong in large number. But in the United States in recent decades, membership rates have declined in trade unions and in medical associations. Participation in employers associations is uneven. Nevertheless, including representatives of trade unions and employers associations on governing boards of sick funds might be justified as recruitment of the only private spokesmen available for the viewpoints of consumers and taxpayers.

Electing the board might not be wise, in the light of past French experiences.[34] Turnouts would be small in the United States and zealous minorities can win, often making a clean sweep of all the seats. A board consisting of appointees from employers, trade unions, and civic organizations would be a realistic and calming force during controversies.

The governing board of a national association of sick funds can be drawn from the officials of member funds (as in Holland) on the grounds they represent the subscribers as well as anyone. If shut out of this chance to participate, the representatives of the public would seek a voice in some other governing board.

Medical profession

The professional association is more concerned with the viability and success of health insurance—and of medical services generally—than is a narrowly focussed trade union of doctors. A union has little purpose other than gaining money for its members, and the leaders are under pressure to deliver more, regardless of the effects on the sick funds or on the national Treasury. A medical trade union can evolve into a professional association—like FMOQ in Quebec—by taking on an association's noneconomic functions. But this evolution occurs only where no professional association exists. A professional association can be recognized under American labor relations laws as if it were a trade union, but it would have to make some changes in its methods of picking leaders and reporting its affairs.

If the medical profession is led by one rather than several associations, the sick funds lose leverage. They lose the chance to put through some policies with the help of one faction and over the opposition of the other. Rivalry among associations produces competitive demands that can increase costs and produces instability that benefits no one. The task of keeping the associations united is so delicate that leaders with such skills may stay on for many years.

If the AMA is confronted by schisms or by rivals, the sick funds should restrain the temptation to make agreements with the small rivals with supposedly binding effect on the entire medical profession. As the French experience shows, such destabilizing tactics do not pay.

Complete facts on the association(s) should be available, including membership totals. Then groups with narrow constituencies cannot make excessive demands. Several policy questions will have to be settled about the relationship between the medical societies and doctors who are not members. Once most doctors belonged to the AMA and its state medical societies, but gradually the proportion has dipped almost to one-half. But the AMA and its state associations will be the bargaining spokesmen. Since the medical associations will be incurring the costs of negotiations from which all doctors profit, perhaps all non-members will be expected to contribute, such as in the "agency shop" of conventional labor relations. If the right of the AMA and its state associations to speak for all is challenged, they would have to collect "authorization cards" from non-members.

The formulation of demands and the negotiation of agreements is a very "political" process. Democratic machinery must be created within the association, to learn about members' grievances, to develop a coherent list of demands that all specialties will support, and to adopt realistic fall-back positions. New kinds of leaders will rise to the top of the associations, skilled in internal compromise and in external negotiations. Bargaining teams will be flexible in composition; when a specialty's interests are being negotiated and jeopardized, its leaders may need to be involved, so that they can reassure their constituents that the association made a conscientious effort.

Structural changes would occur. At present, the basic unit of representation in the AMA is the state association. But under national health insurance, many decisions are made by consensus among specialties. As if it were anticipating the future, the AMA House of Delegates in 1977 added representatives of the specialty associations to its membership, as a second principle of representation. (The House had previously included a few representatives of "section councils" drawn from AMA members in the principal specialties, but the specialty associations are independent organizations, possessing considerable money and power in their fields).

Standing machinery

An organization that manages the negotiations is a good idea. It can bridge bitter conflict, as in Belgium. It can ensure that bargaining remains calm and efficient, as in Holland. Since negotiation between medical associations and sick funds has no precedent in America, one cannot predict whether it will be passionate or congenial; but in either case, standing machinery can be valuable.

With standing machinery, one never need search for arrangements anew, such as the composition of *ad hoc* committees, since the structure is always in place. A secretariat is available to call meetings, eliminating the need for anyone to take the initiative at delicate moments. The secretariat can manage the paper work and can produce neutral facts.

Neutral chairmen are always available and need not be picked anew. They can mediate and sell agreements to the government. A neutral chairman can be indispensable in moderating conflict, carrying messages, and devising compromises, as the Belgian experience shows. The French system's breakdown in the mid-1970s and the occasional deadlocks in Quebec might have been averted by standing machinery and a neutral chairman. One of the most successful parts of the often tempestuous negotiating structure of Britain is the Dental Rates Study Group, organized as a standing committee with a resourceful neutral chairman. Several American industries have had excellent experience with impartial arbiters and with impartial chairmen of labor-management committees.

Standing machinery with a neutral governing board representing diverse social groups may make it easier to tie the payment of doctors into national policies, such as an incomes policy. The governing board of the commission can review bargained agreements, amend them in the light of national policies, or return them to the negotiators. Otherwise an agreement out of line from national policy would have to be accepted or rejected by the government, precipitating trouble in either case: if it is accepted, the government will have repudiated its policy and invited other groups to break through too; if it is rejected, the doctors will threaten strikes or other sanctions, with the tacit assent of the sick funds.

If special standing machinery is not created for doctors' negotiations under national health insurance, perhaps certain general facilities might be available whenever necessary. For example, the Federal Mediation and Conciliation Service has successfully provided boards of inquiry and mediators when strikes have been threatened by hospital employees.[35] FMCS has heretofore specialized in management-labor disputes, and doctors under national health insurance would be free contractors, but the same procedures could easily apply to new situations. However, as British experience illustrates, usually the medical profession prefers specially designed machinery rather than methods that are standard throughout the economy.

Role of government

If the sick funds are government agencies, officials at the higher policy making levels should negotiate with the medical association. Then the doctors will clearly be negotiating with responsible adversaries capable of making decisions. The sick funds would be defined only as administrative agencies that handle money; policies toward providers and labor relations would be planned and implemented higher up. (Of course, it is not likely that the carriers will be nationalized in the United States, particularly at the early stages of national health insurance.)

The role of government is ambiguous and troublesome in most countries with autonomous or private carriers that carry out national health insurance. The difficulties have intensified as governments recently have tried to control costs and inflation. All such countries need to involve government at earlier stages of the negotiations, instead of the present situation, when government must either endorse agreements and pay the deficits or amend them belatedly.

Therefore the negotiating procedures in the United States and other countries should include early meetings among the sick funds, the medical association and government. They might precede or follow the first sessions where the parties communicate their opening positions, but they should certainly precede serious bargaining. The government would report how much subsidy it will provide during the life of the contract and whether it agrees to any increase in the payroll tax. It would report any plans to revise the health delivery system—such as encouragement of prepaid group practices—that might affect the contract and fees under negotiation. The government's representatives could remind negotiators of something they easily overlook: Taxpayers and subscribers should get their money's worth.

During preparation of a government report setting the parameters for the negotiators, the parts of the government would negotiate among themselves, just as the medical profession and carriers do now within their respective structures before bilateral bargaining. All governments would need to work out positions among the Ministries of Finance, Health, and Social Affairs (or whatever Ministry oversees health insurance). In parliamentary systems with weak coalitions, the leading political parties' representative within the Cabinet would be consulted. In the American Presidential (and gubernatorial) system, the executive branch might send the spokesmen to the meetings with the doctors and sick funds, but its positions should be worked out in consultation with the legislature. (This would reduce the recent flurry of episodes in Washington and in some states whereby the executive makes promises and gives assurances to private parties, and the legislature—not having been consulted—prevents them from being delivered.)

If the government is pursuing an economic policy, it should spell it out very clearly when writing to the negotiators. Applying a government's income policy to negotiations over doctors' pay is often puzzling, since negotiators in fee-for-service deal with price per act (i.e., a "tariff system") and do not fix the total income of each category of doctors. Therefore, the government must make clear whether it is regulating prices or total incomes. Doctors' incomes can rise substantially even if the new fees increase only slightly, as a result of high utilization and a different service mix. If the goal is a limit on incomes, the award in fees can be calculated to bring about a target, as the Canadian experiences show. But this implies that the negotiators will also create effective machinery to control excessive utilization and to discourage the substitution of inappropriate but more profitable treatments. If the doctors won't agree voluntarily, government would have to legislate. Government cannot bring about an effective incomes policy by preaching. In medicine, as in other areas, it must be prepared to regulate or legislate, but this—as in other sectors of the social services—requires resourceful negotiations to produce a result that will work successfully with minimum resistance.[36]

Government representatives should probably not participate in the bilateral negotiations between doctors and sick funds. The role of each party and the nature of each stage in negotiations must be clearly defined. If the government's representatives announce their policies at an early session, the situation is somewhat adversarial, with the doctors and sick funds constituting the other side. The relationship cannot be easily reshuffled, with the government as mute "observer" or as consultants in the hard bargaining between doctors and sick funds. However, the negotiators will frequently explore arrangements that might breach the government's plans or call for new government action. Therefore, the negotiating machinery should include methods of consultation. Someone from the government would be available at all times to interpret guidelines, answer questions, and reactivate decision making within government. The negotiators might send written drafts of any clauses calling for higher subsidies, higher payroll taxes, or new regulations, like the memoranda the Dutch negotiators occasionally send to the full *Ziekenfondsraad*.

On the other hand, the government should be able to request progress reports from the negotiators, in order to guard against the freezing of unacceptable agreements. Negotiators everywhere might well adopt the French practice of interim agreements with clauses that are no longer in contention, so that disputes over a few final items do not cause everything else to unravel.

Negotiators from the health insurance funds and (in the case of public carriers) from the civil service should have full authority and the confidence of the political heads of the government. This requires full communication between the civil servants and the staffs of the political leaders in the agencies. If the politicians seem uninformed or have different views, the providers wil try to make "end runs" around the negotiators for the sick funds and obtain more favorable terms from the political appointees.

If the latter are available too easily during negotiations, the machinery cannot work well and no compromise agreement ever is final.

Whatever the role of government should be, it must act decisively. The European pattern is increasingly full consultation among all groups, preparation of a consensus, and then respect for the decision. (Evasion of laws still occurs, but less often than before.) The United States legislates and regulates quite differently: legislation is often passed by majority vote and regulations are often issued by fiat after preparation in secret; instead of negotiation with all groups to produce a straightforward document with the widest support, American laws in the social services are "Christmas trees" of special concessions and exceptions, to satisfy the individual demands of groups who otherwise would fight passage and sabotage enforcement. The result is legislation and regulations that are very difficult to understand and administer and that invite further amendments, either by the legislature, by administrators, or by judicial interpretation. The hesitation of American administrators and the activism of courts mean that implementation is indecisive. Since challenges to administrators are always worth trying, they are constant. If the United States enacts national health insurance, it should also adopt the practice of most European countries of implementing it in good faith. This requires effective democratic government and an acceptance of the "rules of the game" by private parties.

Arbitration

Arbitration has become common to resolve deadlocks in public-sector bargaining in the United States. But it is still rare in national health insurance abroad. In most countries, expiration of the old contract without a new one results in automatic extension of the conditions of service and fee schedule. Prolonged extension of the old fees works to the benefit of the sick funds, as in the experiences of Quebec and Zurich, but only slightly. Doctors can still earn good incomes through higher utilization or (as in Zurich) by persuading the government to raise fees automatically during the interim in connection with an economic index.

If the doctors cannot abide the extension of the old contract, the deadlock becomes embittered and the doctors eventually manage to involve the Minister and the Prime Minister. Usually this works to the advantage of the doctors. In order to avoid such deadlocks and political resolutions, Great Britain created the Review Body, which has worked well. But it does not arbitrate impasses in bilateral bargaining; it has original jurisdiction over pay and operates like a court. Bilateral bargaining without arbitration and with ministerial intervention survives in negotiation of terms of service in Great Britain. But British experience suggests that a neutral Review Body appointed by the sovereign and standing over the government can be a successful alternative to chronic deadlock, provided that the society can recognize and staff neutral machinery.[37]

Bilateral negotiating systems should include arbitration procedures, if only as a standby. West Germany is a good example: Arbitration bodies are provided in the law and always exist, fully staffed and on call. They are hardly ever used, in large part because they are there: The parties know any deadlock will automatically and quickly go to binding arbitration by persons they cannot control, so they would rather write the settlement themselves. German arbitration tribunals have equal numbers of representatives from each side, the members pick a neutral chairman, and the chairman in practice has the decisive vote. Some American arbitration tribunals follow this tripartite arrangement; the presence of the parties during the deliberations educates the arbitrator and often converts him from arbitrator to mediator, trying to work out a consensus. Other American arrangements designate a single arbitrator, who decides.

If the system provides for automatic continuation of expired contracts and standing arbitration methods, the medical association is less likely to walk out of negotiations and threaten a strike. But even if they do, defiance is not action. Strikes are often threatened in medicine abroad, they attract excited newspaper coverage, and almost never do they result in work stoppages. Since doctors are sensitive to accusations of endangering patients, they usually leave official standbys in hospitals and in ambulatory centers, they "scab" in large numbers, and they quickly go back to work. (Only Saskatchewan in 1962 and Belgium in 1964 have had prolonged and widespread withdrawals of service.) Doctors rarely do more than annoy the sick funds and government by refusing to fill out certain forms and by declining extra duty.

Doubtless, national health insurance in the United States will make headlines occasionally with strike threats by doctors and by other health professionals. That is particularly likely if health insurance follows the American style of labor negotiations: serious bargaining only when the contract nears expiration; desperate all-night bargaining sessions just before the deadline; frequent predictions of doom; and last-minute agreement. So far, the Federal Conciliation and Mediation Service has been unable to teach hospital unions to bargain seriously long in advance. But medical care has been one of the more harmonious industries and has lost few days in strikes.[38]

Review of agreements

At present, negotiating systems in Europe and Canada produce an agreement called "advice" or a tentative draft. It must be approved by a higher authority to become a final agreement. But usually this is a fiction:

The approval is *pro forma*. When the higher authority alters the agreement, as in Belgium and (occasionally) in France, an uproar results; the higher authority is intimidated against an early repetition.

But as the Dutch now realize, the separate bilateral agreements result in an incoherent pattern without priorities; and, since the sick funds and government often try to buy peace, the total may be considerably more expensive than a single agreement with all providers. The British Review Body tries to make its awards more coherent by considering them simultaneously and by using the same formula for all, but its jurisdiction is limited to only a few occupations.

A good idea for the United States is a highly visible negotiating body as a final step. The bilateral negotiators for each provider would not produce a final agreement but would refer their draft to the commission. The latter might be bilateral, with the sick funds on one side and all the relevant providers on the other. The government's guidelines about its willingness to raise subsidies, about its willingness to increase payroll taxes, and about other matters would be presented in their original or amended form. Therefore the negotiators would have to work out a total package within the available money.

The negotiating experience would force providers to think about the total health delivery system and about each other to an extent that America has never experienced. They would have to negotiate among themselves in the light of priorities; until now they have followed the custom of allowing each to make unfettered demands on the government and on the patients. The medical profession would be motivated to make the hospital function more economically, since they would be competing for the same money. (Without such machinery for confrontation, doctors are motivated to make hospitals function more expensively.)

Such a coordinating commission has been attempted only in Germany. Designing it would require care and ingenuity. Medical associations usually resist integration into any larger negotiating team that can decide priorities—the role of the Swedish Medical Association in SACO is unique—and the AMA might be skeptical. The distribution of seats on the side of the providers would be delicate: since hospitals spend so much more money than other providers, should they get half of all seats? Standing machinery and a neutral secretariat would have to be created. If the American health "system" will ever develop any leaders, the neutral chairman of this commission would certainly be one. Complications would arise if the separate bilateral negotiations ended at different times during the year. (To make the system work well, presumably their basic contracts would run for the same terms.)

Once the commission exists, it might be less formidable and less time-consuming than one expects. Its mere presence might restrain excessive demands during the earlier bilateral stages. Since the bilateral negotiators will probably be the delegates on the final tribunal, they will be familiar with the issues and with many details, and they will not lose much time over them. But, of course, negotiations among the providers may be prolonged and difficult.

The awards should be accompanied by thorough explanatory reports. This is particularly necessary if an arbitrator made a decision after the parties deadlocked. But the rationale of any award is valuable for the public, for the government, and for the participants in health affairs. When accompanied by its evidence, an award is liable to be less costly. New and controversial clauses about terms of service would be explained and justified. Britain's Review Body regularly justifies its awards with full reports. But at present, in bilateral bargaining, only the negotiators in Holland prepare such detailed reports; they are designed to justify the agreements to the *Ziekenfondsraad,* and the reports are not published.

TECHNIQUES OF NEGOTIATION

Several good books describe the techniques of negotiation in general.[39] Negotiating situations confront national, state, and local medical societies often enough that the American Medical Association has recently created a Department of Negotiations to prepare handbooks,[40] train negotiators, and give advice. Many books in great detail and with great insight describe productive methods of conducting collective bargaining, arbitration, and mediation in the United States.[41]

I shall not recite all possible details here, but I shall merely list a few points that seem particularly valuable for Americans, in the light of experience abroad.

Civility

The most successful negotiations in foreign health insurance—as in American labor bargaining—depend on polite and considerate relations and on respect for the other side. At present in the United States, there is considerable hostility between government and sick funds on the one hand and doctors on the other.[42] This is far from the German habit of referring to each other as "our social partners," but the Americans (as well as certain other nationalities) must learn the same attitudes.

Facts

In most successful negotiating systems, each side prepares detailed economic analyses of its case. (An exception is Germany, where data are more sparse.) In Holland, the papers are exchanged, as in some American collective bargaining. The documentation leads to a calmer debate. It is a good model to emulate in American health insurance negotiations.

Information about utilization, incomes, and costs of practice—derived from bills and tax records—should be calculated and delivered quickly for use by the negotiators. They can then base new decisions on the outcomes of their last awards. North American computing companies have developed such capabilities, which are used by several Canadian provincial insurance plans in deciding their offers to the doctors. Blue Cross and Blue Shield process bills and compute statistics by these methods now and could arm their negotiators similarly.

As the processing of bills and the calculation of statistics are speeded during the coming years, the sick funds will detect aberrations in the fee schedule or in the last award and will be able to reopen negotiations on these points before the next scheduled round. For example, the overpayment of treatment of varicose veins by injection led to overuse by a small number of doctors in Quebec, but several years passed before the defect was realized and the fee schedule was corrected. Excessive amounts were spent on laboratory tests for several years in many countries, until it was realized that multichannel autoanalyzers had made the old fees unduly profitable. In the future, feedback about such anomalies can be quicker, and they can be corrected sooner.

Payments to doctors are supposed to cover both net income and the costs of practice. A fundamental but still unsettled question is the nature of practice costs: should they be averages of doctors' current expenditures, or what doctors woud like to spend to fulfill their definitions of a well maintained practice, or what experts think should be spent in an average well run practice? Sick funds and medical associations usually disagree on the definition, and the upshot is often (but not always) a negotiated compromise without a clear rationale. The explicit or compromised definition of allowable practice costs varies among countries. The United States will need to adopt a definition of practice costs—unless it is consciously left to power bargaining—and a reliable procedure for getting the facts.

The exchange of long statistical documents by negotiators paves the way for an important bridge in bargaining, viz., a joint committee of technicians to produce an agreed set of facts. Such joint committees are created regularly in Holland and occasionally have succeeded in producing reports in French dental negotiations.

Writing a fee schedule is a technical problem, even though fraught with controversial economic implications. Therefore, even though a country has serious divisions over terms of service and money, it can still write and revise its fee schedule in a joint committee of experts. (Only in the most conflict-ridden countries, such as Belgium, is this committee seriously deadlocked.) The United States would have to create such a committee promptly to write and modernize fee schedules, as Europe does now and as Canadian provinces will do soon. Of course, all experts are not equal, and the sick funds will need to develop a knowledge of the costs, clinical necessity, and effectiveness of treatments to participate in these committees as true equals of the medical associations' representatives.

Reasoning in financial awards

As Americans inch toward a prospective payment system, they hope to make it painless and perfect. Each doctor and hospital would charge according to his or its costs and needs. This reasoning was the basis for the unstructured retrospective payment methods that have created inflationary problems for Medicare and for the Blues: It assumes that because each provider is unique, a public payment program should discover these unique features and pay him (or it) according to a unique and tailor-made schedule. Many states maintain hospitals commissions that review each hospital's budget for the next year and fix its rates. A similar method has been proposed for the United States as a whole, under Medicare and national health insurance.

By adopting fee-for-service, capitation, or salary, foreign national health insurance systems standardize the rates for the profession. Calculations are simplified during foreign negotiations, to make the negotiations comprehensible and to make the administration feasible. For example, although Dutch negotiators make very detailed calculations on most matters, they simplify estimation of the rise in practice costs of specialists. Instead of learning differential trends in costs among specialties—which are probably true but difficult to verify—they assume that all rise at the same rate. The fee schedule itself reflects different patterns of practice and costs among specialties.

Adding financial provisions to take individual conditions and individual merit into account is a Pandora's Box: It requires much administration and generates endless controversy. One example is allowing the most expert French doctors to collect extra payments from the patients. Even the simpe criteria listed in the *convention* are subject to interpretation and may have resulted in more approvals than the negotiators intended.[43] Administering the large number of applications has tied up local committees that were supposed to do more important things. Another example is the "distinction awards," permitting higher salaries for Britain's most respected consultants. The criteria have worked out in favor of the staffs of teaching hospitals in the biggest cities, and many persons now favor selection by different principles. But a more discretionary selection process would be more laborious and more disputatious.[44] Once in place, these individualized supplements acquire vested interests and are difficult to change.

Simple economic measures are commonly used abroad, to determine annual increases in fees. A country's index of consumer prices is a favorite. Often the medical association proposes an index of the costs of medical practice, but the sick funds and government usually resist, on the grounds that its components are not commonly agreed upon, providers can affect its movements, and it is not regularly computed by an independent agency. Much research money is invested by Americans to construct indexes that are "objective" and that will make future awards automatic and beyond controversy. Participants in the struggles over national health insurance abroad are skeptical but are certainly interested in whether the Americans succeed. Meanwhile, they will continue with simple measures—if they use any economic indexes at all in the negotiations—on the assumption that supposedly sophisticated indexes are usually debatable and are often unreliable in their data bases.[45]

Once sick funds in several countries paid hospitals much as they paid doctors: An average rate for each day's inpatient costs was calculated, perhaps refined by differentiating it among four or five services. All patients in all hospitals of a certain size in a particular specialty were covered by the same daily payment by the sick funds, without taking account of the peculiarities of each hospital. Although possessing the merit of administrative simplicity, the *per diem* system had several defects: Hospitals could earn large profits by underservicing or by keeping patients for long periods. Therefore, several Canadian provinces for some time and European countries recently have attempted to individualize payments to hospitals. Regulatory offices review and approve hospital budgets, and each sick fund is billed for its share, according to the proportion of the hospital's workload represented by its subscribers. (As a follow-up to the present book, I hope to examine the hospital payment system in Europe and Canada and derive lessons for the United States.)

Budget systems or tariff systems

If a country's entire health service has a single fixed amount of money (i.e., a "budget system" as the first step in deciding payments to providers), that seems a better way to prevent over-runs in costs than committing the authorities to pay all bills, even if the rates are negotiated and regulated. Some proposals for national health insurance in America foresee such a nationwide budget system—particularly the Health Security Bill, to be described on a later page—but their adoption is unlikely. Each sector would have to divide payments within its share of the total budget.

Germany is the only country that ever had a budget system for the services of doctors under national health insurance, as I reported in Chapter VI. The KVs and sick funds once negotiated the size of the lump sum (the *Kopfpauschale*) and the KV then distributed it among the incoming bills according to the relative values in the fee schedule. The Review Body in Great Britain is told the DHSS's prospective budget for the next year, but the figure is not binding on the Review Body. The Review Body is independent, recommends awards to a Prime Minister who is officially left with the decision, and can propose what it thinks best. So, it has occasionally recommended large increases in pay, thereby daring the Prime Minister either to cut the award or to find more money. Overruling the Review Body even in a limited way proved politically fatal in 1970, and Cabinets usually look for new money. Thus a supposedly tight budget system can offer a lever to one group to pry up the lid. A budget system may not be very strict in the United States, as evidenced by the many deficiency appropriations by legislatures.

A "tariff system" (i.e., the first step is to fix the price of each service) might be equally effective if the government announces its financial policies at the start of bilateral negotiations and sticks to them: The government would not offer the sick funds more than a certain subsidy, would not allow higher payroll taxes, and would not allow providers to charge the patients extra money. If the government has never provided a subsidy to the sick funds—as in the financing of the bulk of services in Germany—it is more persuasive than if it says it cannot possibly increase its annual grant. One reason that tariff systems have not strictly limited fees in the past has been the negotiators' confidence that the national government would pay their deficits and would allow higher payroll taxes. The negotiators finally became stingier in the mid-1970s because national governments could not afford higher subsidies—in fact Switzerland cut its grants —and because of fears that payroll taxes had reached their limits. Therefore, budget systems are not inherently stricter than tariff systems: All depends on the determination of the sick funds and government.

If spending on doctors' services and on incomes is restricted—under either a budget system or a tariff system—will the doctors and public feel short-changed? Perhaps they will, but that may not mean that services are poor. The doctors may complain more than the patients, but both make adjustments, as they must in any economically run public service.[46] All would complain even more if medical costs continued to absorb steadily higher proportions of the national wealth, without higher benefits.

Clarity

The negotiators should understand their instructions and must write agreements that anyone can understand. All doctors and administrators of local offices of sick funds must understand the rules. At present, under American Medicare, they do not.

A basic problem is that Americans include social security under the tax laws, and they assume they must enact national health insurance in the same manner. But the tax laws are addressed to regulators and finance officers in government; their arcane style may be appropriate to these specialists and to tax lawyers. A national health insurance law will govern a negotiated set of relationships among many thousands of doctors, administrators, and consumers. Other countries enact national health insurance as a freestanding law in clear prose, and the United States should do the same.

The negotiators must write agreements that anyone can understand, like those in American labor relations. In a field long accustomed to an incomprehensible basic statute and complex and constantly amended regulations, there is a danger that the health insurance negotiators will forget their audience. This will be particularly true if the negotiators try to include in great detail some of the incentive reimbursement formulas which are the present vogue in the United States.

REFORM OF THE HEALTH SERVICES

National health insurance is a way of raising money and paying providers. By itself, it cannot reorganize health delivery or repair serious deficiencies. If medical services work badly, national health insurance will work badly, but insurance cannot be blamed. Therefore, national health insurance can only be one part of a general improvement in American health care.

When Americans discuss prospects for national health insurance, they often justify it as an opportunity for new methods of health delivery. But these ideas are independent. If existing forms of delivering health care seem obsolete or defective, new ones can be devised by government and by private groups. National health insurance can be organized to pay for them and not to obstruct them. But these are independent efforts of the public and private sectors, and health insurance cannot be the agency to create them. For example, if Health Maintenance Organizations (i.e., prepaid groups) have merit, they should be fostered by a specially designed program, but national health insurance should not be written to give them priority over office practice. Any such special clauses would result in the defeat of the bill, since office practitioners allow passage of national health insurance only if their interests are protected.

Several special health activities do not fit the system of paying a provider for therapeutic services and therefore should be organized and remunerated separately. For example, some Americans commend national health insurance as an opportunity to promote preventive medicine. A few preventive acts, such as inoculations fit the usual form of individually billed work by doctors under fee schedules. But much preventive medicine consists of examinations and health teaching and are best done by teams (including many paramedicals) in organizations. Attempts to pay office doctors for the full repertoire of preventive medicine have proved expensive and unproductive in Germany, and most preventive work should be conducted and remunerated separately.

A few services traditionally paid by national health insurance abroad have proved troublesome and therefore should be administered and remunerated separately both there and here. An example is the numerous diagnostic tests produced by multichannel autoanalyzers but billed under the traditional assumption that the pathologist does each one personally. Perhaps routine tests without special medical evaluation can be done most economically by laboratories owned by the sick funds themselves.

One of the reforms needed in American health care should be genuine health planning, instead of vague reports that reflect a consensus among competing providers and consumers. Plans should be implemented by effective prohibition of wasteful uses of resources needed elsewhere, instead of Americans' hopes that small indirect financial incentives will divert anyone from highly profitable acts against the public interest, and instead of the widespread American custom of announcing but not enforcing regulations. Planning can help national health insurance operate more efficiently, but the two are not synonymous. National health insurance abroad coexists with planning efforts of differing scope and effectiveness. They should be coordinated sufficiently so that one does not undo what the other seeks: For example, if health planning tries to transfer care from acute to long-term and home-care facilities, national health insurance should not reward acute care and skimp on the alternatives.

Americans are accustomed to public-utility-type regulation of private facilities, instead of the outright nationalization common in such industries abroad. The American health industry may continue to be privately owned but regulated in detail. National health insurance can continue to pay for care in such facilities, but regulators must coordinate their efforts with the negotiators in insurance. For example, if the regulators are trying to eliminate certain treatments or the use of certain equipment, these acts should be excluded from fee schedules and from allowable costs in hospital budgets.

The maldistribution of facilities and health personnel by specialty and by location can be remedied only by a large effort devoted to that alone. The incentives from national health insurance can have only limited effect. Solving the serious shortages and turbulence of medical services among the urban poor requires even wider improvements in American race relations and reconstruction of the cities.

Effective controls over unnecessary waste and excessive price increases must be applied to the entire medical economy. National health insurance will be in chronic crisis and its cost controls will be subverted—as in Medicare—if the rest of the medical economy is substantial and uncontrolled. Unless the entire medical economy is stable, negotiators for national health insurance will be frequently recalled to amend their awards.

If inflation is a serious and chronic threat, the national government must lead in creation of an effective policy on incomes and prices. Like other policies involving intergroup relations in modern democratic societies, it must emerge from consultations and negotiations. National health insurance cannot work well without general economic stability.

TRANSITION TO NATIONAL HEALTH INSURANCE

Pending bills

The United States seems to have been preparing for national health insurance for forty-five years. Repeatedly it seems to have been on the verge of enactment, but the competing interests deadlock, the Administration and the Congress turn their attention to less controversial and to more understandable areas, and the issue is shelved. Each time, some practical fallout has resulted: the nonprofit and private companies expanded coverage and benefits, to head off the demand for a governmental program; Medicare for the aged and Medicaid for the poor were enacted during the 1960s, in lieu of universal national health insurance.

By the 1970s, the United States was the last country without national health insurance. A feeling of crisis about the mounting costs and complaints about gaps and confusion in nonprofit and in private coverage fueled another round in the campaign for Congressional action. Several bills were drafted, and passage of something was again said to be imminent. Several bills were designed merely to give an interest group *entrée* and a bargaining position in the national debate. They reinforced the sponsoring group's position in the status quo and read very differently from foreign countries' national health insurance laws. (The following paragraphs will discuss very briefly and incompletely the general character of these bills and their references to the medical profession, but a great deal more could be said about their positions on coverage, financing, benefits, administration, and so on.)[47]

Several bills reinforce the existing arrangements whereby employers and trade unions agree on health insurance as a fringe benefit, and the employer negotiates a contract for the employees with a nonprofit or private insurance carrier. The employee need not join. The bills prescribe a list of minimum benefits but vary in the full package. Some bills require workers to contribute part of the premiums, others leave this to labor-management negotiations. Some incorporate Medicare for the aged, others leave it a separate program. Most provide special plans for the poor and replace Medicaid in whole or in part. None mandate prospective reimbursement for doctors; and some explicitly preserve reasonable-charge methods, with all their ambiguity about how to determine payments. None spell out details about the organization of the carriers, the organization of the medical profession, or the methods of any negotiations. Such bills have been sponsored by the American Medical Association (the Hansen-Carter Bill), the Health Insurance Association of America (the Burleson-McIntyre Bill), the American Hospital Association (the Ullman Bill), and the United States Chamber of Commerce (the Fannin Bill). The bills differ in whether employers offer health benefits voluntarily or by requirement; they differ in the roles of state commissions in regulation of reimbursement to hospitals and doctors.

Compared to nearly every other developed country, such bills do not constitute national health insurance at all. Rather, they are methods of regularizing and expanding existing nonprofit and for-profit insurance. By adopting retrospective payment, they omit the extensive clauses about the administration of medical care found in the laws and regulations of other countries. In their voluntary and private character, these bills resemble national health insurance only in Switzerland.

The AFL-CIO has supported for some time the proposed Health Security Act (Kennedy-Corman Bill). It resembles national health insurance in countries with nationalized financing. Benefits and relations with carriers and not by state governments, but by an agency of the national government. All ci·izens would be covered. A payroll tax on employers, a payroll tax on employees, and general revenue would be used for financing, with no cost-sharing by patients. Certain provisions would encourage the development of prepaid group practices on fixed budgets (i.e., Health Maintenance Organizations or HMOs). A fixed budget would be provided for doctors' services and would be divided among them according to bills they render under a relative values schedule. The schedule would be issued by the administering agency after consultation (or negotiation) with the medical association. (Appendix A describes how this method once worked in Germany.) The Health Security Act has a scope much wider than conventional national health insurance and includes other devices to improve health delivery.

Because of fears that costs will strain the national government's budget more than anticipated and because of anxiety about the capacity of any government to administer a complete program, several policy makers introduced proposals to "phase in" national health insurance. The Long-Ribicoff Bill presumes that existing insurance coverage and out-of-pocket expenditures are (or soon will be) sufficient for nearly all care, and it provides special insurance against very large "catastrophic" expenses. Nonprofit and private carriers would administer the program, and doctors would be paid by reasonable-charge methods. Another catastrophic insurance proposal (the Brock Bill) would vary patients' cost-sharing by their incomes.

Several proposals (the Javits and Hart Bills) would pay for medical care for expectant mothers and medical and dental care for children. Although included in the debate over phasing in national health insurance, the "Kiddiecare" proposals are quite different: They would deliver specified benefits to children via agencies of the national government, paid from general revenue. The government might contract administration to insurance carriers, but as fiscal intermediaries and not as underwriters. The government agency would pay according to fee schedules—including possible capitation methods—written by negotiating committees.

Normally a debate over a subject as fundamental as national health insurance is dominated by a proposal by the President. The Nixon and Ford Administrations drafted bills to mark their presence in the national debate, but they did not press for passage, and they did not attract special attention. Their Comprehensive Health Insurance Plan (CHIP) had several parts. One required employers to offer a health insurance plan with extensive benefits. Both employers and employees would pay premiums, but employees could decline to participate. As at present, the employers would contract with nonprofit or private carriers to underwrite health insurance, and doctors would be paid by reasonable-charge methods. The unemployed would be covered under health insurance, with the help of government subsidies, and Medicaid would disappear. The elderly would receive comparable benefits under a program of the national government, replacing Medicare. The several parts of CHIP had different rules about patient cost-sharing, premiums, benefits, public subsidies, etc.

Differences between the American proposals and national health insurance abroad

Most American bills seem very different from the national health insurance systems that have long existed abroad and that are described in this book. Of course, great variations exist both among the American proposals and among foreign systems, so that certain American possibilities are close to selected foreign precedents. However, the following is a brief list of certain features of the American bills that differ from the mainstream of national health insurance abroad.

Several American proposals shrink from mandating coverage of the citizen. Most countries simply require that everyone or nearly everyone is covered and taxed. His option is whether he sees the doctor under his health insurance or privately. Switzerland alone has extensive optional coverage.

Federal systems abroad design national health insurance federally.

The identity and characteristics of the administrators and sick funds are spelled out in most foreign laws and regulations. No special attempts are made to keep the for-profit companies viable. In some foreign programs, the carriers are limited to the nonprofits.

Where several sick funds exist, they are selected by the subscriber and not by the employer.

Benefits abroad are standard among sick funds and among all insured persons. Only Germany has differences among funds in benefits to the subscriber and in payments to doctors for the same benefits. No country has several parts of national insurance with a variety of rules about patient cost-sharing, premiums, benefits, public subsidies, etc., as in CHIP and in several other American bills.

Providers are paid prospectively and not by a reasonable-charge method. Fee schedules are mandated in laws and regulations, along with the methods for negotiating them. Unless the carriers have been nationalized, the government's role in the negotiations is limited, and its approval is *pro forma*. Doctors must follow the fee schedules; if they don't, usually they cannot practice under national health insurance.

The size of patients' cost-sharing is defined and limited in the laws and regulations abroad. Deductibles are avoided, because they are confusing and difficult to administer.

Foreign programs do not attempt to include so much mental health and preventive medicine under national health insurance. These are included under other special programs. They are believed difficult to insure, because their effectiveness is doubtful and they are subject to abuse by providers.

Where national health insurance has been phased in abroad, occupational groups were covered successively. Usually phasing does not occur by benefit. It never occurs by age groups—i.e., the aged are not included first (as under American Medicare) and the children are not added second. No country begins with catastrophic protection alone; national health insurance covers the complete range of low and high bills.

National health insurance laws abroad do not include extensive efforts to reorganize health delivery, such as promotion of HMOs. They include methods of paying the full range of forms of practice that exist. The reorganization of practice is left to other government programs.

Sliding scales by patients' incomes have been abandoned in most countries for premiums, benefits, and cost-sharing.

Steering the United States toward national health insurance

The country could easily continue to drift, as it is doing in several domestic sectors. Discussions about the "health care crisis" are endless and publications accumulate, but the various factions do not try to negotiate a consensus. Instead, each group presents its own position and opposes most others. All groups—and most officials in Washington—hesitate to push any legislation out of the belief that health delivery is difficult and politically dangerous. Continuation of the *status quo* involves yet more costs in money and in administrative disorder.

If Americans are to design and enact national health insurance, an essential requirement is understanding what it is. American discussions of national health insurance are surprisingly fuzzy, and often become diverted over the merits of programs that are not customarily included under national health insurance statutes. National health insurance is not "socialized medicine" or "government control" over health delivery and financing. It does not—or should not—include everyone's pet scheme for making things "better."

If the United States drafts and enacts national health insurance, considerable determination and political bravery will be necessary. First, the White House and HEW will have to solicit the views of many groups—as foreign leaders typically do and, indeed, as HEW began to do during 1977. Then, the White House and HEW must develop a clear-cut and easily understandable plan. Judging from the experience of other democracies, national health insurance is so fundamental and controversial that the Administration must be prepared to do little else for many months. All other controversies should be postponed. The President must go all-out in support, and the Administration must be willing to risk its political life. Lining up a majority will be particularly complicated in the United States because of the separation of powers in the national goverment, the decentralization of power in the federal system, the weakness of political parties, and the immense energy of pressure groups. The Administration must hold fast against excited rhetoric: during legislative fights over national health insurance, doctors often threaten strikes but rarely call them.

Several social forces that bring about national health insurance in other countries are moving somewhat differently in the United States.

This is the reason why the progress toward a program here is more un-even. In other countries, the trade union movement is a powerful and usually unified force on behalf of national health insurance. While several American union leaders are philosophically in favor in the United States, only a few have their own sick funds experiencing cost problems that can be solved (or transferred elsewhere) by creation of an official program with autonomous funds. Much of American labor is covered by contracts with carriers paid by employers. Unlike other countries, it is the American employers who are a growing force for change, since they pay the mounting and apparently uncontrolled bills. Needless to say, American capitalists are cautious about espousing a classical program of the Left. The time is ripe for a collaboration on health policy by labor and management; even if they are not losing money over health now, labor leaders can see problems in the long run, as their Taft-Hartley funds go bankrupt and as their members under employer-paid contracts receive fewer benefits and are pressed for higher cost-sharing.

Several of the principal actors under national health insurance are evolving in directions compatible with their future roles under national health insurance. Blue Cross and Blue Shield are adopting a more adversarial attitude toward providers for several reasons. Employers press them to strike harder bargains with hospitals and doctors, in order to limit the annual increases in their prices. If they don't, the Blues will lose business to private insurance companies, such as the Aetna Life and Casualty Company. National and state government agencies have been pressing the Blues to become more independent of providers, in their antitrust suits. The Blues will probably prepare in other ways for their future roles under national health insurance, such as merging their separate hospitalization and medical care programs, and strengthening their national leaderships.

State medical associations vary widely in their preparations for national health insurance, but the general movement is clear. The AMA's national headquarters has formed a Department of Negotiations, to train members of state societies and to provide participating negotiators. Both the AMA's national office and several state offices have economic research departments to brief negotiators. Several state societies have tariff committees to write and update relative values schedules. Twice a year, the AMA's House of Delegates debates whether it is necessary to have a national health insurance policy at all, but clearly the majority in favor is growing, and the leadership's proposals steadily become more definite. Eventually the AMA will wrestle with such intensely practical questions as whether the national and state associations themselves should conform to the representation and reporting requirements of the National Labor Relations Act, whether the association should create special negotiating affiliates eligible under the NLRA, or whether it should press for a special negotiating system for medicine.

The Blues seem cautiously ready for whatever role the national health insurance legislation provides for them. The survival of the for-profit insurance carriers—Aetna, Prudential, and Mutual of Omaha are the principal health insurers—depends on preserving the existing system. Therefore their proposal—the Burleson-McIntyre Bill—strengthens current voluntary insurance and preserves the carriers' discretion to alter benefits, premiums, and patients' cost-sharing. American companies have much more business than private carriers did abroad on the eve of legislation, they have more at stake, and therefore their determination and political influence are greater. The private firms seem to have no compromise position on national health insurance since—as foreign experience suggests—compromise is not possible. If the private firms lose the legislative battle, and if benefits, premiums and cost-sharing are fixed, they cannot afford to insure for the bulk of care. Thereafter, their health business will be reduced to extra benefits. For the moment in the United States, they are an important adversary of the kinds of national health insurance in operation elsewhere.

In a federal system, possible forms of obligatory and universal health insurance can be tested in individual states. For example, Saskatchewan and British Columbia enacted types of hospitalization insurance and Medicare before Ottawa offered to subsidize plans in all Canadian provinces. While American states have been laboratories for some innovations, such as hospital rate regulation, few have ventured into the politically risky creation of obligatory health insurance.[48] Their unhappy experiences with Medicaid have made most governors and legislators cautious. If state officials ever come to think of medical finance as an opportunity rather than as a millstone, and if Washington remains deadlocked and uncertain about possible schemes, several states might perform a valuable national service by experimenting.

The future of national health insurance

Good health is a mirage: People can move toward it and become better off than before, but the ultimate goal always recedes. Health care is a Utopia: It is never enough. And since national health insurance is a way of organizing payment for services, it is a constant battleground among competing interests, a sounding board for complaints. People protest if services are not available without delay, but they protest also about the costs of the excess capacity needed for stand-by. People think that unfortunate groups—the aged, the chronically ill, children, the poor—should get everything they need without limit, but then protest the costs of the total system. They want authoritative answers and effective therapy, but medicine is still full of uncertainties, and people complain about the ineffectiveness and costs of much of what they get.

In theory, such a troublesome field should be decentralized, with individual consumers making their own choices about priorities and providers. But in practice, humanitarian and life-and-death fields are never organized in this "self-disciplined" and "harsh" fashion. Choices and costs are spread, consumers and providers look elsewhere for help in making decisions and in obtaining resources. American health delivery and financing at present are less organized ways—either "disorganized" or "flexible," according to one's ideological judgment—of sharing these decisions and costs.

National health insurance will simply be a way of focussing the process of making choices and allocating resources. Such forms of national organization for social decisions have become common in other democracies but are still novel in the United States. Americans will have to decide whether their faith in nonorganization continues to be vindicated in health financing, or whether the costs and conflict far outweigh any benefits. If they enact national health insurance, they should not try to "have their cake and eat it"—i.e., it should have a structure and system of making decisions and not merely be national health insurance in name only.

National health insurance will not be the final form of organizing health financing. The demographic trends of developed countries foreshadow problems in its ultimate viability. It is not conventional insurance, with benefits paid from the subscriber's investment, but (like all social security) it is a pay-as-you-go system: Current subscribers, employers, and taxpayers pay for the bills of current patients. In all developed countries, the retired and the invalids (who are heavy users of health care) are increasing at a faster rate than the wage earners (who pay premiums and taxes). Several European countries—Germany, France, and Switzerland—are far along in these trends, and their health insurance accounts are seriously strained. During the late 1970s, policy makers were engaged in desperate patchwork to restrain rising costs and to subsidize the accounts.[49] Eventually, most countries will need to change from premiums to general revenue payments into the insurance accounts (as in most of Canada) or replace insurance by a national health service (as in Great Britain and Sweden). Ultimately policy makers in the United States and elsewhere will have to face the hardest of all choices in a utopian field, how to ration services to the needy. If Americans can make their difficult decision to introduce national health insurance during the coming years, they will be buying time, with even harder choices ahead. But meanwhile, they will have created a system for identifying the problems and for making decisions. And that can be the most valuable lesson the United States will learn from abroad.

NOTES

1. Judith S. Warner, "Trends in the Federal Regulation of Physicians' Fees," *Inquiry*, Volume XIII, Number 4 (December 1976), pp. 364–370.

2. The history appears in Raymond Munts, *Bargaining for Health: Labor Unions, Health Insurance, and Medical Care* (Madison: University of Wisconsin Press, 1976), Ch. 1. Determinations of doctors' fees under these contracts is described in *ibid.*, Ch. 11.

3. In a recent unanimous decision, the United States Supreme Court declared a minimum fee schedule in violation of the Sherman Act. Goldfarb et ux. v. Virginia State Bar et al., 421 U.S. 773 (1975). The federal government then filed an antitrust suit against anesthesiologists for such use of a relative values scale: United States of America v. The American Society of Anesthesiologists, Inc., United States Court for the Southern District of New York, Civil No. 75–4640, 22 September 1975.

4. John Crncich, "The Making of the California Relative Value Studies: The Ideology and Administration of Pricing Policy in the Fee-for-Service Medical Market" (Madison: Center for Medical Sociology and Health Services Research, University of Wisconsin, 1976). The California Medical Association's own account of its procedure appears in *1974 Revision of the 1969 California Relative Value Studies* (San Francisco: California Medical Association, 1974), esp. Appendix IV; and in a series of articles about the RVS in "The Bulletin" [of the California Medical Association], January-March 1970.

5. In Canada, the government offensive was double-pronged. The negotiations gradually claimed jurisdiction over the fee schedules, on the grounds the schedules affected payments. In addition, schedules written and imposed unilaterally by professional associations were made illegal under the Combines Investigation Act. Douglas A. Geekie, "Death of a Fee Schedule," *C.M.A. Journal*, Volume 114, Number 7 (3 April 1976), p. 627.

6. Herman Somers and Anne Somers, *Doctors, Patients, and Health Insurance* (Washington: The Brookings Institution, 1961), pp. 332–333. The scarcity of fee schedules and of other structured prospective payment methods among the Blue Shield Plans and Medicare today are evident in the *Nationwide Survey of State Health Regulations* (Washington: Lewin and Associates, 1974), Ch. 1, pp. 24–25, and Ch. II, pp. 21–25.

7. Theodore R. Marmor, *The Politics of Medicare* (Chicago: Aldine Publishing Company, 1973), pp. 71–72 and 80.

8. Blue Shield's ingenious methods of writing these packages and calculating fees are described in Edward S. Mills, "History of Paid-in-Full Programs" and "Usual Charge Record/Carrier Profile Instrument" (Chicago: National Association of Blue Shield Plans, 1970 and 1973).

9. The unhappy history of payment of doctors under Medicare is summarized in Committee on Finance, United States Senate, *Medicare and Medicaid: Problems, Issues, and Alternatives* (Washington: U.S. Government Printing Office, 1970); Health Insurance Benefits Advisory Council, *A Report on the Results of the Study of Methods of Reimbursement for Physicians' Services under Medicare* (Washington: Social Security Administration, Department of Health, Education,

and Welfare, 1973); and Warner, "Trends in the Federal Regulation of Physicians' Fees," *op. cit.* (note 1, supra). The diverse and often contradictory signals from different parts of the Social Security Administration and the sometimes bewildering changes in viewpoints in particular offices are described in Judith M. Feder, *The Character and Implications of SSA's Administration of Medicare* (Denver: Policy Center., Inc., 1975).

10. The program for civil servants is described in Inez Conley, *Federal Employees Health Benefits Program: Highlights of First Decade of Operation July 1960–June 1970* (Washington: U.S. Government Printing Office, 1971); and Odin W. Anderson and J. Joel May, *Federal Employees Health Benefits Program 1961-1968* (Chicago: Center for Health Administration Studies, University of Chicago, 1971). The early payment of doctors under military dependents insurance—once called "Medicare" and now called CHAMPUS—is described in Paul I. Robinson, "Experience with Medicare," *Journal of the American Medical Association,* Volume 168, Number 12 (22 November 1968), pp. 1630–1633. The replacement of CHAMPUS' early fee schedule by the reasonable-charge methodology of Blue Shield and of Medicare for the aged is described by Frank van Dyke and Robin Elliott, *Military Medicare* (New York: School of Public Health and Administrative Medicine, Columbia University, 1969), pp. 41–43, 47–48, and 71–74.

11. C. Arthur Williams and Peter S. Barth, *Compendium on Workmen's Compensation* (Washington: National Commission on State Workmen's Compensation Laws, 1973), pp. 155–156.

12. United States of America before Federal Trade Commission in the Matter of The American Medical Association et al., Docket Number 9064, 19 December 1975. Soon after this complaint, the FTC announced an investigation of the relations between Blue Shield Plans and medical societies. The state of Ohio filed such an antitrust suit against Blue Shield and the state medical society in 1975.

13. For example, H. E. Frech, "Regulatory Reform: The Case of the Medical Care Industry," paper at Conference on Regulatory Reform, American Enterprise Institute, September 1975; and Clark Havighurst, "Controlling Health Care Costs: Strengthening the Private Sector's Hand," *Journal of Health Politics, Policy and Law,* Volume 1, Number 4 (Winter 1977), pp. 471–498.

14. Mario F. Bognanno, "Physicians' and Dentists' Bargaining Organizations: A Preliminary Look," *Monthly Labor Review,* June 1975, pp. 33–35. The history, organization, and recent activities of the country's oldest and most energetic medical union are described in John Bartlett and David Kuechle, "New York City Doctors' Strike 1975" (Boston: Harvard Business School, 1976, Case Number 9–676–091).

15. On the history and current activities of the medical trade unions, see Philip R. Alper (editor), *Doctors' Unions and Collective Bargaining: Report of Proceedings* (Berkeley: Institute of Industrial Relations, University of California, 1974). On their uneven accomplishments, see James A. Reynolds, "Is the Doctor Union Movement Dead?" *Medical Economics,* Volume 53, Number 17 (23 August 1976), pp. 140–159.

16. One of Europe's most experienced students of the administration of the social services has argued in several publications that the costs of the social

services can be restrained only if the paying agencies are vigilant and bargain vigorously with providers. Philipp Herder-Dorneich, *Die Kostenexpansion und ihre Steuerung im Gesundheitswesen* (Köln: Deutscher Ärzte-Verlag, 1976).

17. John Holahan, *Financing Health Care for the Poor* (Lexington: Lexington Books, 1975), pp. 63–67.

18. For example, the demonstration projects on prospective reimbursement of hospitals, which saved so little money in Clifton R. Gaus and Fred J. Hellinger, "Results of Hospital Prospective Reimbursement in the U.S." (paper at the International Conference on Policies for the Containment of Health Care Costs and Expenditures, Fogarty International Center, 1976); and Harvey Wolfe et al., "Prospective Reimbursement," *Inquiry*, Volume XIII, Number 3 (September 1976), pp. 274–320.

19. The French data are from Blandine Guibert et al., *Chiffres d'affaires des médecins conventionnés du secteur privé* (Paris: Centre de Recherches et de Documentation sur la Consommation, 1973), p. 26; and from Simone Sandier, *Activité, prix, chiffre d'affaires des médecins conventionnés: évolution 1962–1975 en France* (Paris: CREDOC, 1977), pp. 50 and 55. I have calculated German data from the Rheinland fees in *9. Bericht über Erfahrungen mit der Einzelleistungsvergütung in der Kassenärztlichen Versorgung* (Düsseldorf: Verband der Ortskrankenkassen Rheinland, 1975), p. 15; and the consumers price index issued by the Statistisches Bundesamt. The American data are from *Medical Care Expenditures, Prices and Costs: Background Book* (Washington: Office of Research and Statistics, Social Security Administration, 1975), pp. 24 and 58; and from tabulations in the *Monthly Labor Review*. French fees rose faster than American fees during the 1960s, because the French cost-of-living rose faster than the American, but that is another matter. Georges Rösch and Simone Sandier, "A Comparison of the Health-Care Systems of France and the United States," in Teh-wei Hu (editor), *International Health Costs and Expenditures* (Washington: National Institutes of Health, U. S. Department of Health, Education, and Welfare, 1976) pp. 155–157.

20. Charlotte L. Rosenberg, "He Challenged Aetna's Hard-Line Fee Policy—and Won," *Medical Economics,* Volume 49 (11 September 1972), pp. 31–45 passim.

21. David A. Stockman, "The Social Pork Barrel," *The Public Interest,* Number 39 (Spring 1975), pp. 3–30; and Martha Derthick, *Uncontrollable Spending for Social Services* (Washington: The Brookings Institution, 1975). On the organizational weaknesses that prevent America's incentive reimbursement experiment from operating as expected, see Carol McCarthy, "Incentive Reimbursement as an Impetus to Cost Containment," *Inquiry*, Volume XII, Number 4 (December 1975), pp. 320–329.

22. An issue to be resolved in the drafting of national health insurance in the United States is how much legislation and regulation will be done by the national government and how much by the traditional regulators in the state insurance departments. One possible formula—common in Germany—is state enforcement of rules written by the national government. Another solution is the highly controversial occupancy of this field by the national government. Regardless of the formula, more uniformity and less politics will be needed. For a critique by a well informed visitor, accustomed to the greater degree of orga-

nization and stability in modern Europe, see Werner Pfennigstorf, "American Insurance Regulation Seen through European Eyes," in Spencer L. Kimball and Herbert S. Denenberg (editors), *Insurance, Government, and Social Policy* (Homewood, Ill.: Richard D. Irwin, 1969), pp. 453–482.

23. Several state insurance departments have expressed frustration over the lack of any voice by the public over carriers' methods of paying providers, when the results unsettle the carriers' accounts, present the insurance departments with *faits accomplis,* and make it difficult for the departments not to grant higher premiums. For example: In the Matter of a Rate Filing for Community-Rated Business by the Medical-Surgical Plan of New Jersey (Trenton: Department of Insurance, State of New Jersey, Report and Recommendations of the Hearing Officer, 11 July 1975).

24. For a critique of the composition of Blue Shield Boards and the effects on the economic strategies of the Blue Shield Plans, see "The Impact of Blue Shield Boards of Directors on the Cost of Health Care in New York State" (New York: New York State Consumer Protection Board, 1977).

25. Experiences in one state are described in William Averyt et al., "Medical Professionals and the Payment Policies: The Connecticut State Medical Society, 1930–1970" (New Haven, Conn.: Department of Epidemiology and Public Health, Yale University School of Medicine, 1974). Both Blue Shield and Blue Cross at present are trying to think of better ways to manage existing relations with their respective providers. For example, the analysis and recommendations in Robert M. Sigmond and Thomas Kinser, *The Hospital-Blue Cross Plan Relationship* (Chicago: Blue Cross Association, 1976).

26. Contrasts between the United States and other Western democracies in ideological history and in public practice appear in Anthony King, "Ideas, Institutions and the Policies of Governments: A Comparative Analysis," *British Journal of Political Science,* Volume 3, Number 4 (October 1973), pp. 418–423; and in Herschel Hardin, *A Nation Unaware: The Canadian Economic Culture* (Vancouver: J. J. Douglas, 1974).

27. Over sixty organizations have been created by compacts among two, several, or many states. Common in the joint administration of rivers, natural resources, and education, they have not yet been used in health. *Directory of Interstate Agencies* (Lexington, Ky.: Council of State Governments, Revised edition, 1976); and Richard H. Leach and Redding S. Sugg, *The Administration of Interstate Compacts* (Baton Rouge: Louisiana State University Press, 1959).

28. The United States has experienced the same equalizing trends as other countries: once regional economic differentials were very wide, but they have rapidly narrowed. John Shannon, "Making Federalism Work: American Experience," in Russell Mathews (editor), *Making Federalism Work* (Canberra: Centre for Research on Federal Financial Relations, Australian National University, 1976), pp. 15–16.

29. Ted Bogue, *Why Not the Most?* (Washington: Health Research Group, 1977).

30. The very involved and (therefore) often secretive methods of composing national health regulations are described in Drew Altman and Harvey M. Sapolsky, "Writing the Regulations for Health," *Policy Sciences,* Volume 7 (1976),

pp. 417–437. For criticisms of how the regulations work out in practice, see Roger G. Noll, "The Consequences of Public Utility Regulation of Hospitals," in Institute of Medicine, *Controls on Health Care* (Washington: National Academy of Sciences, 1975), pp. 25–48; Patrick O'Donoghue, *Evidence about the Effects of Health Care Regulation* (Denver: Spectrum Research, 1974); and Clark Havighurst, "Federal Regulation of the Health Care Delivery System," *University of Toledo Law Review,* Volume 6, Number 3 (Spring 1975), pp. 577–590.

31. Kay Cavalier, "National Health Planning and Resources Development Act—Summary of Existing Law and Its Implementation" (Washington: Congressional Research Service, Library of Congress, 1977).

32. For example, Richard Simeon, *Federal-Provincial Diplomacy—The Making of Recent Policy in Canada* (Toronto: University of Toronto Press, 1972).

33. Social programs bring national and provincial governments into close collaboration in all federal countries. Either they cooperate as equals—an uneasy and unstable relationship—or the provinces agree to act as administrative agencies for legislation enacted by the national government. Geoffrey Sawer, *Modern Federalism* (Carlton, Victoria: Pitman Australia, second edition, 1976), passim, esp. Ch. 8. Criticisms of the design and administration of American national-state collaborations appear in several recent reports by the Comptroller General of the United States, such as *Fundamental Changes Are Needed in Federal Assistance to States and Local Governments* (Washington: General Accounting Office, August 1975, GGD–75–75.)

34. Henry Galant, *Histoire politique de la Sécurité sociale française* (Paris: Librairie Armand Colin, 1955), Chs. V and VI.

35. James F. Scearce and Lucretia Dewey Tanner, "Health Care Bargaining: The FMCS Experience," *Labor Law Journal,* Volume 27, Number 7 (July 1976), pp. 387–398.

36. A remarkable number of regulations in health seem to work out unexpectedly in the United States. For an example of a highly regarded regulation that could not help but be effective but somehow isn't, see David S. Salkever and Thomas W. Bice, *Impact of State Certificate-of-Need Laws on Health Care Costs and Utilization* (Rockville, Md.: report to the National Center for Health Services Research, 1976).

37. Doubts that the President of the United States can appoint truly neutral arbitrators to resolve disputes between civil servants and federal agencies are expressed in *Employee-Management Relations in the Federal Service: Hearings before the Committee on Post Office and Civil Service* (Washington: U.S. Government Printing Office, 1968), esp. pp. 23–27. A respected organization—the American Arbitration Association—is developing experience in settling disputes involving doctors, including health delivery problems. Irving Ladimer, "Prevention and Resolution of Medical Disputes," in *Legal Medicine Annual 1975* (New York: Appleton-Century-Crofts, 1976), pp. 151–167. Whether the national government would ever accept such private arbitration remains to be seen, but lower governments cooperate.

38. Scearce and Tanner, *op. cit.* (note 35, supra), pp. 393–394.

39. For example, Charles L. Karras, *Give and Take: The Complete Guide to Negotiating Strategies and Tactics* (New York: Thomas Y. Crowell, 1974); and

Gerard I. Nierenberg, *Fundamentals of Negotiating* (New York: Hawthorn Books, 1973). A few provocative theoretical essays have been written about adversarial negotiations, particularly Carl M. Stevens, *Strategy and Collective Bargaining Negotiation* (New York: McGraw-Hill Book Company, 1963); and the collection of papers in the *Journal of Conflict Resolution,* December, 1977.

40. The new unit is described in James H. Sammons, "American Medical Association Explains Negotiations Department," *Hospitals,* Volume 50 (1 June 1976). Its first manual is Seymour J. Burrows, *Physicians' Guide to Negotiations* (Chicago: American Medical Association, 1976). The Department of Negotiations now publishes a periodic newsletter, *Negotiations Update.*

41. For example, Richard J. Fritz and Arthur M. Stringari, *Employer's Handbook for Labor Negotiations* (Detroit: Management Labor Relations Service, Second edition, 1964). Manuals are now beginning to appear about how other professions should negotiate, such as Joseph Garbarino et al., *Faculty Bargainng in Public Higher Education* and George W. Angell et al., *Handbook of Faculty Bargaining* (both San Francisco: Jossey-Bass, Inc., 1977).

42. As in the rhetoric by leaders of American physicians' unions, throughout Alper, *op. cit.* (note 15, supra).

43. J.-P. Alméras, "L'obtention du droit permanent à dépassement," *Le concours médical,* Volume 98, Number 39 (30 October 1976), pp. 5771–5773.

44. Central Committee for Hospital Medical Staffs, "Distinction Awards" (London: British Medical Association, 1972); and Hector MacLennan, "Distinction Awards—The Procedure for Selection," *Health Trends,* May 1973, pp. 24 ff.

45. Therefore, few foreign health insurance system would adopt language like: "It is, of course, contemplated under the bill that the Secretary would use, both initially and over the long run, the most refined indexes that can be developed." *Report of the Committee on Finance to Accompany H.R. 1, The Social Security Amendments of 1972* (Washington: U.S. Government Printing Office, 1972), p. 192.

46. Even during the period of financial stringency of the 1960s, British patients were more satisfied with the National Health Service than were Americans with their care. British GPs were less satisfied than American doctors, but their opinions may have improved lately. Ronald Andersen, "A Framework for Cross-National Comparisons of Health Service Systems," in Manfred Pflanz and Elizabeth Schach (editors), *Cross-National Socio-Medical Research* (Stuttgart: Georg Thieme Verlag, 1976), p. 30.

47. Convenient summaries of each year's crop of bills have been prepared by Saul Waldman and published by the office of Research and Statistics, Social Security Administration. An analysis and critique of the principal bills appear in Karen Davis, *National Health Insurance: Benefits, Costs, and Consequences* (Washington: The Brookings Institution, 1975), Ch. 5; and Peter D. Fox, "Options for National Health Insurance: An Overview," *Policy Analysis,* Volume 3, Number 1 (Winter 1977), pp. 1–24.

48. The few state health insurance initiatives are described in Jordan Braverman et al., papers from a conference sponsored by the Georgetown University Health Policy Center during 1977.

49. The new German legislation addressed to these demographic and financial trends is summarized in *Eine stabile Rentenversicherung und eine gesunde Krankenversicherung* (Bonn: Bundesministerium für Arbeit und Sozialordnung, 1977).

APPENDIX A

Examples of Lessons
from Abroad

SCHOLARS have long studied individual foreign governments and societies, in order to understand them better. More recently, they have suggested principles of social structure by comparing several societies on common dimensions.

Meanwhile, other social scientists have been conducting policy research. They have confined their research to their own countries: since each evaluates his own country's programs or because he suggests methods for his own country, he and the policy makers have always assumed that his data must be drawn only from his own country.

This book and other publications from the present research are designed to make international comparisons useful for policy making. My strategy has been to select problems that face the United States but have no parallels in American experience. The relevant experiences occur in other developed countries. When thinking about how to reorganize an entire country—such as the subject of this book—the only experimental laboratories are in other countries.

Any sort of policy research requires a leap in thinking from examining events to recommending what officials should do. Likewise, cross-national policy research requires mental translation. One cannot merely say that an institution from one country should be copied exactly or avoided in one's own country, since exact copies in another social setting usually—not always—are impossible. Instead, seeing how institutions work in other societies is an exceptionally good way of stimulating the imagination. One can understand features of one's own country previously overlooked or taken for granted. One can think of possible innovations omitted from the domestic debate. Following are examples drawn from the present research about comparative health services, to demonstrate ways that foreign experiences can be valuable for American policy making.

WHETHER TO BECOME LIKE EVERYONE ELSE

Up to now, the most common use of foreign experience for policy making has been negative. Critics of a proposal claim that it has been tried abroad and failed. Usually this is an attack on all possible forms of a program: Nothing is feasible, say the critics.

The mere idea of national health insurance has been discredited several times in American history in this fashion. It was first proposed in the United States in 1915, at a time of enactment in several European countries. It was defeated in large part because medical societies and other critics pinned a "German" and alien image on it.[1]

The abortive attempt to add national health insurance to the Social Security Act in 1935 was defeated in large part because of the AMA's exposé of the weaknesses of national health insurance in Great Britain.[2] Catalogues of the defects of the British National Health Service and of other foreign programs are published in the United States whenever any new proposal for national health insurance is offered.[3]

If a country is considering a fundamental decision, it need not be bound by the experience of others. Even if every known version of a program works badly elsewhere, one's own country might devise a unique solution. Bad foreign experiences should certainly make one think twice. The thinking also should include a better understanding of the foreign situations: Across-the-board dismissals of foreign experiences are usually misleading, since some systems work better than others.

A more constructive approach to cross-national policy research is more selective. One should identify the policy problems of one's own country and then see whether any other society has devices that can be helpful.

TAKING THE EMPEROR TO THE TAILOR

A country sometimes fails to realize that what all others have learned must be an integral part of a program. This weakness is particularly serious in a Great Power—like the United States—that normally believes itself to be the model, not needing to learn from elsewhere. The omissions will prevent one's own country from running certain programs successfully.

A good example is the central subject of this book: In every other country with national health insurance, doctors are paid prospectively and not retrospectively. Nearly all systems use fee-for-service and therefore all must have fee schedules. This requires some sort of negotiating machinery to create the fee schedule, since one group does not impose its decisions on another in a free society.

In contrast to the experience of every other developed country, the United States has been struggling with the payment problem under Medicare for over a decade. It devised an unsatisfactory retrospective payment system and has been patching it ever since. Several American national health insurance bills suffer from the same flaws. The solution is simply to organize in this respect like every other country, since it seems to be a structural imperative of national health insurance.

HOW THINGS REALLY WORK

Foreign countries can display in action the institutions that are merely proposed or have barely begun in one's own country. For example, Americans for several decades have enacted health planning laws, they have created agencies that publish plans, but the plans seem to have had only modest results.

Several other countries can demonstrate planning in action: They not only write plans, but they implement them. One can see the prerequisites for effective implementation, but one can also see the uncertainties and risks.

Implementation of plans

American plans are written by many state and local governmental or semipublic agencies. They contain voluminous and often very detailed information and statements of goals. These passages resemble foreign health facilities and manpower plans; in keeping with the American customs of expensive research and detailed documentation, most American plans are even more elaborate. However, their implementation varies widely among jurisdictions and is often hortatory or indirect, rather than direct orders or direct prohibitions. If a state agency refuses to validate construction or equipment by a "certificate of need," the facility in many jurisdictions may be able to make the purchase or a substitute nevertheless and juggle the financing.[4]

If the United States has great trouble controlling the purchase of buildings and equipment, it would have greater trouble with an even more resistant and politically formidable task, viz., telling doctors where to work. Sweden's efficient planning system does this as well as control construction and equipment purchases. On the grounds that everything in health ultimately is a public service paid by public money, Sweden's planners decide where the money shall be spent.[5]

For many years Sweden has had an overall shortage and an unbalanced distribution of doctors. They have gravitated into specialties and into the hospital staffs in the largest cities. They have concentrated in the traditionally popular fields, such as surgery and internal medicine. Therefore, the country's problem has been how to attract them into ambulatory health center care, into the less popular fields (such as general practice and geriatrics), and into less urbanized areas.

The principal employers of doctors are the twenty-three county councils and three large cities. Left alone, they would compete vigorously for the limited number of physicians. Wages and fringe benefits would be bid up, and the doctors would concentrate in the largest and most prosperous cities.

The system of planning and allocation prevents this. Each year the county councils make their own plans and tell the *Landstingsförbundet* the proposed number of new posts, their locations, and their specialties. The total requests are unrealistically high—they would be even higher if the county councils were not restrained by the existence of the planning system—and the staff of the *Landstingsförbundet* screens them and establishes priorities. The manpower planning staff of the *Socialstyrelsen* has estimated the numbers of young doctors who will be completing their medical education and their hospital residencies during each of the next five years, and these predictions have affected the requests by the county councils and by the *Landstingsförbundet*. The *Socialstyrelsen* has been keeping in mind the policies on medical services enunciated by its own executives and by the Cabinet. Its staff develops specific new recommendations about the direction of services, or it repeats earlier ones.

The allocation of new positions to be filled by the county councils from the next year's crop of new doctors is done by a Medical Planning Committee (*Läkarfördelningsprogrammet-arbetet* or *LP-arbetet*), with representatives from the *Socialstyrelsen,* the Association of University Chancellors, the *Landstingsförbundet,* the *Kommunförbundet,* and the Swedish Medical Association. Every few years, the *LP-arbetet* issues a detailed statement of its goals in medical care, its aims in the employment of doctors, the manpower that is likely to be produced by postgraduate educational programs in each of the coming years, and the posts that shall be available to the county councils in numbers, locations, and specialties.[6] Another committee of the *Socialstyrelsen* with overlapping membership plans the supply: It recommends the numbers and specialties for hospital residencies, so that Swedish doctors will be trained in fields that fit the manpower goals during the coming years. The same manpower planners in the *Socialstyrelsen* do the staff work for both committees and influence the decisions by preparing drafts of the plans.

A county council can fill a post only if authorized under this year's plan or if still unfilled from last year's plan. It cannot offer extra money. The salary scale is negotiated nationally between the *Landstingsförbundet* and SACO, and the ranking of each post is negotiated between the *Landstingsförbundet* and the Swedish Medical Association, as I said in Chapter VIII, *supra*. The arrangements bind all county councils and one cannot take doctors whom other councils might hire by offering more money.

The county councils can bid by offering earlier promotions. A young hospital doctor can rise sooner in a hospital away from the biggest cities and in one of the less popular specialties. The county council cannot snap him up by offering an appointment and the salary of a senior doctor unless he has full specialty credentials. County councils compete by offering doctors the most modern facilities, and therefore Sweden has much underused technology in the hospitals. In order to fill the posts of district medical officer, the county councils are building and outfitting new health centers.

The planning system cannot force the county councils to give up old posts. It can redirect medical services only by its control over new posts.

An important motive for the reform of fee-for-service under national health insurance—described in Chapter VIII, *supra*—was to strengthen the effectiveness of health manpower planning. Private office practice in the biggest cities would become less profitable, and young doctors instead would take the county councils' salaried posts.[7]

The pitfalls of forecasting

Swedish experience demonstrates the optimal conditions for implementation: public authority over construction, purchasing, and hiring; coordination of all spending in these and related programs; the authors and executors of plans have great authority, and community boards advise but do not direct them. (An American might protest that such control is feasible only when government "owns" the facilities, but ownership by "private" or "nonprofit" organizations in health may not be more intractable than ownership by a level of government different from that of the planners. Sweden's county councils have gained considerable independence from the national government in practice.)

Planning is risky. Officials must be willing to take chances, and politicians must be willing to back them up. Implementing manpower and facilities plans is a prolonged process. All participants must be willing to stand by their decisions and not quail in the face of opposition; or, they must have orderly methods of making corrections.

The political risks and administrative costs of forecasting and miscalculating are evident in the confusing history of manpower planning in Great Britain. In several plans, the statistical tabulations and projections about the future appeared methodologically elegant and persuasive, but they were grounded on assumptions that were merely the orthodoxy of the moment. Policy reversed when the assumptions changed and when new facts suggested (as often happens in government) new and unexpected developments that would last forever. One expert committee in 1957 enunciated a then common belief that Britain was educating too many doctors; soon thereafter medical school enrollments were cut. At the first sign of higher emigration and the arrival of foreign doctors, the government panicked and reversed itself.[8] A new Royal Commission then declared that emigration of Britons was excessive, demand was rising, too many foreigners were working in British hospitals, and medical school enrollments must increase greatly.[9] By 1976, several of my informants had become convinced that Britain was educating far too many doctors and that, by the 1980s, will have so many that foreign immigration will stop and some British doctors wil not find posts, either in the hospitals or in general practice.

There is one constant connection between the payment of doctors and this erratic manpower policy: the Review Body must make its awards in the light of Britain's recruitment and retention needs (among other criteria); therefore the BMA buttresses its case for higher pay by arguing that emigration is excessive and will increase without more money. But the Review Body fluctuates, just like the manpower planners. At times its mood is pessimistic and it awards much money; at other times, it pronounces the emigration statistics not so bad, uses other criteria, and gives less money.[10]

IDENTIFYING THE ISSUES

On the eve of any fundamental reform, adversaries predict disasters and influence the terms of the debate. Proponents fear that the critics have discovered a kernel of truth and devote much attention to preventing the problem. One can judge whether a problem is real only by seeing the system in action abroad.

Debunking false problems

Much of the debate over national health insurance today is on how to prevent the government from "taking over" and "controlling" medical care. Opponents try to prevent "political control" of doctors.[11] Proponents apologize that a "government program" and "government control" seem inevitable.

But, as I said in Chapter X, the dichotomy between "government" and the "private sector" in health is false. One does not take over the other, because they merge. National health insurance works with semipublic sick funds handling money and negotiating with doctors. Government plays only a limited part, setting forth basic rules. Doctors are not enslaved by the public authorities. In practice, they dominate national health insurance and earn more money than ever.[12]

Research overseas can show exactly where the predicted event really occurs. For example, government is increasingly active in the hospital sector of national health insurance, in control over construction, in purchase of equipment, and in budgetting.

Identifying true problems

Study of foreign systems in operation can show policy makers what they really should worry about. Therefore, they are forewarned about the provisions that must exist in the statute and in the administration. For example, it is clear that all countries have serious problems of controlling costs, and that all are now searching for new methods. All systems have great cost over-runs during their first year. Therefore, the United States should have in place from the start effective methods to discourage unnecessary utilization, detect waste, and review and approve hospital budgets.

Foreign experience can suggest future problems that Americans do not anticipate. For example, Germany, Sweden, and Britain have experienced sudden large increases in hospital costs, as the junior doctors got "normal" work weeks, full-time salaries that are "normal" for their educational level, and overtime and stand-by pay for extra work and for availability. Americans need to be forewarned that this large increase in their hospital costs still lies ahead.

Often policy makers enact a commendable idea, without realizing that its outcomes can be unexpected and expensive. Foreign events can reveal these. For example, several American national health insurance bills cover dentistry as well as medical care. Adding dentistry to a national health service or to national health insurance—for example, in Great Britain during the late 1940s and in Sweden during the 1970s—uncovers many more untreated cases than anyone suspected. In contrast to medical care, utilization and costs increase much more in dentistry.

SUGGESTING SOLUTIONS

Foreign countries can provide a supermarket of possible solutions to problems that cause deadlocks or indecision in one's own country. Devices that no one thought of during the domestic debate may be operating successfully somewhere else.

The first step—as in all cross-national policy research—is to understand the problems in one's own country, the fears of the interest groups, and the nature of the impasse. One must also develop a sense of what the adversaries might accept. Then one can recognize abroad certain institutions that might be reshaped and recommended for one's own country.

For example, it is not merely the spectre of "government control" that exercises Americans, but centralization under the national government in Washington. (Because of this usage of the word "national", the AMA's House of Delegates in June 1977 renamed its recommended program "Comprehensive Health Insurance" and instructed the Board of Trustees to investigate their proposed law and to assure the next session of the House that the bill would not "nationalize medicine.") Study of other federal systems shows that none organize national health insurance in a unitary fashion, administered entirely by an agency of the central government. Canada and Switzerland have a series of provincial programs that might be too diverse for the United States. Therefore, in Chapter X, I proposed a national-state collaborative structure inspired by ideas from West Germany.

ADMINISTRATIVE MODELS

Most foreign devices cannot be imported exactly, but the analyst must reshape them. However, a few specialized techniques might be copied exactly.

Coordinating agencies

An example from the present research is standing coordinating machinery. This would be an autonomous commission that houses negotiations, prepares neutral and objective research reports, mediates deadlocks between the negotiators, and obtains the cooperation of the government. National health insurance works successfully in Holland in large part because of the *Ziekenfondsraad* and might not be able to function in Belgium at all without INAMI.

Persuading doctors to serve in remote areas

Almost every country has severe rural-urban imbalances. All have tried the same simple list of incentives, viz., extra payments, recruitment of medical students from rural backgrounds, and conditioning scholarships on rural service. But these methods have remarkably little influence.

A few countries have attempted to influence flows by allowing new doctors to practice only in areas designated to have scarcities, but this seems feasible only in a structured national health service.[13] Americans shrink from controls and coercion but hope that voluntary incentives will succeed, without fully realizing that experiences in other countries as well as in the United States by now establish that the simple set of incentives is ineffective.[14]

The need to supplement monetary practice allowances and scholarships with an organized effort are demonstrated by the effective Program for Underserviced Areas of the Ministry of Health, Province of Ontario. Nearly 250 small communities without doctors have applied for inclusion, they have been investigated by the program's director, and 174 have been designated as "underserviced" and eligible for a doctor. The director collects names of doctors and interviews them and their spouses for suitability for service in remote areas. He tries to match community and doctor, to ensure harmonious work and to induce the doctors to stay on. (Most other programs of rural service suffer from high turnover.) Doctors do not practice alone in private offices, but in community health centers with other health professionals. Often the arrangement is collaboration with another doctor.

Financial aid can be a guarantee by the Ministry of a minimum annual income of $33,000. If the doctor does not earn this amount from OHIP fees—an unlikely event—the Ministry pays the difference. A more common device is a practice allowance free of income tax: the Ministry pays the doctor $8,000, $6,000, $3,000 and $3,000 in successive years in quarterly installments each year. The community builds a modern health center and rents it to the doctor at a reasonable rate. The doctor must buy his own equipment, thereby making his own contribution to the arrangement.

In 1976, 262 doctors were serving in 155 communities, and turnover has been low. Important attractions are the varied practice and heavy responsibility. The energetic director of the Program (Dr. William Copeman) constantly visits and communicates with the members, so they are not left isolated.[15]

Symbolic devices

Fights over power and professional status often become very destructive and can be resolved only by great ingenuity. Formulas that enable all sides to claim victory are scarce.

A familiar problem in the enactment of a country's national health insurance is the doctors' belief that direct payment by the sick fund will deprive them of professional freedom. A common compromise is to allow the doctors to continue billing the patients, and the patients are reimbursed by the sick funds. But the public authorities—and often much of the general public—protest on the grounds that doctors should not have opportunities to extra-bill and patients should not be compelled to advance money for no purpose except to appease the medical profession's self-image. Deadlock over this and other matters led to the bitter strike of doctors against the Government of Saskatchewan in 1962.[16]

The solution in Saskatchewan was creation of a "Health Service Agency" that saved everyone's face. Doctors do not send bills to the government nor do they bill the patient. They send their bills to a "Health Service Agency," a private organization that forwards the bills to the provincial health insurance office. The government sends the Agency payment for each act according to the fee schedule, and the Agency pays the doctor. The physician cannot extra-bill the patient. Besides protecting the doctor's image of independence from the government, the Agency helps the doctor by editing his bills and fighting any administrative battles. The Agency business is a sideline of private health insurance companies.

During the years just after the strike, so many doctors wanted to be out of reach of the government that two-thirds of all bills went through the Agencies. By 1977, a new generation of doctors was practicing, nearly all took for granted direct billing to the provincial government, and few bills went through the Agencies.

By then, another country was searching for a compromise between direct third-party payment and burdening the patient with unnecessary and temporary out-of-pocket spending. French doctors had long opposed the authority of the government, and the medical associations had long insisted on a cash benefits system as an article of faith. The national government, trade unions, and many reformers had long criticized this method as a senseless burden on the patient. Some doctors quietly went along with direct payment by the sick funds, to be sure they got their money quickly. Lest their followers stampede in the wrong direction, the leaders of the *Confederation* searched for a compromise method. Apparently without knowing about Saskatchewan's Health Service Agencies they reinvented the same technique, called a *tiers délégué* system of payment. Instead of a private insurance company, a bank was hired to be the financial post office.

If the United States or other countries get into heated fights over direct or indirect billing, the Saskatchewan technique is available as a quick solution. A further lesson is that everyone gets so bored by the method, that eventually all turn to direct billing without qualms.

UNEXPECTED IMPLICATIONS

Some institutions seem attractive and free of trouble when proposed. Difficulties arise after enactment, and then the country may be saddled with a troublesome situation that resists prompt reform. The potential problems might be evident if another country has tried the proposal. It might yield warnings that certain ideas are completely unviable or that certain problems can be headed off by specific reforms. To point to such references, the analyst must understand the full implications of the bills pending on his own country's drawing boards, and also he must be conversant with many foreign experiences.

Fixed budget methods

For example, some Americans hope to design national health insurance with a fixed budget for medical care. An example is the proposed Health Security Act (Kennedy-Corman Bill). Fee-for-service would not lead to cost over-runs: No matter how many medical bills were submitted, the same amount of money would be spent that year. If more bills were submitted that year than the negotiators anticipated, each bill would be paid at less money. The fee schedule would not guarantee payment at par but would be a relative values scale.

A lump sum system for paying doctors presumes an orderly entry of new recruits. German sick funds before 1965 gave a lump sum (a *Kopfpauschale*) to the association of the medical profession (the *Kassenärztliche Vereinigung*), which then distributed it among doctors submitting bills. It is described in Chapter VI, *supra*. The *Kassenärztliche Vereinigung* until 1960 was a closed panel: Only doctors on its list could bill it, and their number was a fixed ratio to the number of subscribers, such as 1:600 between 1931 and 1955, and 1:500 after that. Limitations on entry protected the incomes of doctors admitted to insurance practice; if everyone could treat patients, the *Kopfpauschale* would be divided among an increasing number of doctors, and each would earn less money. Since the number of medical students increased faster than the size of the population, and since free entry into universities was an article of faith in German higher education, there seemed a grave danger of a decline in earnings. But while doctors on the list were protected, those outside had a grievance too: One-fifth of the profession had to scramble for a living without insurance practice, a number went into other careers, the continued expansion of the medical schools would intensify the surplus, and the continued expansion in insurance coverage of the population would ultimately eliminate the outsiders' opportunities in private practice.

Rivalry over the closed panel system had always pitted the unaffiliated office doctors against the KVs. A compromise could not be worked out during the 1950s, and a showdown followed. The unaffiliated doctors filed and won in 1960 a law suit, declaring the closed panels an unconstitutional deprivation of their right to a livelihood. Thereafter, every office doctor automatically belonged to the KV and could treat insured patients.[17]

But now the spectre of rapid decline in incomes had become real. The entire medical profession united in seeking elimination of the *Kopfpauschale* and substitution of payment-in-full for each bill. These changes were made in 1965. As a result, the increase in the number of doctors would not result in the decline of each person's income but would—if the negotiators decided—increase the total costs of national health insurance.[18]

Therefore, a budget system for medical care may be possible only if the number of doctors is limited. If so, this requires control over the number of doctors who are licensed each year. Or, it requires a selective admission to insurance practice by those who otherwise are licensed to practice. Such a closed panel for national health insurance did not survive a constitutional challenge in Germany and might be even more vulnerable in the United States. Obviously a budget system raises many questions that are not evident merely by reading a legislative draft.

HMOs

Many American policy makers hope to promote the organization of prepaid group practices (Health Maintenance Organizations) under special health delivery statutes or as favored sectors of national health insurance itself. Such small closed panels are rare abroad. Where they exist, they are difficult to reconcile with the clauses in the statute that were written during the political compromises with the office practitioners, guaranteeing every doctor the right to see any patient under national health insurance.

For example, closed panel groups existed in Ontario before Medicare and continued thereafter. The Ontario Health Insurance Plan (OHIP) pays lump sums to the groups, which distribute the money in their customary fashion among the physicans. All other doctors are paid by the act according to a fee schedule; they submit individual bills to OHIP. If a panel physician refers a patient to a doctor outside the group, the latter's fees are deducted from OHIP's periodic global payments to the group. Under the law, every subscriber has free choice of doctor and may go to any physician in or outside his group at any time; the cost of these self-referrals also is deducted from OHIP's payments to the group. The groups suffer serious financial problems from this uncontrollable leakage and are believed to discourage outside referrals by their doctors.[19] (However, no interviews or surveys have been done, asking doctors about their decisions.)

While Ontario demonstrates the problems of survival of HMO's under national health insurance, France shows how they might succeed. Persons belong to the *mutualités,* because the organizations' medical panels provide advantages over the individual office practitioners. The patient does not have to pay cash and collect reimbursement from the sick funds; he assigns his claims to his *mutualité,* which bills the *caisse* directly for the care rendered by its employed doctors. The *mutualité* accept the *caisse's* reimbursement as payment in full and does not collect the additional cost-sharing from the patient. The *mutualités* waive cost-sharing to support their employed doctors, because they collect premiums from their subscribers. Their polyclinics offer dentistry, drugs, eyeglasses and other supplies to the subscribers at more favorable prices than the market. The *mutualités* are insurance associations with functions wider than the *caisses,* and they offer additional medical and social benefits, besides the basic services of their medical panels.

ADVISING INTEREST GROUPS ABOUT HOW TO ADJUST

Presenting the parties to a domestic conflict with an image of their futures can show them that a new system is not so threatening and can teach them how to organize constructively. For example, national health insurance of certain types works to the advantage of the medical profession. Therefore, instead of fighting all versions, the medical association can work toward acceptable compromises. (A few leaders of European medical associations have helped to persuade leaders of the AMA that national health insurance can work for the benefit of doctors and therefore the AMA should develop its own plan.)

Studying foreign experience can show interest groups how they must change, to adjust to new situations. For example, in Chapter X, I suggested how the medical association, the insurance carriers, and others might organize themselves—and in fact were doing so—in order to function successfully if national health insurance is enacted.

NOTES

1. Roy Lubove, *The Struggle for Social Security 1900–1935* (Cambridge: Harvard University Press, 1968), Ch. IV; and James G. Burrow, *AMA: Voice of American Medicine* (Baltimore: The Johns Hopkins Press, 1963), pp. 132–134, 142–143, and 147.

2. Burrow, *ibid.,* pp. 198–200.

3. For example, *The Pill That Could Change America: An Up-to-Date Review of Socialized Medicine in the World Today* (Chicago: American Medical Association, 1958).

4. The disappointing history of health planning in the United States is described in Herbert Harvey Hyman, *Health Planning* (Germantown, Md.: Aspen Systems Corporation, 1976). The confusing relations among levels of government at present and the great diversity of practices are analyzed in *Making the National Health Planning Law Work: The State Perspective* (Washington: National Governors' Conference, 1977). The ineffectiveness of the implementation techniques is evident in David S. Salkever and Thomas W. Bice, *Impact of State Certificate-of-Need Laws on Health Care Costs and Utilization* (Rockville, Md.: National Center for Health Services Research, 1977).

5. An excellent summary of all aspects of Swedish health planning is Vicente Navarro, *National and Regional Health Planning in Sweden* (Washington: National Institutes of Health, Department of Health, Education, and Welfare, 1974).

6. *LP 80: Förslag till läkarfördelningsprogram för perioden 1975–1980* (Stockholm: Socialstyrelsen, 1975).

7. Riksförsäkringsverket and Socialstyrelsen, *Sjukförsäkringens ersättningsregler vid privatläkarvård* (Stockholm: Socialdepartmentet, 1973), Volume 1, Chapter 6, pp. 5–8.

8. Summarized in Brian Abel-Smith and Kathleen Gales, *British Doctors at Home and Abroad* (Welwyn: The Codicote Press, 1964), Ch. 1. The methods and miscalculations of British health manpower planning are summarized in Alan Maynard and Arthur Walker, "A Critical Survey of Medical Manpower Planning in Britain," *Social and Economic Administration*, Volume 11, Number 1 (Spring 1977), pp. 52–75.

9. Royal Commission on Medical Education 1965–1968 (Lord Todd et al.), *Report* (London: H. M. Stationery Office, 1968, Cmnd. 3569), esp. pp. 127–162 and 281–291.

10. Review Body on Doctors' and Dentists' Remuneration: compare the pessimistic *Twelfth Report* (Kindersley et. al.), 1970, pp. 13–22; with the *Second Report* (Halsbury et al.), 1972, pp. 5 and 40–44; and with the *Sixth Report* (Woodroofe et al.), 1976, pp. 6–7.

11. Advertisement by the Louisiana State Medical Society in *American Medical News*, 6 June 1977. Speeches on national health insurance before the AMA's House of Delegates, June 1977.

12. Before American Medicare started to operate, I predicted that it would be administered in ways pleasing to the doctors, and they would profit. They gained even more than I expected, since Medicare never acquired the negotiating machinery and the cost controls that are integral parts of national health insurance in all other countries.. Glaser, " 'Socialized Medicine' in Practice," *The Public Interest*, Number 3 (Spring 1966), pp. 90–106.

13. The Swedish allocation method is described on an earlier page of this Appendix. The British system is summarized in John R. Butler, *Family Doctors and Public Policy* (London: Routledge & Kegan Paul, 1973); John R. Butler and Rose Knight, *The Designated Areas Project: Study of Medical Practice Areas— Final Report* (Canterbury: Health Services Research Unit, University of Kent, 1974); and John R. Butler and Rose Knight, "Designated Areas: A Review of Problems and Policies," *British Medical Journal*, 7 June 1975, pp. 571–573.

14. American experiences are summarized in Elliot Long, *The Geographic*

Distribution of Physicians in the United States (Washington: The National Science Foundation, 1975).

15. Copeman has described the program in "177 of 203 Doctors Stay in Underserviced Areas," *Ontario Medical Review,* Volume 40, Number 12 (December 1973), pp. 774–777.

16. Robin F. Badgley and Samuel Wolfe, *Doctors' Strike* (Toronto: Macmillan of Canada, 1967), Chs. 3 and 4.

17. Summarized briefly in Glaser, *Paying the Doctor* (Baltimore: The Johns Hopkins Press, 1970), pp. 123–124.

18. The complex policy struggle—involving the size of medical school enrollments, entry into insurance practice, and the payment system—is described in Willi Thelen, *Numerus Clausus und Ärzteschaft* (Giessen: Verlag Andreas Achenbach, 1974). The pressure to eliminate the *Kopfpauschale* is described at pp. 100–122. The weaknesses of the *Kopfpauschale*—and particularly the incentive for each doctor to maintain his income in the face of declining fees by submitting more bills—are described in Dietrich Maiwald et al., *Ärztliche Praxis: Heute und Morgen* (Planegg vor München: Socio-medico Verlag, 1968), pp. 47–50; and Philipp Herder-Dorneich, *Sozialökonomischer Grundriss der gesetzlichen Krankenversicherung* (Stuttgart: Verlag W. Kohlhammer, 1966), pp. 282–286 and 294–296.

19. Before Medicare, research showed they had few patient self-referrals and few official referrals to outside doctors, but that is not surprising, since internal referral is the *raison d'être* of a panel. The groups had lower hospitalization than other forms of practice, possibly for the same reasons as those usually suggested in evaluations of closed panel groups. John E. F. Hastings et al., "Prepaid Group Practice in Sault Ste. Marie, Ontario," *Medical Care,* Volume 11, Numbers 2 and 3 (March-April and May-June 1973), pp. 92–99 and 177–186. Similar patterns appear in an evaluation after the start of Medicare, but the design was defective and the study did not isolate the effects of financial incentives: *Effects of Delivery Systems and Health Care Resources on Medical Care Behavior* (the "Roth Report") (Toronto: School of Hygiene, University of Toronto, 1975), Parts III and IV. These dilemmas have been experienced also by an American experiment in creating a closed panel of primary practitioners paid by capitation, the Health Maintenance Plan of Wisconsin Physicians Service.

Glossary of Abbreviations and Names

Abbreviation	Name	Literal translation into English	Meaning
CANADA			
TCMP	Trans Canada Medical Plans		National association of health insurance programs sponsored by the medical profession before Medicare
OHIP	Ontario Health Insurance Plan		Medicare insurance program of the Province of Ontario
	Régie de l'assurance-maladie du Québec	Health Insurance Board of Quebec	Medicare insurance program of the Province of Quebec
CMA	Canadian Medical Association		National association of all Canadian doctors
OMA	Ontario Medical Association		Association of doctors of the Province of Ontario
FMOQ	Fédération des médecins omnipraticiens du Québec	Federation of General Practitioners of Quebec	
FMSQ	Fédération des médecins specialistes du Québec	Federation of Specialists of Quebec	

Abbreviation	Name	Literal translation into English	Meaning
FRANCE			
	Direction de la sécurité sociale	Management of Social Security	Office in the Ministry of Health that supervises official health insurance
CNAMTS	Caisse nationale de l'assurance maladie des travailleurs salariés	National Fund for the Health Insurance of Wage Workers	Official sick fund for the large majority of French workers
CCSMA	Caisse centrale de secours mutuels agricoles	Central Fund for Cooperative Agricultural Assistance	Official sick fund for farmers
CANAM	Caisse nationale d'assurance maladie et maternité des travailleurs non salariés des professions non agricoles	National Fund for the Health Insurance and Maternity Benefits of Non-Wage and Non-Agricultural Workers	Official sick fund for businessmen, professionals, artisans
	caisse primaires	Primary Funds	Local units of the official sick funds that deal directly with subscribers and doctors
	sociétés mutualistes; mutuels	Cooperative Societies	Social insurance funds that antedate official national health insurance
CSMF	Confédération des syndicats médicaux français	Confederation of French Medical Syndicates	Principal association of French doctors concerned with economic interests

Abbreviation	Name	Literal translation into English	Meaning
FRANCE (cont.)			
FMF	Fédération des médecins de France	Federation of the Doctors of France	Second association of French doctors
	Nomenclature général des actes professionnels	General nomenclature of professional acts	Fee schedule used for official health insurance
BELGIUM			
	Alliance nationale de mutualités chrétiennes	National Alliance of Christian Cooperative Societies	Association of the Catholic sick funds
	Union national des mutualités socialistes	National Union of Socialist Cooperative Societies	Association of the socialist sick funds
	Fédération belge des chambres syndicales de médecins	Belgian Federation of Trade Unions of Doctors	Principal national association of Belgian doctors
	Confédération des médecins belges	Confederation of Belgian Doctors	Second national association of Belgian doctors
	Algemeen Syndikaat der Geneesheren van België	General Trade Union of Doctors of Belgium	Oldest trade union of Belgian doctors, now a member of the Confederation
INAMI	Institut national d'assurance maladie-invalidité	National Institute for Health and Disability Insurance	Autonomous organization that supervises national health insurance

Abbreviation	Name	Literal translation into English	Meaning
BELGIUM (cont.)			
	Comité de gestion du service des soins de santé	Governing Committee for the Health Care Service	INAMI committee that supervises relations with providers
	Commission nationale médico-mutualiste	National Commission of Doctors and Sick Funds	Negotiating committee between doctors and sick funds
	Conseil technique médical	Technical Medical Committee	Negotiating committee that writes the fee schedule
	Nomenclature des prestations de santé	Nomenclature of Health Benefits	Fee schedule used for official health insurance
THE NETHERLANDS			
VNZ	Vereniging van Nederlandse Ziekenfondsen	Confederation of Dutch Sick Funds	Association of all Dutch sick funds
KNMG	Koninklijke Nederlandsche Mattschappij tot Bevordering der Geneeskunst	Royal Dutch Society for the Promotion of Medical Care	National medical association
LHV	Landelijke Huisartsen Vereniging	National Family Physicians Confederation	Association of general practitioners
LSV	Landelijke Specialisten Vereniging	National Specialists Confederation	Association of specialists

Abbreviation	Name	Literal translation into English	Meaning
THE NETHERLANDS (cont.)			
	Ziekenfondsraad	Council for Sick Funds	Autonomous agency that supervises statutory health insurance
GBZ	Gemeenschappelijk Bureau van Ziekenfondsorganisaties	General Office of Sick Funds Organizations	Administrative staff that handles negotiations between VNZ and the doctors
	Permanente Tarieven Commissie	Permanent Tariff Committee	Negotiating committee for the fee schedule
FEDERAL REPUBLIC OF GERMANY			
RVO	Reichsversicherungsordnung	Imperial Insurance Decree	Statute that created national health insurance
RVO-Kassen	Gesetzliche Krankenkassen	Statutory Sick Funds	Funds that administer national health insurance
	Ersatzkassen	Substitute Funds	Funds that persons can join as an alternative to the RVO-Kassen
BOK	Bundesverband der Ortskrankenkassen	Federal Union of Local Sick Funds	National leadership of the largest association of sick funds
	Verband der Krankenkassen	Union of Sick Funds	Any association of sick funds in a province

Abbreviation	Name	Literal translation into English	Meaning
FEDERAL REPUBLIC OF GERMANY (cont.)			
KBV	Kassenärztliche Bundesvereinigung	Federal Association of Fund Doctors	National leadership of the doctors in fund practice
KV	Kassenärztliche Vereinigung	Association of Fund Doctors	Society of doctors in health insurance practice in each province
GOÄ	Gebührenordnung für Ärzte	Fee Schedule for Doctors	Statutory fee schedule for national health insurance
BMÄ	Bewertungsmassstab-Ärzte	Values Scale for Doctors	Constantly up to date version of GOÄ published by KBV
SWITZERLAND			
	Konkordat der schweizerischen Krankenkassen	Agreement of Swiss Sick Funds	Association of sick funds in German-speaking Switzerland
	Kantonalverband der Krankenkassen	Cantonal Union of Sick Funds	Association of sick funds in each canton
	Verbindung der schweizer Ärzte	Union of Swiss Doctors	National medical association
SUVA	Schweizerische Unfallversicherungsanstalt	Swiss Accident Insurance Institution	National sick fund for accident insurance

Abbreviation	Name	Literal translation into English	Meaning
SWEDEN			
	Socialdepartmentet	Department of Social Affairs	Government Ministry that plans social policy
	Socialstyrelsen	Social Board	Administrative board of the government that supervises health services
RFV	Riksförsäkringsverket	National Social Insurance Board	Administrative board of the government that supervises social insurance
FKF	Försäkringskasseförbundet	Association of Insurance Funds	National association of funds for health and other benefits
LFB	Landstingsförbundet	Association of County Councils	National association of the regional governments
SLF or SMA	Sveriges Läkarförbundet	Swedish Medical Association	Principal association of Swedish doctors
SACO	Sveriges Akademikers Centralorganisationen	Central Organization of Swedish Professional Workers	Federation of associations representing professionals, executives, and civil servants
	Läkarsvårdsdelegationen	Medical Care Commission	Negotiating committee for fees and fee schedules

Abbreviation	Name	Literal translation into English	Meaning
GREAT BRITAIN			
DHSS	Department of Health and Social Security		Government Ministry that administers health and social services
NHS	National Health Service		Hierarchy of organizations and committees within DHSS that provide health care
BMA	British Medical Association		Principal association of British doctors
GMSC	General Medical Service Committee		Governing committee for general practitioners within BMA
CCHMS	Central Committee for Hospital Medical Services		Governing committee for consultants (i.e., senior hospital doctors) within BMA
HJSC	Hospital Junior Staffs Committee		Governing committee for junior hospital doctors within BMA
JNC	Joint Negotiating Committee		Negotiating committee that decides terms of service for hospital doctors. Members from DHSS, CCHMS, and HJSC.

My Informants

I AM deeply indebted to the following persons, who granted much time in interviews. They enabled me to understand their countries and their own roles in national health insurance.

Canada

John S. W. Aldis, William Anderson, Robert A. Armstrong, Marcel Bachand, Robin Badgley, André Beaulé, Georges Boileau, Thomas Boudreau, Jan F. Brandejs, Guy Cardinal, John Carlyle, André-Pierre Contandriopoulos, William J. Copeman, Dorothy E. Daley, Normand P. DaSylva, Eddie d'Souza, Paul Duggan, Robert E. Foster, Peter Fraser, Bruce Gagnon, Gerald Gold, Alice Goodfellow, Harry Gray, G. B. Hill, Harold Hoffman, Martin Laberge, Valentine Larouche, Sidney S. Lee, H. I. MacKillop, Donald MacLean, Pran Manga, D. F. Marcellus, Wiliam A. Mennie, Gabriel Pelletier, Lothar Rehmer, Jean-Yves Rivard, Malcolm G. Taylor, Atam Uppal, Alan Wolfson.

France

Jean Blais, Robert F. Bridgman, Antoinette Catrice-Lorey, J. F. Chadelat, Monique Chasserant, Jacques Colonna, Jean de Kervasdoué, Alain Foulon, Alain Laugier, Georges Lavolée, Philippe Madinier, M. Marçais, Monique Méquignon, Clément Michel, J. Prévost, Georges Rösch, Simone Sandier, Jean Wozniak, Tobie Zakia.

Belgium

Henri Anrys, Jan Blanpain, V. Chevalier, Luk Delesie, Denise Deliège-Rott, H. Halter, R. Laenen, André Maes, Lydia Magnus-Maximus, Yvo Nuyens, Herman Nys, Marie-Louise Opdenberg, Paul Quaethoven, Andrée Sacrez, Jozef van Langendonck, Roger Zwaenepoel.

The Netherlands

L. Andriessen, J. H. Baay, D. J. Brauckmann, C. P. Bruins, C. Dalmeyer-Henneke, J. J. de Bruijn, N. de Graaff, Carel S. de Groot, L. M. J. Groot, H. J. Hannessen, Mr. Helmink, J. P. Kasdorp, H. J. Lammers, Rudy Lapré, F. Luidinga, B. Schultsz, A. R. F. Somers, W. M. J. van Duyne, W. W. M. van der Horst, P. J. Van Leeuwen, Adolf H. Wiebenga, H. Willems.

German Federal Republic

Rüdiger Balthaser, Heinz-Peter Brauer, Siegfried Eichhorn, Wally Esch, Karl-Heinz Frommhagen, Ulrich Geissler, Philipp Herder-Dorneich, Dr. Med Hölscher, Thea Krämer, J. R. Möhr, Dr. Müller, Manfred Pflanz, Romuald Schicke, Anton Schlichtig, Rolf Schlögell, H. G. Schmidt-Jensen, Horst Schumacher, F. W. Schwartz, Fritz Tervooren, Günther Vierbücher, Wolfgang Wichmann, Helmut Wilken, Mr. Wirzbach, Albrecht Wortmann.

Switzerland

Danielle Bridel, Rudolf Gilli, Ervin Gregor, Martin Häfeli, Ulrich Hofer, B. Joss, Peter Kramer, H. Langmack, Ernest Menzi, Ulrich Naef, Hans Ott, Heiner Rittmeyer, F. Roost, Jakob Stöckli, E. von Büren.

Sweden

Leif Åkerblom, Ragnar Berfenstam, Sture Börjesson, Nils Broberg, Ingrid Fägersten, Stefan Hammarqvist, Sture Järnmark, Egon Jonsson, Per-Ove Karlsson, Manfred Kilgus, Rune Lind, Gudjón Magnússon, Karl-Evert Mosten, Ulf Nikolausson, Ingvar Nordin, Olle Orava, Anders Rörby, Ivar Sannefors, Uncas Serner, Björn Smedby, Ulla Takman, Malcolm Tottie, Kurt Wengstrom, Gunnar Wennstrom, Christer Wickberg, Ulf Winblad.

Great Britain

Brian Abel-Smith, G. P. H. Aiken, Alan Amos, D. R. Bagnall, John Bevan, Brian Bicknell, Robin A. Birch, John Butler, Ann Cartwright,

Theodore E. Chester, Roy Cunningham, Kenneth Dawes, C. D. Falconer, Peter Farmer, John Fry, Alan Gilbert, David S. Grimes, John K. Guilor, Rudolf Klein, Robert Kohn, Hugh L'Etang, Michael Lowe, John C. Mac-Kay, Alistair MacKinnon, Miss Macmillan, John Randle, John F. Sharpe, Audrey Simons, Douglas Symes, Ray Taylor, George Teeling-Smith, R. Glyn Thomas, Robert W. D. Venning, Ronald Woods.

I am also indebted to many persons in the United States who helped me specify the problems and issues whose solutions I should seek abroad, and who helped me understand how American health services work.

Washington and Baltimore

Stuart Altman, Brenda Ballard, William Birnie, Martha Blaxall, Ted Bogue, Henry P. Brehm, Lawrence Brown, Ira L. Burney, Inez Connolly, Gerald Connor, Jay Constantine, Max W. Fine, Paul Fisher, Peter D. Fox, William Fullerton, Clifton Gaus, Willis B. Goldbeck, Warren Greenberg, Ruth S. Hanft, Steve Hardan, Robert Hoyer, Lee Hyde, Stanley Jones, John Kern, Mary Nell Lehnhard, Mahadev Mahabal, James Mongan, M. Gail Moran, Selma J. Mushkin, Beverlee A. Myers, Jack Needleman, Karen Nelson, Joseph Onek, Paul Rettig, Dorothy P. Rice, Paul Riesel, Judith Robinson, Bert Seidman, Joseph Simanis, William Sobaski, Lucretia Dewey Tanner, Saul Waldman, Sidney Wolfe, Irwin Wolkstein.

Chicago

Odin W. Anderson, Norbert W. Budde, Edward J. Carels, J. Paige Clousson, John Cnrcich, David Drake, Lynn E. Jensen, John H. Lorant, Theodore R. Marmor, Edward S. Mills, Larry Morris, Tom K. Mura, Ralph E. Schreiber, Eugene Stevens, Jack Werner, Joseph Woosley.

California

Donald Harrington, Roy Howard, Michael W. Jones, Cecilia Richards, John Smillie, Robert B. Talley, Lloyd Ulman, Arthur Weissman, George Williams.

New York

Henry F. Adamy, Alexander Bugsby, John Evanthes, Kathleen Garry, Irving Ladimer, Theodore A. Lutins, Donald Lyons, Mario Menghini, Uwe Reinhardt, David Robbins, Bruce Vladeck, James R. Williams.

Index of Subjects

Index of Names